A Guide through the Theory of Knowledge

A Guide through the Theory of Knowledge

Third edition

Adam Morton

University of Oklahoma

Blackwell
Publishing

350 Main Street, Malden, MA 02148-5018, USA
108 Cowley Road, Oxford OX4 1JF, UK
550 Swanston Street, Carlton, Victoria 3053, Australia
Kurfürstendamm 57, 10707 Berlin, Germany

First published 1977
Second edition published 1997
Third edition published 2003 by Blackwell Publishers Ltd, a Blackwell Publishing company

Library of Congress Cataloging-in-Publication Data has been applied for.

ISBN 1-405-10011-7 (hardback); ISBN 1-405-10012-5 (paperback)

A catalogue record for this title is available from the British Library.

Set in 10/12pt Photina
by SNP Best-set Typesetter Ltd., Hong Kong
Printed and bound in Great Britain
by TJ International, Padstow, Cornwall

For further information on
Blackwell Publishers, visit our website:
www.blackwellpublishers.co.uk

CONTENTS

FOREWORD FOR STUDENTS

This book is meant as a simple introduction to the main issues and theories in the theory of knowledge, also known as epistemology. This is a subject that has many paradoxes and intellectual traps, and touches on some deep and mind-boggling questions. An introduction to the theory of knowledge should not ignore the traps or trivialize the deep questions. But it should try not to wallow in the difficulties or allow controversies about some of the questions to obscure the clear answers to others. So I have tried to find a route through the subject that concentrates on what is clear and definite, while keeping the big questions in view. On some topics I have views which are not shared by all philosophers. (There is no philosopher who has not.) I have tried to make it obvious what is my opinion and what is the consensus of most contemporary philosophers.

At the end of each chapter there are two kinds of questions. *Reading questions* are meant to check your understanding of the chapter. If you find any of them hard to answer you should read the relevant section over again, and if you are still puzzled ask for an explanation in a lecture or discussion group. *Thinking questions* are meant to make links to further topics, to raise doubts about the line taken in the main text, and to provide general intellectual stimulation. They are possible topics for essays. Not being able to answer the thinking questions is definitely not a sign of not having understood the chapter, but trying to think out answers to them will often give you a better sense about the questions behind the questions. At the end of each chapter there is also a list of titles for further reading, and some electronic resources, with an explanation of the relevance of each item. These lists are a good place to start looking for suitable reading matter when you are planning an essay. The electronic resources refer to two sources. The *Routledge Encyclopedia of Philosophy*, version 1.0, is available on CD-Rom and is networked on many university libraries and websites. *The Stanford Encyclopedia of Philosophy*, is available at *http://plato.stanford.edu/*. In referring to articles in the *Stanford Encyclopedia* I <u>underline</u> articles which were available in August 2001, and simply list without underlining articles which are expected to be online in the near future.

At the end of the book there are definitions of technical terms in philosophy used in this book. Many of these words are printed in **bold** when they are first used in the text.

Teachers should notice that there is an appendix for teachers at the end of the book.

Many of the issues discussed here have been fascinating philosophers for centuries. And recent work on them has brought out more of their capacity to intrigue and stimulate. I hope that this book makes the standard problems and theories clear to you; but I will have failed if it does not also make it clear to you why these are still fascinating questions, which every person can gain from considering. The more you think about them the more their fascination grows.

ACKNOWLEDGMENTS

In the first edition of this book I thanked Hartry Field, Gil Harman, Glenn Kessler, Cliff McIntosh, Milly Morton, George Pitcher, and Eric Rosen. Thanks again. I am grateful to Steve Smith, Nathalie Manners, and Jeff Dean at Blackwells for encouraging a second and then a third edition. Five anonymous readers for Blackwells gave extremely valuable advice on revising the book, and Martin Poulter, Andrew Pyle, and Stephen Wilkinson caught a remarkable number of mistakes and bad ideas. My students at the University of Michigan and Bob Stern's at the University of Sheffield gave useful feedback about the second edition, and Martin Montminy gave a wonderfully sharp and practical set of comments after using the book at Ottawa. Susanna encouraged the mooses.

Chapter 1

BELIEFS AND THEIR QUALITIES

1. Defending and Attacking Beliefs

Any person has many beliefs. You believe that the world is round, that you have a nose and a heart, that $2 + 2 = 4$, that there are many people in the world and some like you and some do not. These are beliefs about which almost everyone agrees. But people disagree too. Some people believe that there is a god and some do not. Some people believe that conventional medicine gives the best way of dealing with all diseases and some do not. Some people believe that there is intelligent life elsewhere in the universe and some do not. When people disagree they throw arguments, evidence, and persuasion at one another. Very often they apply abusive or flattering labels to the beliefs in question. "That's false," "That's irrational," "You haven't got any evidence," or "That's true," "I have good reason to believe it," "I know it."

We use these labels because there are properties we want our beliefs to have: we want them to be true rather than false, we want to have good rather than bad reasons for believing them. The theory of knowledge is concerned with these properties, with the difference between good and bad beliefs. Its importance in philosophy comes from two sources, one constructive and one destructive. The constructive reason is that philosophers have often tried to find better ways in which we can get our beliefs. For example, they have studied scientific method and tried to see whether we can describe scientific rules which we could follow to give us the greatest chance of avoiding false beliefs. Rationalism and empiricism and Bayesianism, described later in this book, are constructive philosophies of this sort. The destructive reason is that philosophy has often been caught up in the conflict between one set or system of beliefs and another. For example, people with religious faith sometimes try to find philosophical reasons for believing in God, and anti-religious people sometimes try to find philosophical reasons why it is irrational to believe in God. So the theory of knowledge – or epistemology as it is also called, from the Greek word *epistēmē* meaning "knowledge" – can get involved both in trying to find better ways of acquiring beliefs and in criticizing the beliefs people already have.

This chapter introduces the basic ideas and terminology of the theory of knowledge. It connects the search to improve our beliefs and to referee the conflicts between different systems of beliefs with the fundamental ideas of the subject. The central idea here is the importance of questions about the kinds of beliefs we want to have. The chapter ends with two extreme views, deep skepticism and radical externalism, to show the importance of these questions.

2. Epistemic Ideals

Until recently most philosophers working in the theory of knowledge have not paid much attention to the different ways in which beliefs and the ways we acquire them can be satisfactory or deficient. They have not asked: What qualities do we want our beliefs to have and what qualities do we want them not to have? One reason for this is that philosophers have often thought that the answer was obvious: We want our beliefs to be true and not false. As we will see later (especially in chapter 5) this answer is *not* obvious. But, focusing on the desire for truth, most philosophers until recently have described various ideals for beliefs: ways in which our beliefs and the ways we get them could be perfectly organized. Rationalists described an ideal in which arguments as forceful as those in a mathematical proof could demonstrate the truth of all the beliefs we need to know. Empiricists described an ideal in which evidence from what is seen, heard, or otherwise perceived could give adequate evidence for all our beliefs. A contemporary epistemic ideal, defended by the Bayesian movement in probability theory and the theory of knowledge, aims to describe ways in which we can discover exactly how probable each of our beliefs is, given the evidence we possess.

In the course of this book we will discuss each of these ideals. One important question to ask about each of them is "Are human beings capable of satisfying this ideal: can we have beliefs that are like this?" But another equally important question is "What would the price be for satisfying this ideal: in order to have beliefs like this would we have to lose something else of value?"

A very simple epistemic ideal is that of **coherence**. Coherence is having beliefs that not only make sense individually but which hang together in a coherent pattern. If I believe that all cats are intelligent, believe that my neighbour's cat is a cat, and also believe that my neighbour's cat is stupid, then my beliefs are incoherent. They cannot all be true, and I can start with some of them and give good reasons for disagreeing with others. My beliefs could be incoherent for other reasons too. I might believe many things which amount to strong evidence for something and yet believe the opposite. This often happens when people deceive themselves. Suppose for example that someone knows that their child gets into fights at school, knows that the teachers are afraid of the child, knows that many other children are not permitted to play with the child, and still deceives herself into thinking that her child is a well-behaved little angel. Such a person's beliefs will not be coherent.

Why should we want our beliefs to be coherent? One reason is that incoherent beliefs tend to include many false beliefs. Another is that incoherent beliefs are hard to defend against people who challenge or attack them. So coherence is an ideal that we could set ourselves. We could try to make our beliefs as coherent as possible. This does not mean that any person's beliefs could ever be totally coherent. Every human being will probably always be subject to bad reasoning and self-deception. That's the way we are. But it is an ideal we can try to achieve. It is also an ideal that someone might decide not to aim for, probably because it was thought to conflict with some other ideal, such as the ideal of having interesting new ideas. So even for this very simple epistemic ideal there are questions to answer about what the price of aiming at it is, and how near to achieving it human beings can actually come.

Differences of epistemic ideal lie beneath many disagreements in everyday life. For example, some people have a lot of faith in various kinds of alternative medicine, while others are very skeptical of such claims. A popular book on herbalism may say things like "A man riddled with cancer was told he had four weeks to live. He heard about herb X and decided to drink a quart of X tea daily. Three years later he was still alive." The story may give some people faith in the powers of herb X, while others may refuse to be impressed. The unimpressed people will not only fail to believe that X has curative powers. They will also think that something is wrong with the way that people who are influenced by the story are forming their beliefs. They will think that these people are too ready to believe something on inadequate evidence. They will be loyal to an epistemic ideal according to which beliefs should be related in defensible ways to evidence. A very strong form of this ideal would say that you should only have beliefs for which there is strong evidence like the evidence that supports scientific theories. People who have more faith in alternative medicine are very rarely loyal to any such ideal. They are more likely to be loyal to an ideal according to which a person's beliefs should be part of a pattern that gives meaning to the person's life and fits their own moral and spiritual ideas. These ideals are so different that it is not surprising that people who are loyal to them often find each other's beliefs incredible. The important point for now is that many differences of opinion are the result of different ideals of what a person's beliefs should be like. One task of the theory of knowledge is to provide ways in which these differences of epistemic ideal can be discussed and even resolved.

3. The Basic Concepts

In discussing our beliefs, philosophers use a number of central concepts. It is hard to define any of them in terms that all philosophers would accept, for the definitions are usually tied up with theories about knowledge, just the theories that we have to compare in this book. But if you consider the examples below you will almost certainly conclude that they are concepts that you are already familiar with. Everyone uses them in everyday life, in a general and imprecise way, even if they do not use the words for them that philosophers do. (In what follows I will often write a word in italics to indicate that it is a word worth noticing or in boldface if it is included in the list of definitions of epistemological terms at the end of the book.)

Rational/irrational

George has a date with Shoshana, who is blonde. She decides at the last minute not to go out with George that evening but to stay home and study instead. George is furious, and decides that all blonde women are evil. He will never trust a blonde again. This is especially strange since his mother and sister, who have always treated him with the greatest kindness, are blonde. But from that day on, however friendly, considerate, or helpful a blonde woman is, George always interprets her behavior as evil.

The way that George comes to have the belief that all blonde women are evil is **irrational**. It consists not in careful thinking but in a sudden angry impulse that continues to grip him. Speaking loosely, we may say that the belief itself is irrational. We might say that it was a crazy or a stupid belief, though George may be neither crazy nor stupid. Many philosophers think that a lot of people's beliefs, including beliefs handed down through the generations, are irrational. In some important ways they are like George's belief about blondes. Superstitious beliefs, like for example the belief that it is bad luck to have a black cat cross your path, are good candidates for being irrational. That is, it is irrational to believe that something will cause you harm just because not very well-informed people sometimes say it will, although they can produce no good evidence for this. Some philosophers argue that all religious beliefs are irrational, and some philosophers think that it is irrational to believe in an objective difference between right and wrong. Many other philosophers, needless to say, disagree.

Contrast George with Sonya. Sonya has a cruel father, and her brother is a drug dealer. Neither shows any affection or consideration for her. Indeed, with the exception of two of her teachers in school, all the men who have played any role in her life have been baddies. Yet when asked her attitude to men she says "There are a lot of bad ones. But I've met a few decent ones, so I have some slight hope for them." This does not seem irrational. The way

Sonya gets her belief is **rational**, to the extent that it does not go beyond what the evidence available to her suggests, and leaves open possibilities that are not closed off by that evidence. One conclusion to draw is that very often a rational belief, one that is acquired in a rational way, will have to be more subtly expressed than an irrational one in response to the same evidence. The rational belief will less often say "all" and "never."

True/false

Suppose that there is some mechanism in the universe which ensures that whenever a black cat crosses a person's path something bad happens to that person in the near future. No human being knows of the existence of this mechanism, which works by physical principles which humans will never understand. Then the belief that it is bad luck to have a black cat cross your path is **true**. (So the belief that the probability of bad events is unchanged by a black cat's crossing your path is **false**.) But still there may not be any good evidence for it: the combinations of cat-crossings and bad occurrences are too subtle for us ever to notice them. Then the belief that black cats are bad luck is true even though there is no good evidence for it; true even if the belief that it is true is irrational. So irrational beliefs can be true. That may be a surprising conclusion, but it is clearly right. A less surprising conclusion is that rational beliefs can be false. There can be very strong reasons for believing something although it is false. (Your best friend who has never lied to you before can tell you that your house was not struck by lightning last night, but in fact . . .)

Evidence

Scientists do experiments to find **evidence** for and against scientific theories. Detectives hunt for evidence showing who committed crimes. Evidence can take many different forms. The behavior of animals in a learning task, the pattern of light in the viewpiece of a telescope or microscope, a letter confessing to an action; all these and many others could count as evidence in suitable circumstances. Very often when evidence is produced it is in order to convince someone to change their mind, from belief to disbelief, from disbelief to belief, or from neutrality to either. The evidence then has to be believable by the people who are to be convinced, and in addition has to be such that when they think about it they will, if they are rational, find some tendency to change their beliefs. So evidence produced by the defense in a court case might be testimony that even a juror who was inclined to convict would take seriously. Similarly, evidence for a scientific theory might be the result of an experiment that even someone who believed a rival theory would have to admit did definitely occur and did definitely give the result that it did.

Reasoning and argument

When evidence supports a belief it makes people think that the belief might be true. Because of the evidence they perform some reasoning that tends towards the belief. There are many kinds of reasoning. Sometimes to persuade someone you do not produce any evidence at all but say "Suppose for the sake of argument that . . ." and then go on to draw conclusions. A defence lawyer says "suppose that someone besides my client was hiding in the house that night" and then shows how that mystery person could have committed the crime and planted her client's stolen wallet near the scene. The jury thinks about this, and is led through steps of *reasoning* by the lawyer's *argument*. Then they may conclude "someone else just might have done it" or "if someone else could have got into the house then someone else could have done it." Sometimes reasoning can show that a belief is true without using any evidence at all. For example suppose a student says to a librarian "This book was due on February 1st and it is now March 1st, and the fine is $1 per day, so I owe $29" and the librarian replies "But this is a leap year, so you owe $30." The librarian's reasoning shows that the student's belief is wrong, without producing any evidence they didn't both already have.

Justified/unjustified

Consider Toshiro who lives in Tokyo and knows nothing about North American animals. He has never seen a moose or a chipmunk and does not know what sorts of animals they are His family is taking a trip to Seattle and on the plane they give him a book, in English, with the title *Animals of North America*. In fact the book is a joke and most of the information in it is wrong. In particular, the photo and description of a moose are of a chipmunk and the photo and description of a chipmunk are of a moose. In Seattle he goes to a zoo and sees a moose. He believes that he is seeing the animal called "chipmunk." That is clearly not a silly thing for him to believe, given what he has read and what he sees. On the basis of that information his belief that he is seeing what is called a chipmunk is **justified**. His sister Sumiko, who has much more information about North American animals, looks at the big ruminant with the wide horns and at once thinks "That's a moose," and her belief is also justified. A belief is justified on the basis of information which makes believing it a better strategy for getting to the truth than not believing it. Often people draw conclusions that are not justified by the information they have. For example if Sumiko thinks that since moose have horns and since "mouse" sounds like "moose" then mice have horns, then her belief is unjustified on the basis of her information, unless she also has some reason to believe that animals whose names in English sound alike are similar.

Many theories of knowledge are theories of when a person's beliefs are justified. So they give information about when people are rational in acquiring beliefs. A person acquires a belief rationally when the acquisition is based on or guided by information that justifies the belief. That is the simplest kind of case; there are also more complicated situations in which for example a person acquires a belief irrationally and then later finds evidence which supports it. (A person dreams that they will win a lottery and so goes out next day and buys an expensive car; then that evening their ticket is announced as the winner.) In complicated cases it is simplest to think of rationality as a property of people and their thinking, and justification as a property of beliefs.

Knowledge/ignorance

Toshiro was *ignorant* of the names of North American animals. We are all ignorant of many things: there are many questions we do not know the answers to. Probably no human knows whether there is life on other planets. Probably no human knows how to achieve universal peace. Probably no human knows whether there are infinitely many twin prime numbers (like 3 and 5, 11 and 13, 1,001 and 1,003). There are many people who have beliefs about all these things, and some of their opinions are rational, and some are justified. But it does not follow that any of these opinions count as *knowledge*. To know that there is life on other planets a person would have to have a powerful theory of how life develops or have direct evidence produced by such life. To know how to achieve universal peace someone would have to have a recipe for producing peace and a very convincing reason that showed how and why it would work. To know that there are infinitely many twin primes a person would have to have a correct mathematical proof of this fact. In short and very roughly, to know something your mind has to be linked to the fact, and that link has to be a top quality reliable one. This makes knowledge seem very special and very rare. Yet we talk as if we know many things. Just about every person knows the names of his or her friends, and knows that they have a nose on their face. Most people know that the earth revolves around the sun and that 12 multiplied by 13 is 156. One sign of this is that most people can be relied on to give reliable information about these things. Seen this way, it is not surprising that there are many controversies about knowledge: about what knowledge is and how much knowledge we have. For it is at the same time something that seems very hard to achieve and something that we think we have quite a lot of. (This suggests that disputes between those who want to use the theory of knowledge to criticize the beliefs of others and those who want to use it to understand or improve the beliefs they already have, may go very deep.)

None of these explanations was a real definition. There were too many vague and unexplained terms in them, for example the idea of a "top quality reliable" link between a mind and a fact. Later in this book more precise definitions of some of these terms will be considered. (See chapter 6 for more about knowledge, and see question 16 at the end of this chapter for more about the difference between justified and rational beliefs.) But the explanations probably will have reminded you of enough about these concepts that you can understand them. The important point to grasp now is that all of these words can be used to describe desirable and undesirable, good and bad, features of our beliefs. It is not at all obvious that there is only one kind of desirable feature of beliefs, so these good and bad aspects can cut across one another in complicated patterns. In particular note the following three complications.

A good result can be obtained by a bad method. For example, a true belief can be got by irrational reasoning. You see a spider and because you are scared by its hairy legs you think it must be poisonous. That is bad reasoning, but it may be that the spider is poisonous all the same. There are many examples of this in the history of science. For example, William Harvey in the seventeenth century came up with the theory that the blood in the body circulates, leaving the heart by the arteries and returning by the veins. He got to this conclusion by thinking: The heart is like the sun and the blood is like the earth, so since the earth revolves around the sun the blood must revolve around the heart. This is not very convincing reasoning, to put it mildly, but it led him to a true conclusion. (He later did experiments and found better evidence for his idea.)

A bad result can be obtained by a good method. For example, Toshiro in the example above was not reasoning badly when he thought that the large animal in front of him was called a "chipmunk." Or consider a scientist who tests a million samples of a drug on a dozen species of animals and finds no harmful side-effects. In the absence of contrary evidence she is justified in concluding that the drug is harmless. But it may turn out that in some species under some conditions the drug is fatal. Her justified belief was false. (This example is related to questions about induction, discussed in chapter 4.)

Opposing beliefs can both be justified. Toshiro and Sumiko both had justified beliefs, in terms of the different evidence available to each of them. People thousands of years ago were not stupid when they thought that the earth was flat and the sun revolved around it, just as we are not stupid in believing that it is spherical and revolves around the sun. Relative to the evidence available to ancient people their belief was a sensible one. Note, though, that opposing beliefs cannot both count as knowledge. If the earth is really flat then we are wrong in thinking that we know that it is spherical.

These three complications are similar to complications that arise whenever we are applying several different kinds of good and bad qualities. In particular, they are similar to complications that arise in ethics, when we are trying to understand the good and bad qualities of human actions. There too we find that a good result can be obtained by a bad method, as when someone attacks a rival out of petty jealousy and thereby accidentally prevents the rival from committing a murder. And we find that a bad result can be obtained by a good method, as when a person saves the life of a drowning swimmer who then commits several murders. Opposite actions can also be justified, too, as when two people are in a burning building and one rushes out so that she can survive to take care of her children and the other rushes further in to save some children who are trapped inside.

The analogy with ethics is far-reaching. We apply many of the same labels when evaluating actions and reasoning: careful, sloppy, reliable, clumsy, (in)accurate, (ir)responsible, effective, pointless, and so on. We have in everyday life standards and criteria for both the ways we act and the ways we form our beliefs. And in both cases there is a tension between those who want philosophical reflection to show how often we fail to meet appropriate standards, and those who want it to help us understand our success in meeting the standards we normally set.

4. The Basic Questions of the Theory of Knowledge

Philosophers contributing to the theory of knowledge have been trying to judge how good our beliefs are and how good they could be. They want to evaluate the beliefs we actually have and to suggest ways in which we could get better beliefs. These two aims are obviously connected: if a philosopher thinks that our beliefs are generally rational and true then he or she is less likely to suggest radical changes in the ways we get new beliefs, and if a philosopher thinks that our beliefs are a mass of confusion and falsity then he or she is likely to suggest either very different ways of getting new beliefs, or despair. So there are three central questions that the theory of knowledge tries to answer.

> What qualities should our beliefs have?
> What qualities do our actual present beliefs have?
> What qualities could our beliefs have?

The answers to the first question might seem obvious. We want our beliefs to be true, rational, and based on evidence. But suppose that a philosopher persuaded you that we are not capable of getting very many true beliefs; then you might settle for aiming at rationality rather than truth. Or suppose that a philosopher persuaded you that using reasoning to base beliefs on evidence will result in far fewer true beliefs than some other method, for example relying on the authority of some tradition. Then you might settle for aiming at true beliefs rather than beliefs based on evidence.

Nearly all philosophers want us to aim at both truth and rationality They do differ, though, on the relative importance of these and other good qualities of beliefs. (For more on this see chapter 5.) Philosophers divide, though, into what might be called conservative and radical camps on the question of how much better our beliefs could be than they are. In the early days of the scientific revolution philosophers were very optimistic about the possibilities for human knowledge. They proposed ways of basing beliefs on reason and evidence which they hoped would give beliefs which were both more rational and more often true. (Some of these ways are discussed in chapters 2, 3, and 4.) Many of these philosophers were looking for ways of using reason and evidence which would make it unnecessary to rely on faith or on tradition and authority. Earlier philosophers, and many philosophers writing in more recent times, are less prone to suggest radically new ways of obtaining beliefs. The most radical recent suggestions have tended to come from Bayesian epistemology, discussed in chapter 10.

5. Two Extreme Views

To see how different answers to the three questions above can be combined, consider two very extreme views, *deep skepticism* and *radical externalism*. (**Skepticism** – sometimes spelled "scepticism" – and **externalism** are standard terms in the theory of knowledge. I add the labels "deep" and "radical" to show that I am describing particular forms of these positions.)

Deep skepticism

This answers the question "What qualities should our beliefs have?" with "We should be able to give conclusive reasons which show that they are true." It answers the question "What qualities do our actual present beliefs have?" with "We cannot give conclusive reasons why they are true." And it answers the question "What qualities could our beliefs have?" with "Human beings are not capable of having beliefs which they can know to be true." Deep skepticism thus gives a very strongly pessimistic description of the possibilities for human knowledge; it suggests that we have no, or very little, knowledge. (It is thus a global skepticism, since it covers all of our beliefs. Some milder forms of skepticism might be less pessimistic, in particular they might be local rather than global, applying to just some of our beliefs. For example one might be a religious skeptic, claiming just that we cannot know which of our beliefs about God and immortality are true.)

What reasons might there be for deep skepticism? Here are three arguments for deep skepticism.

Mistakes in reasoning. Most of what we believe is based on evidence. For example we believe that some medicines cure some diseases by reasoning from evidence about particular people with those diseases. But it is easy to make mistakes in reasoning. One small mistake can make a whole chain of reasoning go wrong. One safeguard is to check our reasoning. But this is not really a safeguard as the checking is itself reasoning and can just as easily go wrong. Suppose that there were some profound flaw in the way human beings think. This would spoil all our reasoning, but since it would also spoil the reasoning we use to check our reasoning we would never know that our thinking had gone wrong.

Perceptual illusions. Very often things are not the way they seem. Often when we rely on seeing or hearing we form false beliefs. One reason for this is that there are many illusions: mirages, tricks of perspective and of light, ways in which the human visual system does not work perfectly. (These are discussed at greater length in chapter 2.) And then there are dreams and hallucinations, in which people often think they are perceiving things which do not even exist. We are aware of illusions and hallucinations because they contradict the rest of our experience. But that only means that small errors can be caught. Big errors, in which a large range of our perception is illusory, are much less likely to be caught. (In a dream you usually do not know you are dreaming.) So there could be illusions that permeate right through our perception, which we will never recognize as illusions.

Our poor track record. Humans have often been wrong in the past. We once thought that the earth was flat and now we think it is spherical. The ancient Greeks thought that matter was composed of atoms, and then science thought that it was continuously divisible like a fluid until in the late nineteenth century scientists began to believe in atoms again. Newton, in the eighteenth century, thought that light was composed of particles, but later scientists decided that it was composed of waves instead, until Einstein convinced the scientific world that there are light particles, photons. Any scientific theory will eventually be shown to be false. And the theory that succeeds it will also eventually be shown to be false. Yet scientific beliefs are the ones we have most reason to think true; if these beliefs are false then there is little hope for all our other beliefs. So we have reason to conclude that almost all our beliefs are false.

I shall not evaluate these three arguments. You should, though, consider seriously how convinced by them you are. (See questions 8 and 12 at the end of this chapter.) Instead, I shall describe a very different position, radical externalism.

Radical externalism

This answers the question "What qualities should our beliefs have?" with "Truth is the most important quality of beliefs; other features such as rationality are simply ways of making it more likely that a belief is true." It answers the question "What qualities do our actual present beliefs have?" with "Many of them, especially beliefs about the world around us, are true." And it answers the question "What qualities could our beliefs have?" with "There are many ways in which human beings, individually and in cooperation with one another, can be reliable sources of true information about their environment."

Here are three arguments for radical externalism.

Evolution. Human beings evolved in an environment not too different from the one we now inhabit. Our ancestors lived on the surface of this planet, dealing with objects of roughly the sizes and shapes that we now encounter. Our human and non-human ancestors were sensitive to the same frequencies of light and sound as us. If our senses and our ability to use the information we get from them were not generally accurate we would have died out thousands of years ago. But we are still here, a testimony to our ability to form true beliefs about our environment.

Intuition. When people defend their beliefs with conscious chains of reasoning which they express with words they make many mistakes. But in the course of everyday life we learn many routines of thinking which work well, especially if we do not stop to think about them. For example, people are pretty good at simple arithmetic, as long as it stays simple. (But if you ask a person to state the reasons *why* they believe that $340 - 89 = 251$ they are likely to give a confused and erroneous answer.) Moreover we have skills, such as the ability to find our way from one place to another or the ability to understand one another's moods and facial expressions, which we do not understand very well but which get us satisfactory results. We usually do not get lost on the way home and we usually understand when another person is angry with us. These everyday routines and skills are sources of beliefs, such as the belief that $340 - 89 = 251$, that to get home you must turn left at Elm Street, or that the person you are speaking to is on the verge of violent anger. Since our everyday lives depend on these beliefs and since our everyday lives work reasonably well, we can conclude that the routines and skills we use are fairly reliable sources of true beliefs.

Co-operation. People acting in groups can easily do many things that would be impossible for individual people. This applies not only to hunting and building houses but also to knowing. A member of a society can know information learned generations before and passed down from one person to another. Language is essential to this, and so is the disposition to trust what other people say unless there is some reason to disbelieve them. In modern time a lot of our beliefs depend on very complex networks of co-operation. For example, you believe that television sets pick up radio waves coming through the air, but you probably cannot give a good description of how they do this or even what radio waves really are. And you believe that antibiotics such as penicillin are effective against many bacterial diseases, but if you are like most people you do not have any good idea of how antibiotics are made or how they work against bacteria. But this information is available to you, via your links with other people: you can read books, ask for advice, and consult with experts. So the whole community in a way has a more complete knowledge of many things that individual people do not. Functioning as part of a community, trusting others so that they can put their different bits of information together, an individual person can have a reliable access to many true beliefs. Individual people can rarely have this knowledge using just their individual resources, and they usually cannot give a fully convincing explanation or justification of it. But that does not deny the fact that the beliefs are trustworthy and true.

Deep skepticism and radical externalism are very different views. But notice that they are not simple opposites. For they start from different answers to the first question "What qualities should our beliefs have?" Deep skepticism assumes that the most important quality of our beliefs is that we can be sure that they are true. It then tries to show that we cannot be sure that many of our beliefs are true. On the other hand, radical externalism assumes that the most important quality of our beliefs is just that they are true, whether or not we can be sure of it. (And whether or not the factors that make us capable of having true beliefs are ones we are aware of.) It then tries to show that many of our beliefs are true, even if we cannot be sure exactly which ones. Both deep skepticism and radical externalism may be wrong. But until we have decided which are the most important qualities for our beliefs to have, we should not feel that if one were to be right the other has to be wrong. Given the assumptions each one makes about the aims of belief, they could both be right.

Issues connected with deep skepticism and radical externalism will get more discussion in later chapters. (See especially chapters 5 and 7.) For now the important point is how answers to the three questions shape theories about knowledge. Do we want our ways of acquiring beliefs to produce true beliefs, rational beliefs, beliefs that are true and rational, beliefs that we can be sure are true and justified, or what? How much more true, more based on evidence, or more rational could the beliefs of human beings be? Which of these questions you find important will depend on whether your aim is to criticize beliefs, to find good ways of acquiring them, or to understand the ways we normally acquire them. But whatever the aim, before making elaborate theories it is a wise idea to ask what questions they are supposed to answer.

Reading Questions

(For the distinction between reading questions and thinking questions see the foreword for students.)

1   Section 1 mentioned constructive and destructive functions of the theory of knowledge. It also gave examples of searching for better ways of acquiring beliefs and of criticizing beliefs: which of these was the constructive function and which was the destructive function?

2   Section 2 gives examples of epistemic ideals. It then suggests that we should consider whether they can be achieved by human beings. How might the rationalist ideal not be achieved by human beings?

3   Section 3 claims that rational beliefs will tend not to be wide generalizations expressed with words like "all" and "never." Could we express any rational beliefs using these words?

4   Section 3 had a remark that we should not really say that a belief is rational but instead say that it is rational for a person to acquire a particular belief at a particular time in a particular way. Give an example of a belief that is rational for one person to acquire in one situation but not rational for another person to acquire in another situation.

5   Section 3 said that there can be very strong reasons for believing something although it is false. Give an example of this.

6   Consider the following four cases. (They are all Canadian cases, for no special reason.)

(a) Alberta is enjoying a rare warm break in a cold winter. It is January and she is in Calgary. She is about to travel to Edmonton, 250 km to the north, for a week. She thinks "I'll leave my winter coat behind; it's so nice today it's sure to stay warm."

(b) Victoria is waiting for the ferry from Vancouver to Nanaimo. She is wearing an expensive watch which has never gone wrong and which is reset every noon by a time signal from the British Columbia observatory. She looks at it and sees that it says noon. She thinks "It is noon, so I had better hurry to get the ferry."

(c) Arthur is waiting for the plane to take him from Thunder Bay to Winnipeg. He has a watch which works one day in three. He looks at it and thinks "It is noon, so I have plenty of time before the plane leaves."

(d) William is waiting for the plane to take him from Winnipeg to Thunder Bay. The airport clock says 11:42 a.m. and he thinks "The plane boards at 1 p.m. so I can spend fifteen minutes finishing my coffee and still have more than an hour before I have to be at the gate."

In which of these is the person's belief rational? In which is it justified? In which is it knowledge? Classify them into Yes, No, and Perhaps.

7 Section 4 said that if you thought that we were not capable of getting very many true beliefs; then you might want to have rationality rather than truth as your aim. It also said that you might want to have truth rather than evidence as your aim if you thought that basing beliefs on evidence would result in few true beliefs. Why?

8 In section 5 the second argument for deep skepticism said "We are aware of illusions and hallucinations because they contradict the rest of our experience. But that only means that small errors can be caught. Big errors, in which a large range of our perception is illusory, are much less likely to be caught." Why might someone think this?

9 The epistemic ideals described in section 2 were ones that scientifically minded people could accept: coherence, rationality, truth. But might there not be a price for having beliefs that are rational and aim at being true? Describe some advantages that might come from giving up on rationality and truth.

10 The first argument for radical externalism said "If our senses and our ability to use the information we get from them were not generally accurate we would have died out thousands of years ago." Why might someone think this?

Thinking Questions

11 Consider canny Cassie. She is a great guesser. She has hunches about which teams are going to win basketball or football games; she has intuitions sometimes that a news bulletin or a newspaper headline is false; she often has a conviction about unannounced schedule changes of television programs; and just occasionally she has a terrible foreboding of an impending disaster. We all experience these things; but Cassie is different in that her hunches, intuitions, convictions, and forebodings are nearly always right. When she has a belief about the future it is nearly always true. When she is asked about this she says "I don't know where my beliefs come from and I know no reason why they should be true. In fact, I don't expect that my beliefs about the future are any more reliable than other people's." But she is wrong: her guess-based beliefs are more reliable than other people's.

Suppose you are about to travel to New York by plane. Cassie says to you "Don't take that flight. I don't know why I feel this, but I really don't want you to take that flight." Is Cassie's belief rational? Suppose you take her seriously and believe that you shouldn't take the flight. Is your belief rational? Suppose that while taking Cassie seriously you continue to believe that no person can know the future. Is that belief then irrational?

12   Here is part of the first argument for deep skepticism. "Suppose there were some profound flaw in the way human beings think. This would spoil all our reasoning, but since it would also spoil the reasoning we use to check our reasoning we would never know that our thinking had gone wrong." Is it so clear that we could never tell if there was a flaw that affected all our reasoning? Suppose for example that people always estimate probabilities wrongly. Would we never notice this fact about ourselves? Might there be other kinds of problems about our reasoning which would be forever hidden from us?

13   Here is part of the first argument for radical externalism. "If our senses and our ability to use the information we get from them were not generally accurate we would have died out thousands of years ago." Is this true? Can you think of kinds of inaccurate perception which would not interfere with a species' survival? Might there be kinds of inaccurate perception which would actually increase the survival chances of a species?

14   Consider the ultimate virtual reality machine. It plugs into both your sensory and motor nerves and connects them to a hyper-powerful computer, which stimulates all your senses with exactly the input they would get from a real environment, and changes these stimulations exactly the way they would change if you were really moving your body while interacting with this real environment. Of course the environment the computer simulates is completely different from your actual environment. Suppose you had been in such a machine from birth. Would you have any reason to believe you were not living a real life in the environment you seem to find around you? Would your beliefs (for example that you are reading a philosophy book at this moment) be rational? How does this relate to deep skepticism?

15   How does the ultimate virtual reality scenario relate to radical externalism?

16   In section 3 rational beliefs were described in terms of the way a person acquires the belief at a particular time. Justified beliefs, on the other hand, were described in terms of the relation between the belief and the information on which it is based. Very often rational beliefs will be justified, and rationality and justification will coincide. But not always. Consider two examples. Neither of them makes an open-and-shut case, but discuss their implications for the relation between rationality and justification. (It is worth considering variations on the cases, or different ways of spelling out the details in them.)

   (a) Genevieve wants to know whether the coin in her hand is fair. (That is, whether there are equal chances of heads and of tails if it is tossed.) She tosses it four times and it comes down heads three times. A friend who has a Ph.D. in mathematics tells her that if the coin is fair there is a 2/16 chance that it will come down heads at least three times in four throws. She thinks that since this probability is pretty small the coin is probably biased. In fact her friend is wrong, and there is a 5/15 chance that a fair coin will come down heads at least three times in four throws. Is Genevieve's belief rational? Is it justified?

(b) Genevieve gives a dollar to an old tramp on the street. He gives her a long complicated rambling explanation of why the probability of two people giving him a dollar on a Tuesday is 0.00347. He looks like such a sweet old man that she believes him. In fact he is a once-brilliant mathematician who has had a nervous breakdown and his explanation is completely correct, though Genevieve did not understand it. Is Genevieve's belief rational? Is it justified?

17 Assume that an epistemological theory we may call "traditionalism" is true. According to traditionalism it is rational to hold a belief which many others in your culture believe and have believed, even if there is no strong evidence that it is true, as long as there is no strong evidence that it is false. (Take "strong evidence" to be evidence that would make it rational to hold the belief independently of the traditions of your culture.) Then, as in question 16, we have a way in which it might be rational to hold a belief even though you had no justification for believing it. It all depends on what you mean by "justified." Suppose that a person lives in a culture in which some religious beliefs are widely held. Suppose moreover that there is no direct evidence for the existence of God – no evidence that should convince a determined atheist – and there are no logical arguments proving the existence of God. Contrast the following two definitions of "justified."

(a) A person is justified in holding a belief B if she has evidence that would force anyone who had it to accept B or if she has a logical argument that leads from her present beliefs to B.

(b) A person is justified in holding a belief B if given her other beliefs it is rational to add B to them.

Assume that traditionalism is right. Describe in detail a person's beliefs and the person's situation (evidence, beliefs of other people, etc.) which would make that person's belief in God rational but not justified, according to (a) but not according to (b).

18 At the very end of the chapter we find the remark that different questions we ask about beliefs are related to different purposes in studying belief. Which of the questions listed in the last paragraph of the chapter are most relevant to the aim of criticizing beliefs? Which to improving belief-acquisition? Which to understanding it?

19 Gunther is taking part in a psychological experiment. The experimenters tell Gunther that they are giving him a powerful drug which will make all people look like his mother. Gunther believes them, although the "drug" they give him is actually pineapple juice. The point of the experiment is to test whether he will think that women look like his mother just because he expects them to. Gunther's mother is a telephone repair person and has been called to fix a telephone in the psychology department. By mistake she walks into the laboratory where Gunther is. "Hello mom" says Gunther, for a moment thinking it is his mother, before doubt sets in. Is Gunther's momentary belief that the woman in front of him is his mother justified? Does he know that it is his mother in front of him? (You might have noticed that I said nothing in this chapter about the relation between justification and knowledge. Chapter 6 takes up the question, and chapter 7 focuses on issues raised by this example.)

Further Reading

Accessible discussions of belief, reason, and the aims of the theory of knowledge are found in chapters one and two of Martin Hollis, *Invitation to Philosophy* (Blackwell, 1985), and in chapter one of W. V. Quine and Joseph Ullian *The Web of Belief* (Random House, 1978). Chapters 1 and 2 of Adam Morton, *Philosophy in Practice* (Blackwell, 1996) are also relevant. Chapter 1 of Jonathan Dancy, *An Introduction to Contemporary Epistemology* (Blackwell, 1985) begins with skepticism as a basis for covering some of the same ground as this chapter. Dancy is not an introductory book, though. Issues about how the aims of epistemology have changed during its history are discussed in Mary Tiles and Jim Tiles, *An Introduction to Historical Epistemology* (Blackwell, 1993). Fundamental distinctions between rational and justified beliefs are made and challenged in chapter one of Alvin Plantinga, *Warrant: The Current Debate* (Oxford University Press, 1993), which also discusses the resemblances between standards in morals and in epistemology. Relevant recent points of view are discussed in Michael Williams' "Skepticism," and Keith Lehrer's "Rationality" in John Greco and Ernest Sosa (eds), *The Blackwell Guide to Epistemology* (Blackwell, 1999).

Selections from classic philosophical works relevant to this chapter can be found in John Cottingham, *Western Philosophy: An anthology* (Blackwell, 1996). See part I section 7, David Hume, "Scepticism versus Human Nature," and part I section 10, G. E. Moore, "Against Scepticism." (These are Cottingham's titles, not Hume's and Moore's.)

Electronic resources: *Routledge Encyclopedia of Philosophy*: Epistemology; Epistemology, history of; Rational beliefs; Normative epistemology; Reasons for belief; Skepticism; Certainty; Doubt. *The Stanford Encyclopedia of Philosophy*: reasons; justification vs. explanation; skepticism.

Chapter 2

PERCEPTION

1. The Issues

We have knowledge of many things because we can see, hear, smell, or touch them. So any account of the ways we can and could acquire our beliefs must discuss perception, the use of our senses to learn things about the world around us. There are two central questions in the philosophy of perception. The first is "How do we obtain information about our environment by using our senses, and when is this information accurate?" The second is "What kind of evidence for or against our theories and beliefs can perception give?" These questions arise very naturally when one reflects on two observations. First, people's senses often deceive them and things are often not as they seem to be. Second, one of the marks of science and of responsible thinking is a careful use of facts gathered from unprejudiced observation. In fact, perception seems to be a very special and important source of information. Unreliable as it may sometimes be, it is what we rely on most.

Philosophers trying to answer these questions run into a very basic problem. To understand how reliable perception is we might begin by learning some facts about perception, learning how the eyes and ears work and what kinds of illusions affect them. And to understand how far evidence from perception can support theories about the world we might begin by seeing how perception is related to the world around us, to learn what range of facts connect with the visible spectrum of light reflecting into our eyes, sounds that we can hear entering our ears, and so on. But this seems to run round in a circle. To learn how the eyes and ears work we have to study them scientifically but why should we trust these scientific theories before we know whether the perceptions *they* are based on are reliable? And to learn how perception connects with the world we have to study the world scientifically: but why should we trust this scientific picture of the world? Suppose someone was tempted by the deep skepticism described in the previous chapter. That person might not find their doubts about whether perception gives knowledge answered by a philosophy that used information from perception to explain why perception is reliable.

Contemporary philosophers take this problem less seriously than philosophers in the past have. Since the middle of the twentieth century many philosophers have thought that they can use theories based on perception to study how beliefs can be based on perception, without going round in circles. One of the main purposes of this chapter is to explain why this is so. In doing this I shall describe a number of different philosophical theories of perception, in particular the theories associated with the philosophy of **empiricism**. Some of these theories allow themselves to use facts and theories from the psychology and physics of perception. Other theories, including more extreme forms of empiricism, want to base what they say just on what seems certain, on common sense, and on pure reasoning.

2. The Concepts

Perception is what happens when one becomes aware of objects and situations around one through the use of the senses, such as sight, hearing, and touch. We sometimes describe what someone perceives in *relational* terms. That is, we just say what object or event the person perceives; for example, we might say that someone sees a cat, and hears her, and touches her. Sometimes we also want to say what information about an object has been gathered in perception. We might say that someone hears the cat come in through a window, and sees that she has hurt her foot, and feels that there is a thorn in it. These descriptions are *propositional*; they involve propositions, assertions about what is perceived. It is important to note that we can also say things like "He sees that all his cats are asleep" in a situation in which someone does not get all the information at one glance, but gathers it bit by bit and then puts it all together mentally. One cat may be asleep on the rug, another on the bed, and the third on top of the refrigerator.

As a result, it is quite natural to use the vocabulary of perception, to talk of seeing and hearing and feeling, in cases that involve thinking and remembering as much as they involve the use of the senses. In extreme cases, as when one says that someone sees that torture is wrong or hears that Microsoft has dropped fifteen cents, it seems clear that the use of perceptual terms is purely "cognitive," that is, that it is the head rather than the eye or ear or skin that is doing the perceiving. But in many other cases, such as the example of the person who sees that his three cats are sleeping, it is not clear that we can make a distinction between the cognitive and the perceptual, between pure thinking and pure perceiving. Most perception seems to involve thought as well as the use of these senses.

If we describe a person's perception in propositional terms, we ascribe true beliefs to that person. The person who hears the cat come in through the window and then sees that she has hurt her foot, first believes that the cat is coming through the window and then that she has hurt her foot. When we describe someone's perceptions in relational terms we also assume that the person acquires beliefs about whatever is perceived. However some of the beliefs may be false. For example if a person sees a cat but thinks that it is a bowling ball it is still true that that person saw that cat. And even when we describe a perception propositionally we are not ruling out the possibility that false beliefs are acquired along with the true ones. To someone who sees that a cat is limping it may seem that it is the right front rather than the left front paw that is being favored, and this may be false. The person acquires the true belief that the cat is limping and the false belief that the right front paw is being favored.

The beliefs that are acquired as part of perceiving are called **perceptual beliefs**. There is not an exact line between perceptual beliefs and other beliefs, just as there is not an exact line between perceiving and thinking. But obviously some perceptual beliefs are nearer to pure perception. The belief that there is a gray shape in front of you is *more perceptual* than the belief that there is a cat nearby, which is itself more perceptual than the belief that your cat has come home. The second of these beliefs relies on additional non-perceptual background information, for example the belief that that is what cats look like, and the third belief relies on even more non-perceptual information, for example the belief that this is your cat. This does not mean that there must be completely perceptual beliefs.

Perceptual beliefs can be true or false. (In the examples above one person gets the true perceptual belief that there is a cat coming in through the window, and another the false perceptual belief that there is a bowling ball right in front of him.) The belief that the cat has hurt her foot is a borderline case of a perceptual belief, and the belief that cats are not bowling balls is not any sort of perceptual belief. False perceptual beliefs don't feel any different from true ones. If I look at my cat and I think that she is asleep, she may actually be waiting for me to pass by so she can sneak outside or she may be asleep. It *seems* the same to me in either case. We may also say that I receive the same *visual appearance* whether or not the cat is sleeping. The visual appearance is of the cat lying on the rug with her eyes closed and her legs folded under her and her nose tucked under the tip of her tail. In this case the visual appearance is true to the cat. (Or at any rate the part of it I have described is; we might go on to say that the appearance is, to me, one of a sleeping cat, and this part may be false.) However, visual appearances (also appearances from hearing, touch and other senses) may be quite unlike the facts. It may appear to me that off in the corner of my field of vision a curtain is moving, when actually my cat is tipclawing outside.

Appearances are a fundamental aspect of perception, for humans at any rate. When we see or hear, things look or sound one way or another; they have visual or auditory appearances. Almost every person experiences most of their waking life a rich variety of perceptual appearances from all the senses. Only some of the richness of perceptual appearance is captured in our perceptual beliefs. (To make this vivid: look at any scene you have seen a hundred times. Search and you will find some feature of it which you had not known was there – you had no belief about it – but which was part of the way the scene looked to you.) So appearance and belief are both basic aspects of perception. Yet the relation between them is not simple, as we shall see.

3. Empiricism

One of the most influential movements in the theory of knowledge, and perhaps one of the most influential movements in philosophy, is empiricism. Empiricism was developed by philosophers such as Locke, Berkeley, and Hume in the seventeenth and eighteenth centuries, and has contributed ideas that are still central to philosophy. The most important of these ideas is a picture of the way in which beliefs are justified. According to empiricism a belief is justified when it is connected by good reasoning to evidence obtained by perception. Moreover perception can give us beliefs that are certain enough that they can be the evidence for all beliefs that can be justified at all. (A possible exception is beliefs about mathematics and logic, which are not supported by any evidence at all.)

Empiricism can be seen as giving answers to central questions of the theory of knowledge, described in the last chapter. To the question "What qualities should our beliefs have?" it answers "They should be based on sure evidence obtained by perception." To the question "What qualities do our actual present beliefs have?" it answers "Many of them are not supported by adequate evidence. In many cases the evidence can be found, but in some there is no evidence and the beliefs should be abandoned." To the question "What qualities could our beliefs have?" it answers "We could, potentially, have only beliefs that are based on perceptual evidence." Empiricism is thus both a very down to earth and a very idealistic philosophy. It is down to earth because it aims to base all our beliefs on what we can see, hear, and touch. And it is idealistic because it thinks that human beings are capable of reforming their beliefs so that they are all based on perception.

A theory that gives such a central role to perception must be as clear as it can be about the nature of perception. The empiricist account of perception can be described in terms of the two central questions of the philosophy of perception, introduced in section 1 of this chapter. The first was "How do we obtain information about our environment by using our senses, and when is this information accurate?" According to empiricism when we use our senses we receive distinct units of information, which Locke and his followers called "ideas" but which more recent empiricists call "sense data." These sense data describe the shapes and colors that a person is seeing, the pitches and timbres that she is hearing, and so on. They correspond both to visual appearances (or appearances from other senses) and to beliefs that are as close to pure perception as beliefs can get.

The second basic question of the philosophy of perception was "How does perception provide us with evidence for or against our theories and beliefs?" According to empiricism the ultimate evidence for all our beliefs comes from sense data. There are two features of sense data that make them the ultimate evidence. First, there is nothing that can give evidence for them; they're at the end of the line in terms of evidence. And second, they are certain, they are evidence that cannot be doubted by the person who has it.

Both of these features are controversial, and later philosophers have attacked them energetically. But empiricists did have reasons for assuming them, which arise out of the ways it is natural to defend a belief if it is challenged. Suppose that you think that your cat is on the kitchen counter making "I want to be fed" noises. If someone doubts this belief you will give evidence for it. You might begin by saying "She was here on my lap a moment ago, and then I heard her footsteps going towards the kitchen." If you are challenged to say how you know she was on your lap you would say "But I saw her." Notice how when we give evidence for a belief we move towards describing what we have perceived. But suppose that your questioner still does not give up. "How do you know that you saw her?" "Well," you would say "it looked like her: I certainly saw a black and white cat-shaped figure." Notice how when your perceptual belief is challenged you defend it in terms of a more perceptual belief, and ultimately in terms of appearance, that is, in terms of the way things look or sound or feel to you. Sense data are the information you get from these beliefs, at the end of the line of justification, about your perceptual appearances.

There is a central insight here (which empiricists took over from Descartes). It is that your perceptual beliefs are more certain than your other beliefs, and that your beliefs about your perceptual appearances are more certain than your other perceptual beliefs. In short, you know for sure how things look, sound, and feel to you, and no other person's challenge is going to make you doubt that you are having the perceptual appearances you do have. So sense data are well suited to be the ultimate evidence, in terms of which all beliefs must be justified.

There are two other reasons why we might take perception to be a good source of evidence for beliefs. The first is that perception makes a fairly direct connection between a physical fact and a person. Light reflects off the cat into the person's eyes and causes cells in the retinas of the eyes to stimulate the optic nerve to transmit information to the brain. This process is complicated but reasonably reliable, and probably much less complicated than most of the other ways in which facts affect our thoughts. So it is natural to think of perception as a very basic way of discovering facts. (Note that although empiricists are no doubt influenced by this reason, it is one they have to be careful with, since for them the beliefs about the connection between facts and the brain are among the beliefs that they want to justify using evidence from sense data.)

The other reason to take perception as a source of evidence is that perceptual beliefs are relatively independent of other beliefs. If I come to think that my cat has been abducted by aliens then when I hear her coming in through the window I will think that it is some other cat, but I will still see that a cat is coming in, and she will still look the same way to me. The more perceptual a belief is the less it will be affected by changes in other beliefs. As a result, there is less danger of circular reasoning when using perception for evidence. There is less danger that someone challenging the evidence will be able to say that if you hadn't already held the belief you are finding evidence for you would not have held the belief you are using for evidence.

The appeal of empiricism as an epistemic ideal is clear. It offers us a picture of a wide range of beliefs, including common sense and science, all based on very firm evidence obtained by perception. (This is the appeal of a variety of epistemic ideals and theories, known as **foundationalism**. Foundationalism is discussed in chapter 5, especially section 2.) If we could meet the empiricist ideal we would be able to give reasons for all our beliefs, and though we might not be completely assured that all our beliefs were true, we would have pretty good assurance that they were as true as we can make them.

The appeal of the ideal is clear. But what is its price? And how near to achieving it can human beings come? Unfortunately, after some three hundred years of considering, refining, and arguing about empiricism the consensus among philosophers is that the full empiricist ideal would have a very high price, and is not an ideal that humans can come very near to achieving. There are two main reasons for this.

The first reason is the size of the task that empiricism, taken in its full-strength version, tries to tackle. The project is to show how all of our reasonable beliefs can be justified in terms of pure perception. This means all, so it includes such general and fundamental beliefs as the belief that there is a physical world which is the cause of one's perceptions, parts of which are the tables, cars, and stars that one perceives. And, whether or not they are part of the physical world, the existence of the minds of other people whose reports about the world are a major part of one's evidence about it, is also something that has to be justified. We don't normally look for reasons for these beliefs. We don't normally take seriously the possibility that the world might be an illusion or that other people might be robots. That is because we normally count such things among the evidence for other beliefs rather than things that themselves need supporting by evidence. But a hard core empiricist has to look for evidence for them. For the only evidence hard core empiricists allow is pure perception: sense data, the way things seem. And from the fact that it seems to you that there is a chair in front of you it does not follow that there actually is such a chair. For an empiricist the existence of the chair is a belief, a theory like the theory that there are black holes or electrons, something for which reasons have to be found.

(The problem of showing why it is reasonable to believe that the human beings you are surrounded by have minds like yours and experiences similar to yours is called the **other minds problem**. It is discussed in the first five sections of chapter 8. Note that the other minds problem makes the external world problem harder. For one of the sources of your beliefs in the external world, and in fact of almost all your beliefs, is what other people tell you. But if the words of other people are not the result of thoughts, information and knowledge held by the other people, then you should treat everything that people say to you with great suspicion. The danger is not that other people may be lying to you as much as that their words may not mean anything at all: what you take to be meaningful speech giving you information about the world might just be random sounds. In order to provide evidence for many of your beliefs empiricism would have to give evidence to show why you can rely on what other people tell you about past times, distant places, and experiences you have not had. For it is your links to other people's beliefs and experiences that provide you with most of the evidence you have for most of what you think you know.)

Describing the reasons for believing in the existence of chairs, stars, and cats, so that they sound like good ones, is extremely hard. At this point in this book, I cannot even begin to describe the possibilities, as we have not discussed the kinds of reasoning that lead from evidence to beliefs. (Chapter 4 begins to discuss them; in section 8 of that chapter I pick up the thread I am dropping now.) But to see how hard the task empiricists set themselves is consider the problems that the philosopher Descartes ran into. Descartes tried to assume only that he existed and to prove that his experience was not an illusion but was really the interaction of his mind with a physical world. (An over-simplified parody of his argument could consist of some not very convincing proofs that God exists followed by the claim that therefore God must have put him in a situation where by proper use of his intelligence he could discover the truth.) Very few modern readers are convinced by Descartes' argument. It seems to be full of hidden assumptions and circular reasoning.

The empiricist project is different from that of Descartes. Empiricists allow themselves evidence from the senses, and they do not have to prove their conclusions with certainty. While Descartes wanted to show that he could be sure beyond a doubt that whatever experience he would have he could use it to form beliefs about a physical world, empiricists need only a way of using the experience they actually have as evidence that makes it reasonable to conclude that there is a physical world. Different experience might not have led to this conclusion, and the conclusion need only be reasonable, not proved beyond doubt. But still, the project is extremely daunting. The reason is the size of the gap between the evidence and the conclusion. The kind of evidence from perceptions that empiricism wants, remember, consists of pure perceptual beliefs which do not assume anything except what is purely perceptual. Not the evidence that a cat has come into the room but the evidence that it looks as if a specific round fuzzy shape has covered up some other sharper-edged shapes. From lots of evidence like this it has to be reasonable to conclude that there are cats and rooms, and indeed three-dimensional space, as part of a whole universe of objects completely independent of one's experience.

The evidence seems to be a pretty feeble basis for the conclusion. Suppose that you had just this evidence and no idea of the conclusion you were supposed to arrive at. Would you be inclined to think that experience is caused by a world of physical objects in space and time, rather than being a complex pattern of shapes and colors, or a dream, or a show put on by forces you could not understand? Supposing that you could come up with the "right" explanation, would you be able to find good reasons why it was more likely than the alternatives? (Suppose you had no idea what a movie was, and went into a movie theatre. Would you have any idea of the true nature of what you were seeing? Suppose you were told that you were not seeing real people and objects on screen. Would you have any confidence in any alternative explanations you came up with?) One way of seeing how doubtful it is that the answers to any of these questions are Yes is to reflect on how similar the reasoning would have to be to difficult scientific thinking. In science we often explain the behavior of everyday objects by making theories about very different objects – electrons, genes, black holes – which cause the everyday objects to behave as they do. (Why does the light bulb shine? Because electrons flow through the filament and cause electrons in its atoms to shift orbits, releasing energy as photons, which we see as light.) It is extremely hard to test scientific theories and to know which are the best ones to accept. We certainly are not sure that the theories we now accept are the right ones. The empiricist reasoning from sense data to the physical world would be very similar. We would start not with the behavior of everyday objects but with sense data, and to explain facts about them we would suppose facts about completely different objects: tables, chairs, the earth, the sun, cats, and so on. The reasoning would be just as difficult as in the case of science, we would be just as uncertain that we had got the right answer, and there would inevitably be alternatives to any explanation which it would be very hard to rule out.

The second reason why the empiricist aim of basing all our beliefs on the purest possible perceptual evidence is now considered unworkable concerns the evidence, sense data. Remember that the point of sense data is that they are to represent only what is perceived, with no influence of any belief that the perception might be used as evidence for. So if I see a cat the sense data that I get must be consistent with any possible cause of the situation I am in: hallucination, illusion, fake cat, or real one. This forces sense data to be just records of the way colors and shapes are arranged in a person's visual field, the way pitches and timbres are arranged in hearing, and so on. Now people do have visual fields on which colors and shapes play, and people do hear pitches and timbres as well as violins and howling wolves. But hard core empiricism requires that these sense data be a basis from which a person can reason to recover most of her beliefs. (The ones that she cannot recover are candidates for being abandoned.) So they have to be beliefs, or something like beliefs: when a person sees a cat she has to be able to think "there are shapes and colors of a C-kind, so I conclude that there is a small feline animal approaching me." In describing the basic perceptual belief here I have left the essential content vague, just saying "of a C-kind." But the actual belief would have to fill out exactly what shapes and colors of a C-kind were. And whenever philosophers try to describe how we might do this they fail. (That's a fact, and it may just reflect philosophers' lack of ingenuity or imagination, but it does suggest that it may just be impossible to fill in the specification adequately.) There is no doubt that our perceptual experience has an enormous richness, and that in this richness there is information from which many conclusions can be drawn, but it does not follow from this that we can use this to describe beliefs about pure experience that have the right kind of content to make them evidence for our other beliefs.

You may still find it plausible that most of our everyday beliefs can be justified in terms of sense data. So it may help to separate two ideas: one is clearly true and one is extremely dubious, but it is easy to confuse them with one another. The clearly true claim is that if we take all the sensations that a person has – all the stimuli falling on their sense organs – and describe them as a long list of facts, then among the reasonable explanations of this list there will be the actual physical facts that caused those sensations. The presence of the cat is among the possible causes of your having cat sensations. But note what this does not say. It does not say that this long list of facts is something that any person could use in any kind of reasoning. It does not say that the list describes the way that the scene seems perceptually to the person. And it does not say that the actual physical facts will be alone, or even have any special position among, the reasonable explanations of the list. The world as it is causes and explains our sensations; this does not mean that anything like sensations is sufficient evidence for our beliefs about the world.

4. Some Experiments

We can get some more insight into why the empiricist ideal is difficult to attain by considering some facts about perception. In this section I summarize five psychological experiments which suggest interesting conclusions about appearance in visual perception.

Experiment 1: seeing as

In figure 1 there is a drawing of a duck. Look at it. It is easy to see the duck in the drawing.

Actually, the picture can also be seen as a rabbit (see the duck's beak as the rabbit's ears). If this paragraph had begun by saying "Figure 1 is a picture of a rabbit," you would have seen it as a rabbit when you first looked at it.

The picture does not look the same when it is seen as a duck and when it is seen as a rabbit. One thing this shows is that some visual impressions are not determined by the image on the retina of a person's eyes (since the image on the retinas, the sensitive regions at the back of the eyes, is the same when a person sees a duck in the drawing as when the person sees a rabbit in it). It also shows that some visual appearances cannot be completely described in a simple geometrical way, as the distribution of light and dark points in space. For in these terms too there is no difference between the duck-appearance and the rabbit-appearance. A visual appearance is not a picture. (It is perhaps a picture plus some sort of explanation of the picture.)

This experiment also shows that our expectations influence how what we see appears to us.

Experiment 2: perspective

In this experiment subjects observe circles from various angles. They are asked to draw the visual impressions that they have of these circles seen at these angles. (They are asked to draw what they look like, not what they think they are.) Some subjects draw all the circles as circles except those which are seen at extremely great angles. Other subjects draw all the circles as ellipses except those which are seen at extremely small angles. But all subjects draw less eccentric (more circular) ellipses than those which the corresponding circles will throw on their retinas. Moreover, the less sophisticated subjects, especially those with less knowledge of psychology or of perspective drawing, draw the rounder ellipses, and the more sophis-

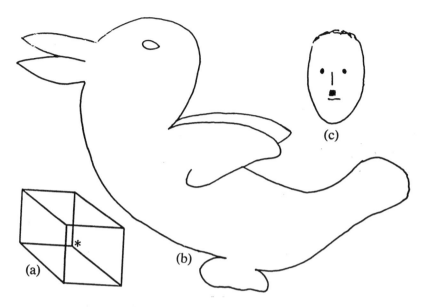

Figure 1. Pictures that change their meaning. The duck-rabbit (b) is particularly striking, because it is perfectly placed between two kinds of examples (a and c). At one extreme is the reversing cube (a), which can be seen two ways, each of which represents a different geometrical configuration – is the starred corner at the front or the back? At the other extreme are figures that vary in terms of their expressive meaning; (c) looks like Charlie Chaplin or like Hitler. The duck-rabbit shares with examples like (c) the feature that its changes of meaning are not simply changes of the geometrical figure it represents, and shares with examples like (a) the feature that its meanings clearly differ in what it is seen as, and not in the way one reacts to it. It is thus ideally suited to illustrate the moral: appearances are not uninterpreted pictures.

ticated subjects draw the flatter ones. But even the most sophisticated subjects do not draw the ellipses as flat as they should have been according to the rules of true perspective drawing, or as they should have been if their visual appearances corresponded to the images on their retinas.

The conclusion here is that people's beliefs about a situation, in this case the belief that the figures are circular, influence their perception of it. We make the appearance resemble the way we think the reality is. (The conclusion can be resisted, see thinking question 16.)

Experiment 3: the upside down world

Subjects spend a period of days, or sometimes weeks, wearing glasses which turn the image upside down. At first it looks as if everything is upside down:

the sky is beneath and the earth above. Then there is a fascinating transitional period in which some things at some times appear inverted, and some things do not. Finally the subject says that things look normal: the sky seems above and the earth beneath. Then the subject takes off the glasses and everything seems upside down again!

This is an intriguing experiment, and hard to draw firm conclusions from. It certainly shows that a person's visual impression of the world is not just a matter of the input from their sense organs. It suggests also that the input from the sense organs determines the visual impression, in a way that depends in part on the beliefs and tendencies to behavior that they produce. Thus as long as subjects had not learned to use their senses to guide their actions when they were wearing the glasses they had an upside down impression, but when they had learned how to get around wearing the glasses and manipulate objects properly then the world stood on its feet again. There is a lot more that can be said about this experiment, and others like it; more detailed descriptions and analyses of them are well worth reading. (For one thing, it is not perfectly clear how the world does appear to someone who has got used to the inverting spectacles; I have glossed some things over.)

Experiment 4: wise babies

Modern technology allows us to make observations of young babies that would have been impossible not long ago. One recent technique is to monitor babies' eye movements to see what features of their environments they dwell on. It then turns out that even very young babies do a surprising amount of structured looking. They tend to look much more at unexpected objects and situations than at expected or familiar ones. In one experiment infants as young as two and a half months watch a ball roll behind a screen which is then lifted revealing the ball at rest at an end wall. Then when they are familiar with this they see two kinds of event. In one, the "possible" event, a box is placed in the path of the ball, the screen is lowered, the ball rolls, and the screen is raised revealing the ball at rest by the box. In the other, the "impossible" event, a box is placed in the path of the ball, the screen is lowered, the ball rolls, and the screen is raised revealing the ball at rest by the end wall, as if it had passed through the box. Infants looked longer at the impossible event, suggesting that it was surprising, and thus that at the age of two and a half months they are on the way to thinking of the world as containing solid objects which can not pass through one another. The important fact here is how young the children are: it is as if some information about the structure of the physical world is not derived from sense-data but implicit in the structure of the visual system.

Experiment 5: blindsight

People sometimes become blind as a result of damage to the visual areas of their brains. A very small number of people who have this kind of damage have capacities which make it very hard to classify them as either simply blind or simply sighted. They think of themselves as blind, because they are not aware of seeing anything. The world looks to them as it does to a blind person: they have no consciousness of any colors or shapes or the location of any objects. Suppose such a person is facing a screen on which bright dots are projected. They are asked to say where the dots are, and they protest that they cannot, since they cannot see the dots or anything else. The experimenter insists however that they guess by pointing in a direction every time a dot is projected. Then to the person's amazement, they very often point in the direction of the dot. In fact, although they make mistakes they perform at much better than chance. In some sense they know where the dots are, although they are not aware of having any visual sensations at all.

Some of the visual pathways in the brains of these people seem not to have been damaged, with the result that visual information about the location of events is available for them to act on. It is however not available to consciousness. So although the person can learn to form beliefs that could be described as perceptual (they think "the dot is 45 degrees to the left" because that is where they are inclined to point), they have no visual appearances. Their perceptual beliefs are not linked to ways the world seems visually or looks to them.

5. Evidence without Certainty

Empiricism, at least in the traditional form in which it was described in section 3, gave us no good account of how perceptual beliefs are justified. It led us into a swampy maze. The five experiments I have just described suggest why. They suggest that empiricism makes a false assumption about perceptual appearances. In assuming that all our perceptual beliefs can be based on sense data empiricism supposes that when we perceive something we first start with information about appearances and then use this as evidence for a belief about what we are perceiving and what it is like. These experiments, and others described in the psychology of perception, suggest that this is wrong.

The experiments do not suggest that there is nothing to the notion of an appearance, for they rely on subjects being able to describe how things look to them, and express in other ways what visual impressions they have. If we take appearances to be specifications of how the world looks, sounds, and so on, to people – which they report when asked about their impressions –

then there clearly are appearances. But what the experiments suggest about visual, and presumably other, appearances is that they are not purely collections of information gathered by the senses, and that perceptual beliefs are not obtained solely by reasoning from them. For the way a person's environment appears to the person at any moment depends also on that person's previous state, their beliefs and desires and habits, just as the acquisition of perceptual beliefs does. For example, in the first experiment (seeing as) the figure looks like a duck or like a rabbit depending on what the person looking at it believes they are going to see. In the second experiment (perspective) people represent the appearance of what they are seeing in ways that make them more like the shapes they know the things they are seeing really have. And in the third example (upside down world) the appearance that information from the senses leads to is shaped in part by the practical purposes the information is going to be used for. Experiment 4 (wise babies) suggests that we arrive at the outlines of some beliefs about how things really are so early in life that they are in effect shaping our perceptions from the very beginning. And experiment 5 (blindsight) suggest that with some people information gathered by the senses has no connection with appearance. It thus makes it more likely that in all people some sensory information, perhaps information vital to our beliefs and actions, does not show up as appearance.

Perception thus begins with sensory inputs or patterns of stimulation, which are probably not beliefs of any kind, and by combining these with beliefs that the person already has makes perceptual beliefs *and also appearances*. Appearances are not produced at the boundary of the mind; they are produced by a complex interaction of sensory input and pre-existing belief. They are thus not very well suited for the role of ultimate basic evidence since they depend on beliefs themselves. To people with different beliefs the same things will appear different, so the appearances cannot always provide impartial evidence to settle their differences.

There are several possible reactions to this situation. The empiricist ideal of absolutely certain evidence based on the sense data of individual people which will give good reasons for our beliefs is impossible. So we could try for a less demanding ideal. We could want evidence that was less than certain. We could want evidence based on something other than perceptual appearances. We could want perceptual evidence that gave reasons for less than all our beliefs. Nearly all contemporary philosophical theories of knowledge retreat from the full empiricist ideal in all these ways, to a greater or lesser degree. Before asking exactly how much we should retreat in each way we should remember the point made in chapter 1, that there may be many different qualities we want our beliefs to have, and it is far from clear that a single ideal can meet them all. Do we want beliefs that are completely beyond doubt, or beliefs that fit neatly with scientific knowledge, or beliefs that we can use in everyday life? Beliefs that a community of people can use for their combined scientific and practical projects, or beliefs that a single person can use to gain as much knowledge as she can all by herself? Different kinds of perceptual evidence may be right for these different purposes.

Behind the details of empiricism there was a vaguer ideal, of holding beliefs because they are supported by evidence that can be seen, heard, or otherwise sensed. The nearer we can get to this ideal the more confident we can be that we are not holding beliefs just because we have been taught them in childhood, or because they are written in textbooks, or because other people believe them. How much of this vaguer ideal could remain if we retreat from full-strength empiricism? How much can we expect our beliefs to be shaped by our perceptions, if we accept that how we interpret our perceptions – how things seem to us and what perceptual beliefs we form – is always going to be influenced by the beliefs we already hold? To see how different from the official empiricist account of perception this can be consider two further conclusions.

First, *evidence arises in context*. The evidence on which scientific theories are based is rarely absolutely certain. For example the chief source of evidence for theories in astronomy is observations made through telescopes. Astronomers try to make these as carefully as they can, and to make as few unnecessary assumptions as possible when describing their observations. But they are not totally certain. When an astronomer says that she has seen a new star appear at given co-ordinates in the sky it is always just possible that she has instead seen some optical malfunction of the telescope, or has been hallucinating, or that some activity by extra-terrestrials has caused a bright light to appear at the appropriate spot in the sky but much nearer the earth than it appears to her. And even when the evidence takes the form of a photograph of the light collected by the telescope a lot of interpretation has to be added before the photo can be used as evidence. Is this really the film that was at the telescope's focus at the time in question? What direction was the telescope pointed when the light was collected? Which marks on the film represent light focused down the telescope and which represent either light from other sources or effects of the film's development? Were atmospheric conditions above the telescope distorting the paths of light rays to it? All these questions can be answered if there seems to be serious doubt about them. But answering them usually involves other sophisticated equipment and other not completely certain observations.

The point is that in science the technique for finding evidence is to use unusual situations and complex experimental apparatus to find tell-tale effects of natural processes. Doubts about the evidence are resolved by other evidence and other experiments. This will not answer all possible doubts. It is not meant to; usually in science some particular theory has to be defended against doubters who support some other particular theory, and the evidence has to be chosen so that both of these sides can take it seriously, but not so that non-scientists or skeptical philosophers will be impressed. So if astronomers are debating the origins of quasars they need evidence that will be interpreted in the same way by astronomers who believe in steady state and big bang theories of the origin or the universe, who believe in different theories of the evolution of stars, the distribution of mass in the universe, and so on. But they do not have to worry what doubts or inter-pretations will occur to mystics who believe that the stars are angels dancing around the earth with messages for mankind, or to skeptics who suspect that telescopes produce images of things that do not exist.

This is very different from the technique suggested by empiricism, which aims to qualify the content of observations until they could not be doubted by anyone, no matter how little they know or what other beliefs they hold. The ultimate certain evidence, according to empiricism, is not "there is a supernova at time t at co-ordinates r, θ" or "there is a bright event at t, r, θ" but "it seems to astronomer p that at time t she saw a bright light at what she thought was location r, θ, and which she assumed to be produced by light from beyond the earth." When you appreciate the difference between this kind of evidence and the evidence that is actually used in science you cannot feel very optimistic for the empiricist aim of basing all our beliefs, particularly scientific ones, on absolutely certain sense data.

The second way in which living up to the empiricist ideal in practice tends against official empiricist doctrine can be summed up as *more certainty means weaker evidence*. That is, if we try to make evidence completely certain we find that we can support our beliefs less well. Suppose that you are an empiricist and you take the best evidence to be your sense data, information about how things look, sound, or feel to you. You want to use this evidence to support beliefs about the world around you, beliefs such as the belief that you are on the surface of planet earth, occupying a human body and sur-rounded by other humans. On the way to these beliefs or as a consequence of them you will want to find evidence for the belief that there is a physical world around you which causes your sense data by stimulating your senses. But very basic beliefs like these are not easy to justify in terms of sense data. In effect, it is not easy for an empiricist to show why the deep skepticism discussed in section 5 of chapter 1 is not right. By asking that all beliefs be supported by absolutely certain evidence empiricism may be guaranteeing that very few beliefs will be supported.

6. What is Special about Perception?

If we pay attention only to what is over-stated in empiricism we are likely to lose the sense that there is anything special about perception as a source of beliefs. But that would be a mistake; perception is clearly our most useful and reliable source of information about the world. My own explanation of the central importance of perception traces it to two facts: direct causal linkage and conscious awareness. Let me explain. (Not all philosophers would agree with all of this.)

Direct causal linkage consists in the simple effects that many kinds of events in our environment have on our perceptions. A blue bird flies in front of us and we see blue, it sings and we hear high notes. Sometimes the linkage amounts to tracking: as an object changes location or a note changes pitch our perceptions change accordingly. By saying that the effects are simple I do not mean that the process that leads from something happening to a person's perceiving it is simple. These are complex processes that evolved over millions of years in order to represent the environment accurately. I mean just that we can state simple rules to sum up the patterns, such as "If there is a blue object right in front of a person in normal light and the person is looking then usually they will see the object as blue." Moreover the direct and simple connection is aided by the limited effect that beliefs can have on perception. Although, as experiments 1 and 2 show, what you believe can affect what you perceive, there are definite limits to this. No amount of persuasion that a red object is blue will make it look blue when seen under good conditions; many perceptual illusions work just as well on people who know that they are illusions. (One aspect to the resistance of perception to belief is that the richness of perceptual states goes beyond the stock of concepts that enter into our beliefs. Some philosophers express this by saying that perception requires "non-conceptual contents." Where perception and belief do not mesh it is harder for either to influence the other.) Although this limited responsiveness to belief means that we cannot fine-tune our perceptions to avoid some persistent illusions, it also means that perception can give us truthful surprises. You may expect the litmus paper to turn blue, but when it turns pink you know that the experiment is producing an unexpected result.

But perceptual processes are not infallible, there are many little gaps and slips and perhaps some large systematic biases. These are compensated for by conscious awareness, the fact that when we perceive we are usually consciously aware of how things seem to us. (Usually, not always, as experiment 5 shows.) As a result, when we acquire beliefs by perception we often know that we are perceiving, which sense we are using, and what kind of a sensory experience we are having. To see the importance of this consider an imaginary intuitive capacity by which a person might just come to have beliefs about, for example, when their loved ones were in danger. A person with this capacity would just find herself thinking "Mother is in trouble," and accepting it as a fact. If the capacity was not infallible, the result would be that very often false beliefs were acquired and integrated into the person's stock of beliefs without their having any chance to check them. With perception, on the other hand, when one acquires a belief one typically knows that one is doing so, because one is conscious of the appearance presented to one, and thus has the opportunity to check or hesitate. One can consider whether this is a situation in which this kind of perception is not reliable, and one can consider whether there is some other way of interpreting what one is seeing. ("What, a pink elephant dancing on the roof of the car? Can't be, look again.") The difference in content between perceptual states and beliefs is an advantage in this. For what one is consciously aware of – the way things seem – is easily distinguished from the beliefs that one may be tempted to derive from the situation.

If this is correct, empiricism was right to stress the importance of appearance in perception. But empiricism was wrong to think that the importance is a matter of certainty, of the impossibility of being wrong about how things appear to one. The importance is instead a matter of checkability: because one knows when and how one is perceiving one is able to control, check, and delay the acquisition of perceptual beliefs. Because perception is accompanied by appearance we can – to some extent – accept or reject the beliefs that it suggests to us.

Reading Questions

1   Suppose that I write a book in which I say "everyone should believe anything that Adam Morton says." The book has other surprising claims in it too. Someone doubts whether the book is a trustworthy source of information and another person says "the answer to that question is in the book too: in chapter 1 it says you should believe what it says." What is the problem here, and how does it relate to the issues in section 1?

2   Which of the following beliefs are more perceptual and which are less perceptual?
    (a) A blind person's belief that grass is green.
    (b) A person's sudden realization that another person is very angry.
    (c) An experienced hunter's belief that there are moose droppings at his feet.
    (d) A musician's belief that her instrument needs tuning.

3   Why might beliefs about mathematics and logic be exceptions to the empiricist claim that all beliefs are based on perception?

4   Which of the following is nearer to being a report of a person's sense data?
    (a) I see a moose.
    (b) I am experiencing a shape in front of me with a central brown region and below it four vertical regions and above it a head-shaped region connected to yellow-grey spreading areas.
    (c) It smells like moose.

5   Consider the example in section 5 of doubts about the interpretation of photographic evidence in astronomy. One doubt was whether the image in the film was caused by light coming down the telescope. How might this doubt be resolved, and how would this require other equipment and other observations?

6 Why is there a problem for empiricism from the fact that, as section 3 expresses it, your links to other people's beliefs and experiences provide you with most of the evidence you have for most of what you think you know? You hear what people say and you see what they write: is this not empirical evidence?

7 Why is it important in experiment 1 that if the description had begun by saying "Figure 1 is a picture of a rabbit," you would have seen it as a rabbit when you first looked at it?

8 Why does experiment 3 show that a person's visual impression of the world is not just a matter of the input from their sense organs?

9 Why might the conclusion of experiment 4 be difficult for an empiricist to accept?

10 (a) "You may expect the litmus paper to turn blue, but when it turns pink you know that the experiment is producing an unexpected result."

   (b) "One can consider whether this is a situation in which this kind of perception is not reliable, and one can consider whether there is some other way of interpreting what one is seeing. ('What, a pink elephant dancing on the roof of the car? Can't be, look again'.)"

   How can these both be true?

Thinking Questions

11 In section 2 a person sees a cat and thinks it is a bowling ball. How wrong could you be about something and still be perceiving it? Suppose that someone thinks that the black spot at the edge of her visual field is a floater in her eye, when actually it is the image of her cat in the half-light. Is she seeing her cat? Suppose that there is a row of identical buttons along the top of a chair and placed among them is the nose of a cat hiding on the far side of the chair, the only part of her that is visible. A person sees the row of buttons and takes the nose to be simply another button. Does he see the cat?

12 Some beliefs are more perceptual than others. But, according to section 2, there do not have to be completely perceptual beliefs. Supposing that there are not infinitely many beliefs, does not every person have to have some beliefs that are their most perceptual beliefs? And are these not then completely perceptual for that person?

13 Is it true that your beliefs about what things look like are more certain than your beliefs about how things really are? Consider this story. A bank employee catches a very brief glimpse of the face of a robber. He cannot give the police any usable description of what the robber looked like. A week later he sees a woman for an instant through closing elevator doors. He knows that she was the robber he saw. But again he cannot give any definite description of what she looks like.

14 Is it true that you know for sure how things look, sound, and feel to you? Consider these possible counterexamples.

   (a) A person wonders why he finds a portrait in a gallery disturbing. It looks to him both attractive and angry. In fact the portrait closely resembles his mother, to whom he has a very complicated attitude. He does not know what it looks like to him.

(b) A person goes into a restaurant and has the best meal of her life. She tries to reproduce the special taste of that meal at home. But she finds she cannot because although she remembers the meal very vividly she does not really know what it tasted like.

(c) A person is trying to describe a singer's voice. "She has a very high soprano" she says. "No" someone else says, "it is not high; its just squeaky. You don't know what it sounds like."

15   See the film *The Matrix*. What alternative hypotheses to account for the patterns in our sense data does it suggest?

16   The conclusion drawn from the second experiment is that we make the appearance resemble the way we think the reality is. Describe some alternative interpretations of the experiment that block this conclusion. (Suppose for example that the link between sense-data and the way people describe their experience is more complex.)

17   The conclusion drawn from the fourth experiment is that two-and-a-half-month-old babies are on the way to thinking of the world as containing solid objects which can not pass through one another. Describe an alternative interpretation of the experiment that blocks this conclusion.

18   The example of the astronomical observations depended on the fact that astronomy uses complicated equipment such as telescopes. Can similar points be made for sciences, such as field biology, which do not need sophisticated equipment?

19   Suppose that, as argued in section 5, evidence in science does not refer to the experience of particular people. Could an empiricist still argue that scientific evidence is only valid when it is based on the experience of particular experimenters? After all, each experiment is performed by a particular person at a particular time, and the report of the experiment depends on what that person experienced.

20   Section 5 suggests three retreats from the empiricist ideal. We could look for (a) evidence that was less than certain or (b) evidence based on something other than perceptual appearances or (c) perceptual evidence that gave reasons for less than all our beliefs. And it also suggests that we might associate these retreats with the search for (i) beliefs that are completely beyond doubt, or (ii) beliefs that fit neatly with scientific knowledge, or (iii) beliefs that we can use in everyday life? Which of (a), (b), (c) would be a suitable means for getting beliefs of which of the kinds (i), (ii), (iii)?

21   Section 5 also suggests that we could look for (1) beliefs that a community of people can use for their combined scientific and practical projects, or (2) beliefs that a single person can use to gain as much knowledge as she can all by herself. Which of (a), (b), (c), described in the previous question, are suitable means for getting beliefs of kinds (1) and (2)?

22   The last section of the chapter argues that the fact that perception is normally accompanied by appearance allows us to block perceptual beliefs when we know that they are illusory. How could we come to know this, except by perception? Perception is being used to regulate perception. Can this be a safe way to procede?

Further Reading

A very readable introduction to issues about perception, covering both philosophical and psychological theories, is Robert Schwartz, *Vision* (Blackwell, 1994). There is a very simple discussion of the philosophy of perception in chapter 9 of Adam Morton, *Philosophy in Practice* (Blackwell, 1995), which focuses on empiricism. A good collection of philosophical papers on perception is Jonathan Dancy (ed.), *Perceptual Concepts* (Oxford University Press, 1988); the papers by Lewis, Dretske, Armstrong, and Grice are most likely to be helpful to a non-advanced student. Chapters 10 and 11 of Jonathan Dancy, *An Introduction to Contemporary Epistemology* (Blackwell, 1985) discuss perception from a more advanced level than this book. Recent work is summarized in William Alston, "Perceptual knowledge" in John Greco and Ernest Sosa (eds), *The Blackwell Guide to Epistemology* (Blackwell, 1999).

Accessible texts in the psychology of perception are Lloyd Kaufman, *Sight and Mind* (Oxford University Press, 1974) and Irvin Rock, *Introduction to Perception* (Macmillan, 1975). Iona Rock, *Introduction to Perception* (Open University Press, 1978) is an extremely clear and helpful exposition in two short volumes. Experiments on the perceptual skills of small children are described in chapter 3 of J. Gavin Bremner, *Infancy* (Blackwell, second edition 1994).

Two stimulating books on the overlap between philosophy, psychology, and art theory are Richard Gregory, *Eye and Brain* (McGraw Hill, 1966) and E. H. Gombrich, *Art and Illusion* (Pantheon Books, 1960).

For the views on perception of the British empiricists see David Hume, *An Inquiry Concerning Human Understanding*, chapters 2, 3, 7, 12, and John Locke, *An Essay Concerning Human Understanding*, books I and II. For discussions of the empiricists see Roger Woolhouse, *The Empiricists* (Oxford University Press, 1988), chapter 10 sections A and B of John Cottingham, *Rationalism* (Oxford University Press, 1988), Barry Stroud, *Hume* (Routledge, 1988), and chapters 6 and 10 of Jonathan Dancy, *An Introduction to Contemporary Epistemology* (Blackwell, 1985).

Selections from classic philosophical works relevant to this chapter can be found in John Cottingham, *Western Philosophy: An anthology* (Blackwell Publishers, 1996). See part I section 3, Aristotle, "Demonstrative Knowledge and its Starting-points," and part I section 5, John Locke, "The Senses as the Basis of Knowledge."

Electronic resources: *Routledge Encyclopedia of Philosophy*: Empiricism; Perception, epistemic issues in; Phenomenalism. *The Stanford Encyclopedia of Philosophy*: perception; perception, epistemological problems of; qualia; sense-data.

Chapter 3

APRIORI BELIEFS

1. Knowledge Just by Thinking

Suppose you have three kittens and two baskets, and you are going to put some of the kittens in one basket and some in the other. How many ways are there of doing this? You could find out by trying all the ways and counting them. Or you could find out by thinking. You could reason as follows: Consider the first kitten, it could go in either the right basket or the left one. That gives two ways of starting. Each of them can be continued by putting the second kitten in either the right basket or the left basket. So that makes two times two or four ways of going on. Then the third kitten can be put in either the right basket or the left one, giving four times two or eight ways of distributing the kittens between the baskets.

This could be a fact about three particular real kittens and two particular real baskets. And you can see that it is true without having to collect evidence. You know in advance, prior to any evidence, what the answer has to be. Philosophers refer to knowledge that we can have in advance of any evidence as **apriori** knowledge. ("*A priori*" is the standard term. It comes from Latin words meaning prior to the evidence. Students find the term confusing since it sounds like it is talking about a thing called a priori. So this book will join a small trend of writing "apriori" as one word.) The opposite of apriori knowledge is **aposteriori** knowledge, knowledge which can only be gained after, posterior to, seeing the evidence. (Traditionally two words, "a posteriori.") Mathematics, as in the mini-proof about the kittens and the baskets, is one of the main sources of apriori knowledge. Or, to put it more carefully, mathematics gives many examples that philosophers use when explaining their theories about apriori knowledge. But there are many examples which do not come from mathematics.

Suppose for example that someone tells you that they have a moose in their pocket. You find this hard to believe, and challenge them to produce it. They reach into their pocket and bring out a pebble. When the person claims that this is a very unusual moose you are more than skeptical. You know the person must be either joking, or lying, or crazy, or mean something very different by the word "moose." You do not need to consider any further evidence to know that a small piece of stone cannot be a large mammal. If you did not know things like that you would not be able to understand any evidence.

Or suppose that you are mixing some paint in order to decorate a friend's kitchen. She is very particular about colors, and so you show her the yellow shade you plan to use. She says to you "It's not red enough yet." You go to mix in some more red paint and by mistake mix in blue. So the result is a greenish yellow instead of an orangeish yellow. You apologize but she says "No, that's great, the more blue you put in the more orange it gets." Here too you know immediately that something is drastically wrong with what she is saying: a yellow colored object cannot get redder (more orange) and bluer (more green) at the same time. Either this person is not serious or they are very confused.

Notice that in both these examples although there was a belief which did not need to be supported by evidence, someone could have got the belief from considering evidence. Someone could just notice that when you mix paint it never gets more orange and more green at the same time. And although it is harder to imagine how someone could just notice that moose never happen to be stones, someone could go around collecting evidence that moose are never pebbles. (They could, but it would be a waste of time.) Evidence might also help one to get the concepts of orange, green, and moose, to understand what these things are so that one can then know – apparently without evidence – that more orange means less green and that moose are not pebbles. So apriori beliefs are beliefs that *can* be acquired without evidence from experience, once one understands well enough what they are about.

The issues here are in a way the opposite of those of the previous chapter. One main question there was "How many of our beliefs can we base on evidence from what we perceive?" The contrasting question here is "How many of our beliefs can we base on reasoning rather than on evidence from perception?" This chapter discusses some ideas about beliefs based on reasoning, involving the concepts of **apriori**, **analytic**, and **necessary** beliefs. These ideas have a long history in philosophy, and contemporary philosophy is profoundly influenced by challenges to traditional views of them begun by W. V. Quine. The chapter ends with a conclusion that some of the traditional ideas survive the challenge, though with very significant changes.

2. Apriori, Analytic, Necessary

There are different ways in which a belief can be independent of perceptual evidence and it is important not to confuse them. Apriori knowledge has already been mentioned. Consider now two similar but different kinds of belief.

Analyticity

Consider again the moose example of the previous section. You know that a moose is not a stone just because you know that "moose" means "large North American mammal of the deer family" and you know that no stones are large mammals of the deer family. (A complete definition of "moose" would have to say more: this is only part of the meaning of "moose.") So you can know that a moose is not a stone just by understanding the meaning of the words you use. Philosophers have considered many similar examples. "All bachelors are unmarried," "All sisters are female," "Your mother's mother is your grandmother" are all examples that have been suggested. In all of these it is hard to see how someone can doubt the belief as long as they understand what the words mean. All of these are **analytic** beliefs. (The sentences that express them are called analytic truths, or analytic propositions.) Analytic beliefs are apriori, because knowing how to speak a language makes it unnecessary to consider evidence for them. (Beliefs that are not analytic are called **synthetic**.) In the next section we consider whether all apriori beliefs are analytic, or whether some are synthetic.

A special case of analyticity is **logical truth**. Suppose you believe that it will either rain or snow and that it will not snow, but you do not believe that it will rain. Then there is something very wrong with your beliefs, because anyone who understands the meaning of the words "and," "not," and "or" knows that if it will either rain or snow and it will not snow then it will rain. This is not a fact about the weather but about logic. There are many similar examples. You can know that either all moose are chipmunks or there is a moose that is not a chipmunk, without ever having seen a moose or a chipmunk. In all these cases knowing the meaning of a few words, "logical" words such as "and," "not," "or," and "all," allows you to know that very many beliefs must be true.

Another way of approaching logical truths is through the idea of a **deductively valid argument**. Consider the following argument: It will either rain or it will snow; and it will not snow; therefore it will rain. Logicians call arguments like this "deductively valid"; their defining feature is that the conclusion of the argument ("it will rain") will always be true if the premises ("it will rain or it will snow," "it will not snow") are true. In fact, not only will it always be true that it will rain, given that it is true that it will either rain or snow and also true that it will not snow, any other argument of the same general form will work the same way. "I have either left my car keys in my jacket pocket or they are in the fridge. They are not in my jacket pocket. Therefore they are in the fridge." is an equally valid argument. Any argument of the form "*p* or *q*; not *q*, therefore *p*" will lead reliably to a true conclusion ("*p*") as long as the two premises ("*p* or *q*," "not *q*") are true.

There are many forms of deductively valid argument. Another is "If all As are Bs; all Bs are Cs; therefore all As are Cs." Logicians study the many forms of deductively valid argument. For each deductively valid argument there is a special belief, a logical truth. "If it will either rain or snow and will not snow then it will rain," "if all cats eat mice and all mice are rodents then all cats eat rodents." Indeed, since each deductively valid argument is just one of a whole family of arguments with the same form, logical truths also come in whole classes. "If I have either left my car keys in my jacket pocket or they are in the fridge, and they are not in my jacket pocket, then they are in the fridge." "If all philosophers are boring and all boring people are stupid, then all philosophers are stupid."

The result of the link between logical truths and deductively valid argument is that as long as a person can understand deductively valid arguments they can know that logical truths are true. As long as you can reason from the assumptions "All cats eat mice and all mice are rodents" to the conclusion that "All cats eat rodents" you know that if all cats eat mice and all mice are rodents then all cats eat rodents. So to know logical truths we can rely, it seems, not on evidence but just on our ability to reason and argue.

Both analytic beliefs and apriori beliefs are often connected with the concept of **necessity**. This is not a central concept in the theory of knowledge, but it is worth saying something about it since issues about apriori knowledge are closely connected to issues about necesssity. Necessary beliefs are beliefs that not only are true but have to be true. They could not have been false. (Notice that the discussion of the moose example in section 1 said that you know that a small piece of stone *cannot* be a large mammal, and the discussion of the paint example said that something *cannot* get redder and bluer at the same time.) Many beliefs that are known apriori are also necessary. It is necessary that $2 + 2 = 4$ or that a set with three members has eight subsets. However the universe had been, from the very beginning, it could not have developed so that $2 + 2$ was anything other than four, or that moose were pebbles, or red was blue.

It is very easy to get confused here, though. When we say "Without consulting the evidence you can know that $2 + 2$ has to be 4" we can mean two things. We can mean that we *have to think* that $2 + 2 = 4$, or we can mean that $2 + 2$ *has to be* 4. These are only the same if the things that we have to think are things that could not have been false. And there are good reasons for doubting that this is so. Consider two examples.

The first example needs a single person who is known by two names, such as the writer Mark Twain (author of *Huckleberry Finn*) who was originally known as Samuel Clemens. Mark Twain could have lived a different life so that he was never given the name "Samuel Clemens." But that person, Mark

Twain, could not have ever been different from himself, Samuel Clemens. So the belief that Mark Twain is the same person as Samuel Clemens is necessary; the fact that it refers to could not have been otherwise. But it is not apriori; it is something that we have to learn, on the basis of evidence. (In fact, we could learn that all the books are wrong in saying that Mark Twain was Samuel Clemens.) So necessary truths are not all apriori.

Just as not all necessary truths are apriori, not all apriori truths need be necessary. Or, at any rate, this can be argued quite strongly. First suppose that human beings come with an inbuilt idea of space which makes us think, without considering the evidence, that space has three dimensions and is organized in the way it is (so that, for example, if a region A is contained within a region B and region B is contained within region C, then C is *not* contained within A). Suppose now that although space is like this, it does not have to be. Perhaps events within the first millisecond after the big bang determined that space would have three dimensions and the kind of organization it does have, but if those events had occurred differently then space would have been different. Then our beliefs about space are apriori but not necessary.

Another example comes from Descartes. Suppose that Descartes, wondering whether he could be wrong even about his own existence, reassures himself by reasoning "I'm wondering about this, so I am thinking, so I exist." He can know just by thinking, without any evidence from perception, that he exists. So his belief that he exists is apriori. (It is apriori for him. *My* belief that Descartes existed is not apriori.) But it is certainly not necessary. Descartes could easily not have existed. (Or consider the belief "I am here." That is apriori in that I know in advance that here is where I am. But I could easily not have been here, but on the beach instead.)

There are also analytic beliefs that are not necessary. Here is a simple though rather artificial example. Define the word "pouce" to mean "the length of my thumb today, July 8, 2002." Then it is analytic that my thumb is one pouce long today. But it is not necessary: my thumb could easily have been a bit shorter, because of malnutrition or some accident.

Neither of these arguments, the argument that some apriori truths are not necessary nor the argument that some necessary truths are not apriori, is accepted by all philosophers. There are some objections to them worth thinking seriously about. But they do show that it is not at all obvious that "apriori" and "necessary" mark the same property of beliefs. Later in this chapter we will have to wonder what the connection is between a belief being apriori and its being true.

3. Kant on the Synthetic Apriori

All analytic beliefs are apriori. But what about the other way round? One reason for thinking that all apriori beliefs are analytic comes from thinking, as empiricists do, that evidence from perception is the main source of knowledge. For suppose that we make the empiricist assumption that what perception does is to link our minds to the facts in the world that our beliefs are about, through the experiences that are evidence for those beliefs. Then it follows that no beliefs about anything in the world are apriori. For all of these beliefs depend on evidence from perception. The only apriori beliefs then can be beliefs that are not about anything in the world. Suppose that the only thing that beliefs can be about except the world around us is the meanings that we give to words in our minds. Then it follows that apriori beliefs are based on the meanings of words, that is, are analytic.

This argument makes several big assumptions. It assumes that the only reasons we have for beliefs about the world come from perception. And it assumes that all beliefs are either about the world or based entirely on meanings. Neither of these assumptions is very convincing. (But this does not have to mean that the conclusion – that all apriori beliefs are analytic – is false. There might be a stronger argument for it.) To see how we might challenge these assumptions and the conclusion they lead to, consider three examples of beliefs which some philosophers have thought were apriori but not analytic.

First consider beliefs about color, such as the belief that as a yellow color gets more reddish it cannot also get more bluish. Or the belief that if something is red it is not green. It is hard to see why these have to follow from the meaning of color words. The belief that green is a color might follow from the meaning of "green" and "color," but the fact that when a yellow object becomes more orange it becomes less greenish seems to be just a fact about colors. Yet it is a fact that we can know without considering any evidence. As long as we know what colors are we know that it is true. Or so some philosophers have argued.

Next consider beliefs about mathematics. A good example is the belief that there are infinitely many natural numbers, that the series 1, 2, 3, 4, . . . goes on for ever. (Or, another way of expressing it, that for every natural number there is another one which is greater than it.) If we know that arithmetic is true we know that this belief is true. But it is hard to see how it is part of the meaning of the word "number." However you define "number" it does not seem to follow that there are infinitely many of them.

Thirdly, consider beliefs about cause and effect. Suppose that some person thought that there was never a reason why things happened. One billiard ball rolls into another and the second starts moving, he thinks, just for no reason, the fact that it is immediately after the collision being a pure coincidence. Plants that get no water die, but he just thinks: Some plants die and some do not, there's no reason. If we ask this person to investigate why something happened, he does not even understand the question. Perhaps such a person could collect basic evidence from perception, though it is hard to see how he could survive long enough to perceive anything interesting, but he could not use the evidence to support or refute any beliefs about why events occur, since he does not think any such beliefs could be true. This points to the importance of beliefs about causes: beliefs that there are causes to be discovered in the world, that very often something that happens does so because of some other event, and that we can learn the connections between causes and their effects by considering evidence about them. These seem to be beliefs that we have to have before we start considering evidence about the causes of particular events.

None of these examples is completely convincing. Philosophers who believe that only analytic beliefs are apriori can find replies to them. But they do make the beginning of a case for non-analytic apriori beliefs. What is needed to make the case stronger is a general pattern which would show what the examples have in common. One such general pattern is described in the work of Immanuel Kant (1724–1804), especially in his *Critique of Pure Reason*. Kant pointed out that collecting evidence for or against our beliefs is something that itself needs to be guided by beliefs. For example, someone who had no beliefs about distances in space would not be able to begin to use a telescope, or interpret what she saw through it. And someone who had no beliefs about numbers and counting would not be able to make or use any measurements, and so would be unable to understand almost all scientific experiments. So, Kant reasoned, behind our ability to collect evidence through perception for our beliefs there must be a body of fixed beliefs, which we have to assume in order to get the enterprise of finding and interpreting evidence started. Kant called these beliefs *synthetic apriori*.

Kant's own list of synthetic apriori beliefs included arithmetic and geometry, the belief that events have causes, the belief that there are laws of nature that we can discover, and the belief that people and physical objects persist through time. We can see how these explain the examples about cause and arithmetic at the beginning of this section. It is not so clear how they fit the example about colors. One way of fitting that example into Kant's picture would be to argue that if we are to describe the endless variety of colors and shades in the world with a few fixed terms like "red" and "green" then we will have to think in terms of degrees of red and green (and other colors) so that we can capture all the in-between shades. But to do this we will have to relate the colors into a single structure, which means making assumptions like "more red is less green." So here too the same Kantian idea can apply: before we can begin to describe the world we have to make some assumptions.

Kant had a lot more to say about the assumptions we must make before we can begin to describe and understand the world. The central problem that he tried to answer was why these assumptions should be true. Why should the fact that we have to have some beliefs before we can begin to collect and consider evidence give us any confidence that these beliefs are true? His answer was that they are true because we make them be. (So he was inventing a kind of idealism: he thought that the mind makes some aspects of the world) They are not true because of the way the world around us is, but because of the way our minds are. Some later philosophers have thought that this was a very deep insight into the relation between thought and reality. Others have thought that it was mistaken. The important point for us is the claim, accepted by most philosophers now, that without some prior beliefs we could not even begin to describe what we perceive. We have to have some beliefs before we consider evidence.

4. Quine on the Analytic/Synthetic Distinction

W. V. Quine, writing in the 1960s, made a claim that at first seems the opposite of Kant's. Yet when we consider Quine's full position, it turns out not to be so very different from Kant's. Quine's claim was that there is no fundamental difference between analytic and synthetic beliefs. No belief, according to Quine, is true simply because of the meaning of words. All beliefs are true because of the way the world is and the meaning words have, and we cannot separate these two components.

Consider some standard examples of analytic beliefs: the belief that all bachelors are unmarried, the belief that cats are animals, or the belief that people are born before they die. If these really were a special kind of beliefs, argues Quine, it would be impossible to find any evidence against them. But in fact we can imagine circumstances in which we might even begin to doubt whether they were true. Suppose, for example, that a sect of mad fanatics insist that all females over the age of 16 must be married. If they discover that any woman is not married they kill her. In order to prevent this, every young woman at the age of 16 marries a young man of the same age. This is not a "real" marriage; the couple do not live together or act as man and wife, and when either of them wants a "real" marriage with someone else they divorce and begin relationships more like marriage as we know it. Suppose now that young men in their twenties, looking for young women to share their lives with, describe themselves as "bachelors" if they are only married in this 16-year-old fanatic-forestalling way. It would then be very natural to call these men married bachelors.

Someone might argue against this as follows: "bachelor" means "unmarried man," so if we ever come to think that there are married bachelors we have simply changed the meaning of the words. Quine has a reply to this. There are many definitions we could give for "bachelor" that fit the way we use the word equally well. For example we could define it as "man who is not in a relationship with a woman which late twentieth-century people would think of as marriage." The differences between these definitions do not matter for us, but they would be significant differences for the people in the situation described. To think that we can tell definitely when a word's meaning has changed is the same kind of mistake, according to Quine, as to think that there is a definite distinction between analytic and synthetic beliefs.

It is important to see that Quine is not claiming that any belief can be abandoned at any time. To abandon the belief that bachelors are unmarried, or even to be in a position to think there might be evidence against it, we would have to be in a very different position than we are now. The example two paragraphs above describes one such very different position. So Quine is not denying that it is reasonable to treat the standard examples of analytic beliefs as if they were apriori, believing them without considering evidence from perception and using them when we consider evidence for other beliefs. He is just pointing out that the situation may change so that it no longer makes sense to treat some of them as apriori.

One particular kind of change of situation is particularly important, on Quine's way of thinking. That is change of our beliefs. Quine emphasizes that beliefs are linked to one another in a vast network, which he calls the "web of belief." For example, the belief that the earth is round is linked to the beliefs that compasses point north, to the belief that light travels in straight lines, to the belief that the same sun rises every day, and to many others. To consider evidence for or against any of these we would have to take the others into account, either assuming them or at the same time considering whether the evidence told for or against them also. In this web of beliefs some beliefs are nearer the edge and some are nearer the center. Perceptual beliefs are nearer the edge in that they are linked very much to experience and comparatively little to other beliefs. These beliefs are fairly easy to change given new evidence. Other beliefs are nearer the center in that they are linked very much to other beliefs and only very indirectly, thorough long chains of other beliefs, to perception. These beliefs change very slowly as we get new evidence: they are insulated from evidence by the beliefs that surround them. Moreover they can rarely be refuted by contrary evidence since instead of abandoning such a belief we can nearly always instead abandon some other belief to which it is linked. (For example instead of abandoning the belief that bachelors are unmarried the people in the story above we could instead have abandoned the belief that everyone who had gone through a marriage ceremony was married.)

5. Conceptual Truths

Quine's conclusions and Kant's are different in an obvious way. Quine is saying that no belief is safe: it might be reasonable to abandon absolutely anything we believe; while Kant is saying that some specific beliefs have to be maintained in order to make any sense of our experience. But underneath this difference there are important ways in which Kant and Quine agree. Both philosophies agree that we cannot make sense of what we perceive without some beliefs that interpret and link perception to thought. So both break with the empiricist idea that we can get evidence for and against our beliefs simply by describing our experience. And both agree that it is structured patterns of beliefs rather than single beliefs that allow us to think, consider evidence, and explain the world around us. In the long run these similarities are more important than this difference.

One difference is very important though. Kant's conclusion was that there are beliefs that everyone must have in order to make sense of their experiences, while Quine's conclusion was that that everyone must have some beliefs that are at the center of their web of belief. To translate Kant into Quine's terms, he is saying that there are beliefs that must always be at the center of the web of belief, while Quine is saying only that there must always be a center, though different beliefs can be there. There are many subtle connections between these two positions, but both agree that for any person at any time the web of belief will always have a center. There will always be beliefs that the person needs to make sense of what they perceive, and which are not for that person at that time supported or challenged by any evidence. So in what follows I shall follow out the consequences of this weaker conclusion.

At this point it is important to distinguish concepts from beliefs. In order to have a belief you need to have the concepts involved in it: to believe that cats eat mice you have to have the concepts of "cat," "mouse," and "eat"; to believe that no moose weighs more than six tons you have to have the concepts of "moose," "weight," "six," and "more than." Nearly all simple apriori beliefs can be used as tests for having concepts. If you think that orange is more blue than yellow you do not have the color concepts that the rest of us have. If you think that cats are a kind of pebble then something is unusual about your concept of cat or of pebble. (Note that these tests come by combining simple apriori beliefs: the belief that orange is redder than yellow; the belief that as a color gets more red it gets less blue; the belief that cats are animals; the belief that animals are not stone; the belief that pebbles are stone.)

So the web of beliefs is also a web of concepts. When someone has a belief, for example that cats are generally smaller than moose, they will also have other beliefs involving the concepts involved in it which give the beliefs meaning and allow there to be evidence for and against it. So the beliefs that cats are small carnivores and that moose are large herbivores allow explanations of why cats are smaller than moose, and beliefs about what cats and moose look like allow everyday perceptions of cats and – if you're lucky – moose to give evidence for the belief. A well-functioning web of beliefs will link all of its beliefs both with perception and with apriori beliefs, the first to provide evidence and the second to provide clarity.

There are many ways to have a well-functioning web of beliefs. Empiricism suggests that we should have a stock of concepts which are specifically for gathering evidence from perception. Call these **experiential concepts**; they would include concepts like those of color and shape and sound. These would provide evidence for beliefs involving **theoretical concepts** with which we explain and understand the world. Concepts such as those of mass, energy, gene, virus, and the structure of space and time would be theoretical concepts.

Most concepts are not purely theoretical or purely experiential. For example, one aspect of concepts of animal species, like the concepts of cat, moose, and fish, consists in their links with perception, since we know what cats, moose, and fish look like. But another aspect is theoretical, since we think of these animals as fitting into a complex system of classifying living creatures. As a result of this second aspect we do not think that everything that looks like a cat, a moose, or a fish really is one. There are fake moose, and it may not be easy to tell just by looking. And not everything that has fins and swims in the water is a fish. Whales and scuba divers are mammals and not fish. In our contemporary system of beliefs and concepts almost all concepts are linked both to perception and to theories.

One result of the two-way linkage of most concepts is that the beliefs that give us our understanding of concepts – the apriori beliefs – often change. Only a few centuries ago the concept of a fish was so closely linked to having fins and swimming in the water that whales were thought of as fish. Now we connect the concept of a fish to being cold-blooded, having gills, and being related to other fish by a common evolutionary history. So we do not think that whales are fish. While it may once have been an apriori belief that anything that has fins and spends most of its life underwater is a fish, now we think that this is false. A clear example of this occurs when someone introduces a new word for a specific concept. Suppose that I invent the word "infoCD" and define it as "Compact Disk with a computer program on it." Then the belief that infoCDs have computer programs on them is an apriori belief *when the concept is first introduced.* But after that other people may use the concept for their own purposes, the web of belief takes over, and anything can happen. Perhaps all the infoCDs have information stored on them in a different way to music CDs, and this is the same way as CDs with information that is not in the form of programs. So then people may take this as the defining characteristic and it may no longer be apriori that infoCDs have computer programs. Or perhaps we cease to think of all programmable digital devices as computers, so that the very objects I originally named as infoCDs are no longer used to program what we then think of as computers. The important conclusion is this: *we always have apriori beliefs, but at different times we treat different beliefs as apriori.*

6. The Uses of Reasoning

This chapter began with a mathematical example. It was meant to support the idea that simply by reasoning we can know facts. That question led us to a discussion of apriori knowledge which focused on beliefs which are needed in order to have particular concepts, beliefs without which we would not be able to communicate or consider evidence. Most of these beliefs were pretty simple, bordering on the trivial. This might make them uninteresting. But to think this would be to ignore one of the most basic and amazing features of human thought. That is, by reasoning from trivial assumptions we can get to non-trivial conclusions. In fact, we can often get to non-trivial conclusions surprisingly quickly. Among the many ways we can reason from the trivial to the amazing, three stand out. Call them destruction, exploration, and accumulation.

Destruction

Often a philosopher takes assumptions which, at the time she is writing, would be accepted by everyone as being so obvious that anyone who doubted them must be joking or confused, and from these assumptions derives very surprising conclusions. Very often the conclusion is something that is hard to believe, so that the result is a paradox. For example, the ancient Greek philosopher Zeno started with simple assumptions such as "in order to move from one point to another you have to pass through all the points in between" and "between any two points there is another point" and came to the paradoxical conclusion that motion is impossible. (Zeno's argument ran as follows. To get from A to B one will have to pass through the halfway point – call it h_1 – between A and B, and then through the point – call it h_2 – halfway between h_1 and B, and then through h_3 halfway between h_2 and B. And so on: one will have to pass through infinitely many points to get from A to B, however near they are. And one will have to do this in a finite amount of time. But passing infinitely many points in a finite amount of time, Zeno thought, was clearly impossible.)

Paradoxical conclusions like this can be used to argue that something is wrong with the apriori beliefs that they assume. Obvious though they may seem, a little reasoning shows that some of them may be false. But when it begins to seem that apriori beliefs are false we begin to loose our grasp of the concepts involved in them. For the philosopher who says that, for example, perhaps you can move from one point to another without passing through all the points in between, is a bit like the fool or the confused person who simply does not have the concepts needed to grasp this belief, and does not understand what "point" or "move" mean. With an important difference, though. The philosopher is usually trying to show that there is something wrong with the concepts she is making trouble for. She is in effect saying "If this is what we mean by 'motion' and 'space' (for example) then we should consider using other concepts instead." So within philosophy one important purpose of reasoning from apriori beliefs is to show problems and limitations of our concepts. The effect is not only destructive; very often the aim is to get clearer or better concepts, which will be linked to different sets of apriori beliefs.

Exploration

Sometimes we think something is obvious when a little reflection shows that it is not. Sometimes we think that anyone who has a particular belief must be confused and then a little reflection shows that the belief is not so confused after all. For example you might think it was obvious that the fairest way of dividing food or other goods between people is to give each person an equal share. Then you might think a bit further and wonder whether this was fair when some people had more to start with, or when some people would get more satisfaction from their share while others would have no interest in it. (Suppose that two tourists fresh from their luxury hotel are walking in the desert and meet a starving man who has not had food or drink for two days. They propose to split an orange three ways. Is this fair?) As a result you might try to formulate a more subtle definition of fairness, in terms of the situations of the people before the distribution and the benefits they would get from it. In doing this you would be formulating new apriori beliefs to define the concept of fairness. But they would not be entirely new. You would probably be trying to find beliefs that you and others had implicitly held all along, without being able to express them clearly. This too is a major philosophical activity, to find better ways of articulating beliefs which lie behind the concepts that we use all the time.

Accumulation

Instead of generating paradoxes or digging out implicit beliefs, reasoning can begin with apriori beliefs and lead to more apriori beliefs. Much of mathematics is like this. We can begin with assumptions so obvious that they seem completely uninteresting, like "$0 + 1 = 1$" and "for every number there is another distinct number which is greater than it by one," and by deducing consequences from them we get to completely unexpected interesting conclusions, such as that to add up a sequence of consecutive numbers you can ignore all but the first and the last (since the sum of the whole sequence is the first plus the last, multiplied by the number of members in the sequence and divided by two). The remarkable thing about mathematics is that when we deduce consequences from apparently apriori beliefs in this way we do not very often get paradoxes or find we have to dig out further implicit beliefs. At any rate this happens less often in mathematics than in the rest of our beliefs. Although paradoxes and problems about what assumptions are the right ones do crop up regularly, mathematicians seem to be able to handle them in such a way that the body of mathematical theorems keeps accumulating. Philosophers disagree about the best explanation of this. Some point to the special non-perceptual intuitions that are used in mathematics, whereby we can "see" numbers and geometrical structures in our minds and reason about them. Some point to the rigorous nature of proofs in mathematics. Some point to the place of mathematics in the web of belief, as central as any beliefs could be. None of these explanations is completely convincing.

Reading Questions

1   Which of the following beliefs are apriori beliefs and which are aposteriori (all Australian beliefs, for no particular reason):
    (a) Australia is bigger than New Zealand.
    (b) Australia is in the southern hemisphere.
    (c) If you have two koalas and three kangaroos, you have five animals.
    (d) If Perth is west of Adelaide and Adelaide is west of Sydney then Perth is west of Sydney.
    (e) Perth is west of Sydney.
2   Which of the following beliefs are analytic, which are logical truths, and which are necessary:
    (a) Kangaroos carry their babies in their pouches.
    (b) Kangaroos live in Australia.
    (c) Kangaroos are mammals.
    (d) If George is the brother of Sam and Sam is the father of Frederika, then George is the uncle of Frederika.
    (e) If George is the uncle of Frederika and George is a kangaroo, then Frederika is a kangaroo.
3   Kant thought that "There are infinitely many numbers" does not follow just from the meaning of the word "number." Consider the following definition of "number": the number of any set of things is the result you get when you count them. Say why this claim of Kant's is plausible if we use this definition. Is it obvious that this is the right definition?
4   Tell a story in which people come to abandon the belief that "cats are animals" (similar to the story in section 4 in which people come to abandon the belief that bachelors are unmarried).
5   Near the beginning of section 5, Kant's and Quine's positions were contrasted by saying that Kant claims that there are beliefs that must always be at the

center of the web of belief, while Quine claims that there must always be a center, though different beliefs can be at the center. Which of the four claims below is a restatement of Kant's position and which is a restatement of Quine's?

(a) Given a person and a time, there must be beliefs which are at the center of that person's web of belief at that time.

(b) There are beliefs which at any time are at the center of the web of belief of any person.

(c) Given a person and a time, there must be beliefs which are not only at the center of that person's beliefs but of any other person's too.

(d) There are beliefs which are at the center of any person's web of belief at a given time, and given a different time or a different person there are beliefs which are at the center of the web for that person and that time too.

6   Which of the following are experiential concepts, which are theoretical concepts, and which are not clearly either: middle C, pain, causation, evolution, democracy, television, electro-magnetic radiation, triangular.

7   Suppose that a philosopher is arguing that the right action for any person at any time is the one that causes the greatest amount of happiness for that same person. Suppose that she argues for this by arguing that concepts of duty and obligation to others lead to conclusions we do not want to accept, such as that each person should give all their money to famine relief. To what extent is her project best described as destruction, exploration, or accumulation?

Thinking Questions

8   In section 1 it was claimed that if someone says that a pebble is a moose they must be joking, lying, crazy, or mean something very different by "moose." Describe a situation in which a pebble could really be a moose. Suppose we came to think that this situation could actually occur, what other beliefs (besides "No moose is a pebble") would we have to abandon?

9   To explain Kant's idea of synthetic apriori beliefs three examples were used. The example about colors is in several ways unlike the other two. Suppose that you are watching a sunset and have no words for colors but a good understanding of physics. How will your description of what you see differ from the description a person with a normal color vocabulary might give? How will your explanation of what is happening be different? How does this relate to the example in the text?

10   There is an example near the beginning of section 3 of a person who believes that there is never a reason why anything happens. The opposite of such a person is one who believes that for every event there is a cause which determines that exactly that event and no other has to happen. To the first person there is no regularity or system to the world; to the second person the world seems completely regulated by cause and effect. In section 3 it was argued that the first person would have such trouble understanding the world that they would not be able to gather or understand evidence that might show them they were wrong. But what about the second person. Might she not be locked into a mistake too? Consider how such a person might gather and consider evidence

about coincidences (such as finding that four people at a party have the same birthday) or (if you have enough knowledge of them) about random physical events such as radio-active decay. What problems might come from the second person's convictions?

11   To support his picture of the web of belief Quine uses an argument from the French philosopher Duhem. Duhem argued that evidence never shows conclusively that any belief is true or false, since there is always some other belief that can be accepted or refuted instead. For example if you believe that the earth is flat you do not have to abandon your belief when you learn of people flying due west and eventually returning to their starting point. Instead you could conclude that following a compass does not lead to traveling in a straight line, or that at the western edge of the world there is a mirage of the eastern edge and a hyper-fast air current that takes one eastward. This idea can be used to argue that any belief could be abandoned, too. Suppose that we discover that the things we take to be cats are the fruits of a kind of fungus that flourishes in cat-litter trays. We could use this as evidence for either (a) cats are not animals, or (b) some animals are fungi. What *other* beliefs might we have to consider abandoning in deciding to accept either (a) or (b)?

12   Section 5 said that nearly all simple apriori beliefs can be used as tests for having concepts. To see why only simple apriori beliefs can be used this way, give some examples in which someone might deny a complicated apriori belief, one that they might not deny if they thought more about it, without showing that they are confused, insane, or misunderstand the meaning of some word.

13   Suppose that someone is confused about whether a complicated apriori belief is true. For example, suppose that someone thinks that 13 cubed is 2,199 when it is actually 2,197. Suppose that they have calculated this result very carefully but made a mistake. Should we describe this belief as reasonable or unreasonable, justified or unjustified? Discuss the difficulties of applying these labels to cases like this. (It may help to look back to question 16 of chapter 1.)

14   Suppose that someone's use of the word "fish" is like that of most English speakers 300 years ago, so that she insists that whales are fish and argues with people who tell her that they are not. Is her belief unreasonable?

15   Suppose that instead of the definition of "number" used in question 3 we use the following definition: one is a number and two is a number and anything that is got from a number by adding one is a number. Is the belief that there are infinitely many numbers now analytic?

Further Reading

Expositions of some basic ideas about apriori and analytic beliefs are found in chapter 4 of W. V. Quine and Joseph Ullian, *The Web of Belief* (Random House, 1978). Quine and Ullian make very few connections with standard philosophical ideas and terminology, though. Quine's exposition of his ideas in "Two dogmas of empiricism" and other essays collected in *From a Logical Point of View* (Harvard University Press, 1955) is stimulating, though not always easy. Many of the papers in Paul Moser (ed.), *A Priori Knowledge* (Oxford University Press, 1987) are clear and helpful, especially Richard Swinbourne's "Analytical, necessary, and *a priori*."

More advanced papers, including Saul Kripke's "Identity and necessity" are in A. W. Moore (ed.), *Meaning and Reference* (Oxford University Press, 1993). A personal favorite is Marcus Giaquinto, "Non-analytic conceptual knowledge," *Mind*, 105 (1996), 247–68. Kant's views are found in his *Prolegomena to any Future Metaphysics that can Qualify as a Science*, and in part I of his *Critique of Pure Reason*. Both are very difficult. Straightforward expositions of Kant are found in Stephan Korner, *Kant* (Penguin, 1955), and Ralph Walker, *Kant* (Routledge, 1978). For introductions to the philosophy of mathematics, see Hugh Lehman, *Introduction to the Philosophy of Mathematics* (Blackwells, 1979), or S. F. Barker, *The Philosophy of Mathematics* (Prentice Hall, 1964), or the introduction to the second edition of Paul Benacerraf and Hilary Putnam (eds), *Readings in the Philosophy of Mathematics* (Cambridge University Press, 1983). Hempel's paper and the symposium between Carnap, Heyting, and von Neumann, in Benacerraf and Putnam, are particularly suitable for beginners.

Selections from classic philosophical works relevant to this chapter can be found in John Cottingham, *Western Philosophy: An anthology* (Blackwell, 1996). See part I section 1, Plato, "Innate Knowledge"; part I section 6, Gottfried Leibniz, "Innate Knowledge Defended"; part I section 8, Immanuel Kant, "Experience and Understanding"; and part VI section 7, Imanuel Kant, "Causality and Our Experience of Events." Recent positions are described in George Bealer's "The a priori" in John Greco and Ernest Sosa (eds), *The Blackwell Guide to Epistemology* (Blackwell, 1999).

Electronic resources: *Routledge Encyclopedia of Philosophy*: A posteriori; A priori; Rationalism; Innate knowledge; Kant, I. *The Stanford Encyclopedia of Philosophy*: a priori justification and knowledge; Zeno's paradoxes; modality, metaphysics of; Quine, Willard van Orman; truth, necessary vs. contingent.

Chapter 4

INDUCTIVE REASONING

1. Simple Induction

110011011001101100110110110

There is a pattern to this sequence of zeros and ones. After a moment's thought, you can see the pattern and continue it. If the zeros and ones were data about some natural phenomena, for example the number of accidents at some busy intersection on successive days, then when you saw the pattern you might predict that it would continue in the same way, that the next four days would have 1, 1, 0, and 0 accidents.

Many philosophers have thought that a large proportion of our knowledge is obtained by a process rather like this. We observe patterns in the world around us; by understanding them we are able to predict how they will exhibit themselves in cases that have not yet been examined. Call this process simple induction. Sometimes this term is applied to an even simpler kind of reasoning, in which all the observed instances are the same in some respect and we conclude that all unobserved instances are the same in that respect. This comes to pretty much the same. For example, in the history of human observation night has been followed by day in every twenty-four-hour period, so we expect night to be followed by day in the future. (Ignoring what happens in the arctic and antarctic.) We can see this pattern as the constant repetition of the single phenomenon "night and then day" or as a pattern of two phenomena "night, day, night, day, . . ." It isn't essential that the prediction be about the future: we predict data that we have not yet obtained, but the data can concern the past as well as the future. The term induction, without the "simple," is used by some writers for reasoning that goes from a particular set of data to a general conclusion about future data (not necessarily asserting that some pattern found in the data will be repeated). Others use it for any reasoning that does not claim to be deductively valid. I will only discuss simple induction.

The idea that much of our knowledge can be got by starting with observations and reasoning by induction is attractive. For reasoning by induction is modest and careful; it does not seem like wild speculation. To put the point more carefully, the conclusion of a piece of inductive reasoning is meant to go as little as possible beyond the data on which it is based while yet describing a general pattern which will allow us to predict more data. The conclusion contains no concepts not found in the description of the data, and asserts no more than that the pattern of observations will continue. In the example, you do not speculate why two days with accidents are always followed by a day without an accident, why this accident-free day is sometimes followed by another and sometimes by a day with an accident, or why there is never more than one accident per day. You just look at the data and see where they are going.

Unproblematic as induction may seem, there are troubling questions about it. Two of them are basic and very hard. The first is, what reasons do we have to believe that the conclusion of simple induction is true? The other is, what inductive inferences do we actually make and treat as supporting their conclusions? These two questions are closely connected. I shall discuss each and then their connection.

2. Hume's Problem

David Hume first raised sharp uncomfortable questions about whether it is reasonable to be influenced by inductive arguments. (See question 8 at the end of the chapter for more on what questions Hume may have thought he was asking.) Hume's argument is complicated and subtle, but the issues turn around a single simple fact about inductive reasoning.

The premises of an inductive argument can always be expanded to include additional information. We can find out the number of accidents on the next few days; we can watch the sun rise yet another morning. The added evidence may strengthen the argument; it may give more reason to believe the conclusion. But it can also weaken it; it can produce an argument that gives one less reason to believe the conclusion. Sometimes, additional evidence can turn an inductive argument for a conclusion into one against it. Suppose that the sun does not rise tomorrow; if I add this to the evidence I will have an argument showing that the sun does not always rise. Hume's point can now be put as follows: since additional evidence, not yet discovered, may weaken an inductive argument, or even establish the opposite conclusion, and since one cannot be sure that such additional evidence may not turn up, one can easily doubt that the conclusion is true. Some have supposed that Hume went on from this to the further assertion that an inductive argument gives one no reasons to believe in its conclusions. It is not at all clear that Hume believed anything like this. Just as well, for it is not at all clear that anything like this is true. (See question 8 for more on what Hume may have meant.)

The reason that the further assertion is more doubtful is that although Hume's argument shows that a conclusion obtained by induction can be doubted, it may yet be certain. That is, given the evidence it may be perfectly reasonable to treat the conclusion as being true and to act accordingly, while remaining ready to suspend belief or even to believe the opposite if contrary evidence should be found. It could be reasonable to expect the accidents to continue according to the same pattern; it would be crazy not to expect the sun to rise.

Many particular instances of inductive reasoning are completely convincing. It would be irrational not to be convinced by them, to wait for some more powerful assurance that their conclusions are true. It would not be irrational, however, to wonder why inductive reasoning can be so compelling, to ask where its force comes from. (Why, after a million sunrises, do we expect more of the same, rather than thinking that the universe must soon be running out of them?) To think about this in any systematic way we have to know which inductive inferences are the convincing ones. Nelson Goodman was the first to realize how hard it is to know this.

3. Goodman's Problem

Goodman made an important discovery about the inductions which we regard as reasonable. He discovered that we have very little idea which they are. Goodman's argument rests on the fact that a finite sequence of events or observations or items of evidence can always be taken as conforming to a great many, in fact infinitely many, different incompatible general patterns. It cannot be reasonable to believe that all these patterns are realized; the data cannot continue in accord with more than one of them. And it is very hard to see what makes one pattern more plausible than another.

The sequence of 0s and 1s that I began the chapter with could have been taken as exhibiting the pattern: blocks of two 1s and two 0s and blocks of two 1s and one 0, alternating. This may be the way most of us would most easily think of it. But it is not the only way. We could have taken the series as consisting of blocks of ten digits, first 1100110110 then 0110110011, then 0110011000, then the first again, and so on. Then the series would continue 0011 instead of 1100. Or we could have taken it as consisting of 110011011001101100110110000110 followed by itself backward, then forward again, and so on. Then the next four digits would be 0110. There are an infinite number of possibilities.

Goodman pointed out that this fact about sequences applies to all simple inductions. A sequence of past sunrises is just as much in accordance with the pattern "sun rises every 24 hours until April 22, 2045, and then no more" or "sun rises every 24 hours until April 22, 2045, and then every 37.8 hours" as it is in accordance with the pattern "sun rises every 24 hours forever." Evidently there can be no rule of simple induction which says if you observe a large number of instances of a pattern, assume (until contrary evidence turns up) that the pattern will continue. For such a rule would lead to wild and contradictory results. (Quite how wild the results would be is shown by question 11 on the famous "grue" example.)

Another example tending in the same direction is due to C. G. Hempel and is known as the *ravens paradox* Sitting by my desk looking around my study and seeing the books and the pictures, the cat, and the curtains closed in front of the windows, I notice that many of these things are not black. Moreover all of the things that are not black are not ravens. I check to make sure of this and yes, every single non-black thing is a non-raven. This makes me remember that every thing I have ever seen in my life that was not black was not a raven. So, reasoning by simple induction, I conclude that all, absolutely all, things that are not black are not ravens. Then I remember some logic: "Everything that is not B is not R" is equivalent to "Everything that is R is B." (Sometimes it takes a bit of thought to see that this is so. Just think: if I know that all cats eat mice then I know that if it won't eat mice it's not a cat; and if it's really true that if an animal won't eat mice then it's not a cat, then this must be because all cats eat mice. Pause for a moment until this becomes clear.) So if I am concluding that everything that is not black is not a raven, I should also conclude that everything that is a raven is black. But this is an outrageous conclusion. It is not outrageous that all ravens are black, of course; but it is outrageous to think that I could find evidence for this belief by looking around my study, where there is not a single raven. Armchair ornithology, as Hempel puts it, should not give us beliefs about real birds in the wild.

The relation between the ravens paradox and Goodman's problem is this: in both cases we have a possible pattern "All As are Bs" and a body of data which fits it since it consists of As that are Bs but which does not give us reason to believe that the pattern holds for all cases. Seeing the sun many times before April 22, 2045 does not make us believe that the sun will rise every day till April 22, 2045 and never thereafter, even though the data fits this pattern. Seeing many non-black things that are non-ravens (and no non-black things that are ravens) does not make us think that all non-black things are non-ravens. In both cases simple induction leads to conclusions that it should not. In fact the close connections between Goodman's point and Hempel's can be seen by reflecting that all the days that you (or anyone) has experienced which have had a sunrise have been not after April 22, 2045. So reasoning by simple induction you should conclude that all days with sunrises are not after April 22, 2045. But this is equivalent to concluding that all days that are after April 22, 2045 do not have a sunrise. Combine this with the conclusion, also coming from induction, that all days before April 22, 2045 do have a sunrise, and you have Goodman's problem.

We should *not* take these problems to show that induction is not a good way to reason. As Hume pointed out, an enormous proportion of our beliefs are supported by induction. Why else do most people believe that the sun will rise tomorrow? (Astronomers may have complex theories to back up their belief, but the rest of us expect a sunrise every day because that is the pattern we have always known. And the astronomers' theories themselves depend in part on reasoning by induction.) Why else do most people believe that bread nourishes, water quenches thirst, and fire burns? Instead, we should realize that inductive reasoning does not consist in taking any data that fits any regular pattern and supposing that the pattern holds generally. Induction consists in taking the right data and the right pattern, data and pattern that fit together in the right way, and in the absence of any contrary evidence supposing that the pattern holds generally.

What is the right way for data and pattern to fit together? You might think that all that is required is for the pattern not to be a peculiar and complicated one like "The sun rises every 24 hours before April 22, 2045 and every 27 hours thereafter." So the question may seem trivial, for it may seem perfectly clear which inductions are reasonable and which are not, hard as it may be to find a formula that exactly captures the distinction. But the question is far from trivial and the distinction far from obvious. Often there is a real practical problem of telling which features of the evidence should be used as a basis for inductive reasoning. Suppose that in the traffic accident example all the data refers to days in which the sun was shining. Should we use the data to predict the number of accidents on future rainy days? We might or might not, depending on all sorts of other factors. Philosophers have suggested ways of discovering irrelevant features of the evidence, in order to reveal the true pattern and the causal law behind it. (One of the most influential has been J. S. Mill in the nineteenth century.) But none of these methods is obviously right and none applies in all cases. Goodman's puzzle is a way of making one see how fundamental the problem is.

4. Sampling

There is a very general connection between Goodman's problem and a basic tool of scientific reasoning, inference from a sample to a population. Simple induction takes a sample of events of some kind (the sunrises or accidents that have been observed) all of which have some property, and projects to the conclusion that all events in some larger population (all sunrises or all accidents at that location) will have that property. But most often all the events in the sample do not have the property; usually only some of them do. Then we can notice what proportion of events have this property, and we can consider what conclusions to draw about the proportion of events in some larger population that have the property. For example, we might have a coin that has been tossed ten times and come down heads four times and tails six times. Suppose that these tosses are part of a long series of, say, 1,000 tosses. Should we conclude that in the long series the coin will come down heads 400 times and tails 600 times? Probability theory tells us that in fact the coin is very unlikely to fall in exactly these proportions in the long run. It is very likely, though, to fall in *roughly* those proportions. If the proportion in the sample is near to half heads and half tails, then the proportion in the population is likely to be near to half heads and half tails; if the proportion in the sample is biased to tails, then the proportion in the population is more likely to be biased to tails than to heads. So in this example it would be reasonable to conclude that in the longer series the coin will come down with roughly equal number of heads and tails and that if it has a bias it is more likely to be to tails than to heads.

The connection with Goodman's problem is that while in the particular case in which all the members of a sample have some simple property we may be tempted to think that we have to conclude that all members of a larger population have the property, the temptation is much less in the more general situation in which some members of the sample have the property and some do not. In the more general situation we see that some properties can be projected to the larger population, and some other properties cannot. For example, the property of having roughly equal numbers of heads and tails can be projected and the property of having some precise proportion of heads and tails cannot. So the question "Which properties can be projected to the population, with which degrees of confidence?" is a very serious one. We can't evade it if we want to get practical conclusions about any matter where the data is more complicated than "all As are Bs." But this is exactly Goodman's problem. Goodman's problem shows us that even in the simpler case in which all the members of a sample have a property, the question of whether this is a property that we should confidently project to a larger population is a serious one. We tend not to see how serious it is in the simpler case because we usually consider examples in which it seems obviously reasonable to project from sample to population.

We can draw two conclusions here. The first is that reasoning by simple induction is just a special case of inductive reasoning in general. There are many links between data about samples and conclusions about populations in which the conclusions are not absolutely certain given the data but are certain enough that it is reasonable to give them some degree of belief. The general study of such links is statistics, which is a central part of the scientific method. (Not that statistics can answer all the philosophical questions about induction. The questions raised in this chapter are parts of the philosophy of statistics, which is a hard and important subject, just as statistics itself is.)

The second conclusion is that questions about what properties to project to larger populations will not go away. Suppose you want to know how a coin will land in a large run of tosses. Should you be thinking in terms of exact proportions of heads and tails, or rough averages, or tendencies to deviate one way or another from some norm, or what? Should you take into account the way the coin is constructed, or just the data about its previous tosses? Which of these lead to examples of inductive reasoning which are reasonable and which do not? Goodman's problem is all around us.

5. Solutions to Goodman's Problem

Philosophers have suggested many solutions to Goodman's problem. Nearly all of them have one feature in common. That is, they point out that we do not do inductive reasoning in a void. Before we reason from any particular data to any particular general pattern, we already believe many general patterns, some of which we will believe from earlier instances of inductive reasoning and some for other reasons. Consider, for example, someone who sees many instances of sodium making an orange flame when it is burned and concludes that sodium always burns with an orange flame. This person will already believe that sodium is a chemical substance with regular and predictable properties, and will probably already know of other substances that have the same color flame whenever they are burned, about which there may be much more data than there is for sodium. So this person's beliefs will have described "being sodium" as the kind of property that could fit into a general pattern, in particular one about color of burning, and will have described colors of flames as the kind of pattern that can be expected to continue.

There are many ways of elaborating on this point. For there are many features of the situations we find ourselves in that could be emphasized. Goodman himself emphasizes the fact that no instance of inductive reasoning is ever the first. So we can look at the terms in which the evidence is described and the pattern stated and see how these have fitted into previous cases of induction. Suppose that we can describe the evidence as a large number of cases of objects of kind K (ravens or mornings) having some property P (like "black" or "having a sunrise") where K and P are terms used in many earlier inductions, which have not led to false conclusions. Then, Goodman suggests, we may select the hypothesis "all objects of kind K have property P" as stating a likely pattern and take it to be supported by inductive reasoning from this evidence It is hard to evaluate this suggestion, for no one has ever made a thorough study of a large number of inductive inferences, to see if the natural ones can be differentiated from the unnatural ones by this criterion. Also, it is not clear how the idea is to be applied to hypotheses more complicated than those of the form "all objects of kind K have property P."

Another suggestion, found in the writings of Carnap, Jeffrey, and others, is that even before considering any evidence we are more inclined to believe some hypotheses than others, and that the extent to which a pattern or hypothesis is selected depends upon the extent to which we are inclined to believe it before taking account of the evidence. This suggestion, too, is hard to evaluate, and for similar reasons. A realistic analysis of actual inductive practice in terms of it has not been performed, although philosophers of science working in the Bayesian tradition (discussed in chapter 10) have done a lot of relevant work. And the suggested explanations – of the degree to which a person is inclined to believe a hypothesis – only apply to fairly simple hypotheses.

A third suggestion is a more general version of this second one. It is that when we make an inductive inference, we do so against a background of a large number of beliefs besides those about the evidence for the inference. Many of these beliefs are about the sort of regular patterns that we can expect to find in the world. We believe such things as: objects left alone tend to remain in existence and change few of their characteristics; natural processes that occur with a regular periodicity tend to continue with that rhythm, and if interfered with gently tend to change their periodicity rather than become nonperiodic; animals of closely related species tend to have similar characteristics. Given the evidence for an inductive inference, those beliefs do not enable us to deduce the conclusion as something indubitable, but they do help select the hypothesis to be supported by the inference from those which it does not support. The hypothesis selected is the one that describes a pattern of events, a uniformity in nature, of a kind which according to one's general beliefs is likely to exist.

Opinions about the possible causes of a body of evidence do affect how we are inclined to generalize from it, and provide some support for this position. Roughly, the harder we find it to imagine what kind of process could result in a general pattern of events, the less willing we are to look for or believe it. The fallacy of "charting" the stock market is an illustration of this. It is foolish to expect a stock to be worth $20 per share tomorrow just because it has been worth $14, $16, and $18 on the three preceding days. A wise investor knows that most of the factors that affect future stock prices are not represented in the graph of past prices. The pattern alone doesn't mean much. You can imagine the prices of a stock following some mysterious pattern so long and so consistently that we were forced to conclude that the pattern might continue, having no idea at all how this pattern was produced. But the evidence would have to be mighty impressive. On the other hand, if you can see how business conditions and the company's reputation and the financial climate could easily produce such a pattern, you will soon expect it to continue, as long as these conditions remain. To do otherwise, to ignore the possible causes and use induction in a purely formal manner, would be pure superstition.

6. Justifying Induction

The first question about induction was "What reasons do we have to believe that the conclusions of simple inductions are true?" I didn't answer this question. Some philosophers have tried to give reasons why it is reasonable to believe the conclusions of inductive inferences, and some have argued that it is only out of confusion or misunderstanding that one could think that any such reasons were possible or necessary. I think that Goodman's problem about induction shows that it would be wrong to argue along either of these lines.

For how can we make an argument showing why we should believe the conclusions of inductive inferences when we do not know which inferences have the believable conclusions? No good argument could convince us that we should follow the general rule, "On seeing a large number of instances of a general pattern, suppose that the pattern will continue," because, as we have seen, this rule is not one that anyone in their right mind would follow. Until we know more about what our habits of induction actually are, we cannot say very much about whether they are reasonable. But for the same reason it is not right to decide that they are all reasonable; if we knew which inductive inferences we actually make, we might find that some of them are rather less sensible than others.

For example, many people believe that if a coin has been tossed very often and always comes down heads, then it is very likely to come down tails the next time; such people also tend to believe that standing beside a tree that has been struck by lightning is safe, because lightning very rarely strikes twice in the same place. There is a general principle behind such inferences (sometimes it is misnamed the law of averages, philosophers often call it "the gambler's fallacy"); it is something like "If you see a large number of instances of a pattern and you believe that the pattern is very improbable, then assume that it will not be continued." Now this principle is *not* rational; a little thought should convince one that a coin that has come down heads a large number of times is at least as likely to come down heads again the next time. This principle is not accepted by many people. Yet it is perfectly possible that among the inductive inferences we are accustomed to make there is a group of inferences which can be seen to be unreasonable when considered in the light of the purposes of inquiry, of the other inferences we make, of our beliefs about the world, and of common sense.

There is one other fact that has to be mentioned here. Explanations why induction is reasonable must be careful not to be too ambitious. They must not try to show that even the best kinds of inductive reasoning, using the right kind of evidence to support the right kind of general belief, will always give true conclusions. For, as Hume pointed out, this is wrong. The best of inductive reasoning will sometimes give false conclusions. Tomorrow we might find some kind of water that does not quench thirst, some circumstances when sodium does not burn with an orange flame, even a lead weight that rises when released, or a free lunch. All that a justification of induction can do is to give reasons how often some kinds of inductive reasoning will give true conclusions. Some philosophers, such as Hans Reichenbach and Wesley Salmon, have tried to argue that inductive reasoning will give true conclusions more often than other methods of reasoning from the known to the unknown. They have tried to show that induction is more reliable than believing the first thing that comes into your mind, or believing what fits the patterns in your tea leaves. Other philosophers have tried to assess the reliability of induction in terms of facts about probability, some of which are discussed in chapter 10. None of these attempts give a complete and satisfying treatment of the question, but they are the kinds of theories that respect the two basic facts about induction: that it must go from the right kind of data to the right kind of generalization, and that however well-fitted data and generalization are there can be no guarantee that the result is not a false conclusion.

7. The Safeness of Induction

How safe is induction? Much of what I have said suggests that induction is not as safe as it appears to be. I pointed out that many inferences that have the outward form of simple induction are totally unreasonable, and I suggested that when induction is reasonable it is because of its congruence with a background of previous inductions, assignments of probability, and beliefs about nature. Presumably when these things are mistaken an induction is not to be trusted.

But induction is safer than many other methods. Without getting into delicate issues about whether one can give a reason for trusting inductive reasoning, one can give reasons why inductive reasoning will less often result in false conclusions than various kinds of noninductive reasoning. The safeness of induction lies in the fact that it does not risk speculating about the causes of the patterns it predicts. Compare the inductive generalization that the traffic accident data will continue to show the pattern one would naturally find in them with the following hypothesis about the causes of the data. The road in question is used only by trucks serving a construction project. On Monday the drivers drive enthusiastically and there is an accident. This doesn't inhibit them and there is another on Tuesday. However the experience of two accidents makes them drive more carefully on Wednesday and Thursday and there are no accidents. But by driving carefully for these two days they have gotten behind schedule and have to drive furiously on Friday and Saturday in order to have even one day's holiday, Sunday. So there are accidents on Friday and Saturday. There are never two accidents in a day, because after the first accident the drivers slow down for the rest of that day. Every week is the same.

This hypothesis might be right; it might be wrong too, and one can easily think of a number of rival hypotheses incompatible with it. It would be hard to choose between the hypothesis and some of its rivals on the basis of evidence one would be likely to have. Yet many of these rival hypotheses would also predict that the accidents will continue in the 1100110 pattern. The inductive generalization asserts only what these bolder, farther reaching, more interesting hypotheses have in common; it is true as long as any one of them is true.

Induction is modest, it makes no guesses about the causes of events. It is therefore less risky than other parts of the enterprise of hypothesizing about the nature of nature (and less interesting, too). We could not reason inductively, I think, unless we also made hypotheses about causes, and our choice of inductive generalizations may depend on the causal hypotheses that we make. But the truth of induction's conclusions does not require that our causal hypotheses be true. We can be right about the patterns found in the data, and wrong about the reasons why they are found there.

8. IBE

The safeness of induction might give a misleading impression. It might make us think that when we go beyond apriori reasoning we either go one careful step beyond, and reason by simple induction, or we take a large risky speculative step, and indulge in wild hypothesis-making. And indeed many philosophers have written as if this were the case. But more recent philosophers have seen that it is not at all obvious that simple induction, or anything similar to it, has to be the first stage of reasoning beyond the apriori. The more complicated picture that emerges is best presented in terms of an alternative way of reasoning about the world, sometimes called ampliative reasoning, or abduction, or the **inference to the best explanation**. IBE for short. Begin with an example.

Suppose that you come home expecting to find your friend there. She is not home, and you notice that her bicycle is gone. Moreover you remember that she had said that she was near to finishing a story that would have to be sent to a magazine in a hurry. So you suppose that she has gone to the post office on her bike. You set off in that direction to meet her.

The reasoning that leads to the belief that she has gone to the post office is an example of IBE. You begin with the facts that the bicycle is gone, that she was finishing the story, and that the story needed to be mailed to the magazine, and you see that they all fit together if you also suppose that the reason the bicycle is gone is that she took it to go to mail her story. This belief explains these facts, and that is why you believe it. We reason like this all the time. The example is typical of IBE reasoning in several other features too.

First, there could be other explanations. The bicycle could have been stolen and she could have gone to report the theft to the police. She could have been abducted by terrorists who then disassembled the bicycle and hid the parts under the floorboards. And so on. The conclusion that she took the bike to the post office is the *best* of the explanations available to you at the time, but that does not make it the only possible explanation.

Second, you do not have to believe it. You would be irrational to believe an inferior explanation, like the one about abduction by terrorists, given the facts. But you could refuse to venture any explanation at all. You could say "She's not here. Could be many reasons. I'll wait and see." That would not be irrational. But it would leave you with no course of action if you wanted to see her.

Third, the reasoning can be rephrased in terms of probability. The various hypotheses about her whereabouts are not all equally likely even before considering the evidence about the missing bicycle. So their conditional probabilities on the evidence could be considered, as will be described in chapter 10. It would turn out that the hypothesis that she had taken her bicycle and gone to the post office with it was the most probable one. The most probable among those that you had thought of and had the kind of attitude that could translate into a prior probability, that is.

Not all examples of IBE show all three of these features. Some important examples miss some features. Consider for example beliefs in the existence of a world of physical objects around us, interacting with each other and us via chains of cause and effect. The simplest forms of these beliefs are assumptions of continuity: when you turn your head and then look back you assume that the things you now see are the same ones that were there before you looked away. Some epistemologists argue that the rationality of such beliefs come from the way that they explain our experiences. We need to suppose that there is a world around us, they say, in order to make sense of the data we get through our eyes and ears. And the option of refusing to accept any explanation and believing only in our experiences is not really open to us since these beliefs would be too complex for us to handle. So, some argue, we have no alternative but to accept the existence of the physical world as the best explanation of our experience. But it is also the *only* available explanation, we don't really have any worked-out alternatives. (Philosophers' fantasies of brains in vats and evil deceiving spirits are not detailed enough to count.) So the first feature is missing: the existence of a physical world is not the best of a range of alternative explanations.

The third feature – the link with probability – can be missing or at any rate hard to discern in some cases of scientific reasoning. This happens when a novel scientific explanation requires a new concept. Suppose that we have an explanation in physics which refers to concepts, like curved four-dimensional space-time or subatomic particles that are both waves and particles, which are new with the theory. Then we have no degree of belief, no probability, for the explanation before it is invented. We have to assign it a probability, or at any rate decide how much we believe it, and the obvious way to do this is in terms of how well we think it explains the evidence. Something similar happens when new social attitudes bring with them new words to describe states of mind ("laid back," "uptight," "spaced-out" in the 1970s) with which to explain people's behavior. There is no previous set of beliefs in terms of which to judge how probable these explanations are; we just have to see how well they handle the data.

It is when explanations involve novel concepts that the inference to the best explanation becomes really interesting and controversial. Should we believe that the space around us really is part of a curved four-dimensional continuum, just because that is the only adequate explanation we can come up with for our observations in physics and astronomy? Would it not be more reasonable to hedge our bets and accept the hypothesis temporarily as the best we can do, without putting too much faith in it?

9. Safeness Reconsidered

Simple induction is just one way of reasoning from limited data to general conclusions. There is also the inference to the best explanation. And there are the generalizations of simple induction like those discussed in section 4 on sampling. Statistical reasoning from samples to population and simple induction share the feature that the conclusion is expressed in the same terms used to describe the data. If the data concern accidents or sunrises then the conclusion is also about accidents or sunrises. Inferences to the best explanation, on the other hand, often have conclusions that use quite different concepts from the data. The conclusions can be about the factors affecting drivers' alertness or about the structure of the solar system. As a result it is tempting to suppose that an inference to the best explanation will always involve a greater risk of being wrong than a narrower, sample-to-population, kind of inductive reasoning. To be more precise, for any inference to the best explanation consider the consequences of its conclusion which can be expressed in the same terms as the data. Call this the *reduction* of the conclusion. For example, the reduction of the conclusion that the planets revolve around the sun in the way that astronomy suggests is that their future positions in the sky will fall into a certain pattern. Now consider the inductive inference which runs "The sample data fit the pattern described by the reduction of the conclusion, therefore we can suppose that observations in a larger population will also." The conclusion of that inference can be true even if the main conclusion – the "best explanation" – is false. So it seems that this narrower inductive inference is safer than the corresponding inference to the best explanation. That is a more careful statement of the conclusion of section 7.

This conclusion is right. An inference to the best explanation can go wrong in ways that do not affect the sample-to-population inferences that can be derived from it. (So one possible attitude to a scientific theory is always to say: I believe its predictions but I will remain neutral about whether it provides a true explanation of them.) But this fact should not hide two other facts, which make it a less important point than it may seem.

First, it may not be easy for us to state the pattern in question. Suppose that we come to believe that a particular disease is caused by a particular virus, though we don't have sure microscopic evidence of the virus. The symptoms of the disease may be caused by other causes too, and diagnosing the disease may be very difficult. And the circumstances in which infection with the virus will occur will be ones in which other diseases, or no disease at all, may be acquired. Treatments for the virus may overlap with treatments for other viruses. And so on. The result is that although we have a useful and informative theory about the disease we cannot sum it up as a tidy set of predictions and rules about things we can observe. If we could, the result might be a safer thing to believe than the theory we have, but we can't. A more far-reaching example is that of our beliefs about other people's minds, which we use to explain their actions. No one has ever succeeded in stating the purely observational consequences of these beliefs, so that we have no real choice but to accept that other people have desires, emotions, and memories, if we want to explain what they do. (The ambition to find the patterns in our actions that we could use to understand one another without the "theory" that we all have minds, is behaviorism, discussed in chapter 8.)

The second reason is Goodman's problem (again). Once we have a theory that explains some evidence we may go and make a reduced theory that fits the evidence but does not mention anything not found in the evidence. (Once we have a theory of the solar system we can deduce when eclipses will occur – when the earth and two objects in the system will be in a straight line. And then we can write down a table of these eclipses that does not mention gravitation or the shapes of the planets' orbits.) And we can then see that the reduced theory could be got by sample-to-population inductive reasoning from the observations we have made. (The table of eclipses includes the eclipses that we have observed.) But that does not show us that the inductive reasoning would be *good* reasoning. If we only had the data and their projection we might not know that the inference was more reasonable than the perverse examples that make Goodman's problem vivid. (Suppose that our observations of eclipses include just one example where Saturn is eclipsed by Mars, and the table of eclipses includes many such Saturn-Mars eclipses in the future. Should we really think that this way of projecting from a single case to one among the infinite number of possible future patterns is worth trusting?) Moreover, according to many solutions to Goodman's problem, the facts that determine the reasonableness of inductive reasoning include just the kind of things that figure in the best explanations of data. They include facts about causation and laws of nature. (The reason we trust the inference from the one observed eclipse to the many future ones is that it is part of an account of how the planets move that itself fits with a general picture of how things happen in the universe.) So although the reduced induction-supported theory might be a safer thing to believe than the full explanatory theory, we would not know that it was safer unless we also believed the explanatory theory.

The conclusion to draw can stand as the conclusion of this chapter. We cannot form non-trivial beliefs about the world without inductive reasoning. But there are many forms of inductive reasoning, and many subtle connections between them. No one form can be evaluated apart from its connections with the others.

Reading Questions

1 Which of the following are instances of reasoning by simple induction?
  (a) Mary likes chocolate, Sally likes chocolate, Rosanne likes chocolate; all the women I have ever met liked chocolate; therefore all women like chocolate.
  (b) All human beings die, for example Socrates died, Joan of Arc died, Bertrand Russell died; therefore I too will die.
  (c) When this ball is dropped it accelerates downwards; when a bird stops flying it falls; if you lose your balance at the top of the stairs you end up at the bottom; therefore there must be a force of gravity.
2 The following are both features of deductive argument:
  (a) When B follows deductively from A and C follows deductively from B, then C follows deductively from A.
  (b) When B follows deductively from A then B follows deductively from A and C, for any C.
  One of them is not true when "follows deductively" is replaced with "follows by simple induction" and this is an important difference between deduction and induction. Which?
3 Find another two ways of continuing the series of 1s and 0s, besides the three mentioned in section 3.
4 Astronomers, according to section 3, may have reasons for believing that the sun will continue to rise besides reasoning from simple induction. Why? Who besides astronomers could have non-inductive reasons for believing this? Why does section 3 say that "most people" believe that bread nourishes, water

quenches thirst, and fire burns on the basis of inductive reasoning, instead of "all people"?

5   Describe a situation in which someone predicting the stock market solely from the pattern of the data, ignoring all information about the causes of the data, could loose a lot of money.

6   Suppose that two people are betting on the tosses of a coin. Theodora sees it land heads six times in a row and then puts all her money on the bet that it will land tails the next time. Elena sees it land heads six times in a row and then puts all her money on the bet that it will land heads the next time. Explain which one is more likely to be the richer one afterwards. How does this relate to the issues in section 6?

7   The discussion in section 9 of the virus explanation of a disease lists some reasons why the reduction of the explanation to a pattern in the data may be difficult, and then says "and so on." Continue the list.

Thinking Questions

8   Read Hume's discussion of induction in his *Inquiry Concerning Human Understanding*, chapters 4 and 5 (or his *Treatise on Human Nature*, book I, part 3 (2, 3, 4)). Hume may be taken as arguing for any of the following: (a) induction does not have the force of deduction, the conclusion of an inductive argument can be false though the premises are true; (b) when we reason inductively we are assuming that the future will resemble the past, and we can never justify this assumption; and (c) when we reason inductively we are blindly following a way of thinking that cannot be shown to be reliable. Produce evidence for at least one of these interpretations of Hume. Can you find evidence for more than one?

9   Consider the following reasoning. "All the evidence that has ever been produced has been consistent with the theory that objects fall because there is a gravitational force between them and the earth. Therefore all future evidence is likely to be consistent with this theory. Therefore we should accept this theory." How does reasoning like this complicate this chapter's contrast between inductive reasoning and reasoning to the causes of phenomena?

10   John Stuart Mill, in chapter 8 of book III of *A System of Logic* (first published in 1843) described four methods for determining what the causes of a phenomenon are. For example his "first canon" is "If two or more instances of the phenomenon under investigation have only one circumstance in common, the circumstance in which alone all the instances agree is the cause (or effect) of the given phenomenon." By this Mill means that if you observe that P occurs under many conditions which always include a factor F, and you observe that when F occurs without any other factors P is also observed, then you can conclude that "P whenever F" is a law of nature. Find examples like those of section 3 to show that this rule is too simple.

11   Nelson Goodman's example to illustrate his point was the following. Define an object to be *grue* if it is either green and we see it before April 22, 2045 or blue and we see it after that time. Now we have seen many samples of green emeralds, and none that was not green. But they were all grue, since they were seen

before April 22, 2045. So all the emeralds we have ever seen have been grue. So, reasoning by simple induction, we may conclude that all emeralds are grue. But this means that emeralds seen after April 22, 2045 will be blue, which is crazy.

The advantage of making the point with a special word like "grue" is that the weird general principle "all emeralds are grue" is then expressed in language that is just as simple as the non-weird principle "all emeralds are green." What are the important differences between "green" and "grue"? Here are three possibilities:

(a) "Grue" refers to a specific point of time, and "green" does not.

(b) We can tell by looking whether something is green, but we cannot tell whether something is grue just by looking.

(c) "Green" is a word of ordinary English, and "grue" is not.

For each of these show that there are words which have the characteristic of "grue" which can be used to make general principles which can be supported by simple induction. What is the relevance of this to Goodman's problem?

12 Suppose we have some data and a theory that explains the data. We can reason as follows: "All the data up to now have been explained by the theory, so all the future data will be explained by it." Does this show that simple induction can do everything that the inference to the best explanation can do?

13 Suppose we have a sample from a population and some property of the sample which we project to the whole population. We can divide the sample into subsamples and reason "all sub-samples up to now have had the property, so all future sub-samples will have it, and so the whole population will have it." Does this show that reasoning from sample to population is a special case rather than a generalization of simple induction? (Consider examples.)

Further Reading

Simple introductions to issues about induction are in chapter 9 of Robert M. Martin, *There are Two Errors in the the Title of this Book* (Broadview, 1992), chapter 5 of Adam Morton, *Philosophy in Practice* (Blackwell, 1995), chapter 8 of W. V. Quine and Joseph Ullian, *The Web of belief* (Random House, 1978), and chapters 2 and 3 of Merilee H. Salmon, *Introduction to Logic and Critical Thinking* (Harcourt Brace Jovanovich, 1984).

The relation between probability and induction is explored in chapters 1 and 2 of Brian Skyrms, *Choice and Chance* (Dickenson, 1966). More advanced topics are developed in chapter 13 of Jonathan Dancy, *An Introduction to Contemporary Epistemology* (Blackwell, 1985). The best way to learn about Goodman's problem is by reading chapters 3 and 4 of Nelson Goodman, *Fact, Fiction, and Forecast* (Bobbs-Merrill, 3rd edn, 1973). See also Gilbert Harman, "Induction: enumerative and hypothetical" and Richard Fumerton, "Inference to the best explanation" in Jonathan Dancy and Ernest Sosa (eds), *A Companion to Epistemology* (Blackwell, 1993).

Personal favorites are R. C. Jeffrey, "Goodman's query," *Journal of Philosophy*, 63 (1966), 281–8; Mary Hesse, "Ramifications of grue," *British Journal for the Philosophy of Science*, 20 (1969), 13–25; and David Johnson, "Induction and modality," *The Philosophical Review*, 50 (1991), 399–430.

Selections from classic philosophical works relevant to this chapter can be found in John Cottingham, *Western Philosophy: An anthology* (Blackwell, 1996). See part VI section 5, David

Hume, "The Problem of Induction"; part VI section 8, John Stuart Mill "The Uniformity of Nature"; and part VI section 6, David Hume, "The Relation between Cause and Effect."

Electronic resources: *Routledge Encyclopedia of Philosophy*: Induction, epistemic issues in; Goodman, N.; Quine, W. V. *The Stanford Encyclopedia of Philosophy*: Hume, David.

Chapter 5

MIDDLEWORD: FALLIBILISM

We are now halfway through. This is the middle chapter of the book and marks the point where the most fundamental distinctions and ideas of epistemology have been introduced. The topics in the second half of the book are more specific, and in preparation for them this chapter draws together some threads from the first half. The general thread-drawing theme is that of **fallibilism**, the idea that anything we believe, however good our reasons for believing it, could be wrong. This is a controversial idea, and before seeing the reasons for and against it we must think carefully what it really means. Some versions of fallibilism are wild implausible positions, verging on lunacy. Others are safe and responsible positions, verging on platitude. I shall try to describe an intermediate fallibilism, strong enough to be interesting but weak enough to be believable. In doing this I shall allow my own opinions to show more explicitly than in any other chapter except chapter 11. You should read this chapter warily, not accepting what it says unless it really convinces you.

1. Error versus Ignorance

In the first four chapters the topic of risk kept recurring. In chapter 1 truth was listed as a basic desirable quality of beliefs, but with the worry that there might be a price to pay for aiming only at true beliefs. Chapter 2 asked whether reasoning from perceptual beliefs meant taking a risk of arriving at false conclusions, and discussed the empiricist aim of gaining true beliefs without running any risk of acquiring false beliefs along with them. In chapter 3 we asked whether there were any beliefs – apriori beliefs – which ran no risk of falsity. And in chapter 4 induction was described as a method of reasoning which went minimally beyond the evidence: it gives novel beliefs at a minimal risk of falsity.

The risk in all of these is risk of falsity. The reason is that the ideas in these chapters all come ultimately from the philosophies of the seventeenth and eighteenth centuries, when philosophers and scientists were searching for a method of acquiring beliefs which would replace what they saw as the ramshackle falsity-ridden edifice of our traditional beliefs with a more reliable and more confidence-inspiring structure. Philosophers were looking for a method that was guaranteed to produce truths and so the danger of getting false beliefs was foremost in their minds.

But falsity is only one possible danger. Call the danger here **error**. Fear of error is fear of having false beliefs. Consider another danger, which we can call **ignorance**. Ignorance is the danger that we will not have the beliefs that we need to understand the world and live our lives. Ignorance and error are not the same. For example if someone has no beliefs at all they run no risk of error, but their ignorance is total. And if someone only believes certain or apriori beliefs, such as the belief that $38 - 12 = 26$ or that moose are animals, their risk of error is very small but their ignorance is still very large. So we should ask what the important kinds of risk are. No doubt there are many possible dangers in acquiring beliefs. (For example, there is the danger that you will come to believe something that makes your friends think you are crazy.) But in general they lie along three dimensions. There is the error/ignorance dimension: Do we want to avoid having false beliefs, or do we want to avoid having enough true beliefs? There is the long term/short term dimension: Do we want to maximize the number of true (or useful) beliefs we will get if we continue investigating for ever, or do we want to maximize the number we will get in a shorter time? And there is the true/useful dimension: Do we want to get true beliefs or beliefs that will allow us to carry out various important projects? All these dimensions interact, and trade-offs between them often involve all three: for example we may have to decide how many false beliefs we can accept as the price for having useful beliefs in the short term. It would be nice not to have to make these trade-offs, to be able to minimize risk along all dimensions and get a body of beliefs which, both in the short and long term, contains few falsehoods and many useful truths. But we would have to be very optimistic to be sure this is possible. (After all, a good approximation to the truth is often more useful than the absolute literal precise truth, but being too easily satisfied with an approximation can mean fewer truths in the long run.) The early rationalists and empiricists were extremely optimistic; they hoped for a way of acquiring beliefs which will give us as many true beliefs as we can get on any topic we consider. Now philosophy is older and wiser, and we suspect there is no such method. When you realize you can't have everything, you begin to consider trade-offs between the things you can get.

2. Foundationalism versus Holism

Consider two extreme ways of setting priorities among these kinds of risk. The first would be extreme error-avoidance, avoiding at all costs acquiring any false beliefs at any stage of trying to understand the world. The other would be the choice that contrasts most dramatically with this, extreme ignorance-avoidance, and avoiding at all costs having a shortage of the beliefs we need to live with one another and have comfortable lives. No doubt anyone who made either of these extreme choices would try to argue that other kinds of risk were not as risky as they might seem. The extreme error-avoider would argue that if we build our beliefs up carefully, avoiding getting any false ones, we will eventually get true and useful beliefs on any topic we investigate. And the extreme ignorance-avoider would argue that beliefs that contradict the evidence are not going to be useful, so that in trying for useful beliefs we will end up with beliefs that are as near to true as makes no practical difference.

Extreme error-avoidance has been very influential in philosophy, though few contemporary philosophers would agree with it. It is most clearly shown in a family of epistemological theories called **foundationalism**. Foundationalist theories assert that there is a class of beliefs called **basic beliefs**, which do not require any evidence. A person is justified in holding a basic belief just by having and understanding it. For many foundationalist theories, beliefs about what one is perceiving and some kinds of apriori beliefs are basic. A foundationalist theory will also describe ways of reasoning it approves of, which when used to reason from basic beliefs will give true conclusions as often as possible. By reasoning from basic beliefs we can justify non-basic beliefs. So all beliefs are justified when (and only when) they can be got by approved reasoning from basic beliefs.

Different foundationalist theories will suggest different basic beliefs and different kinds of approved reasoning. The most influential foundationalist theory is classical empiricism (as discussed in chapter 2). It suggests as basic beliefs each person's beliefs about their own perceptual appearances, plus analytic beliefs (as discussed in chapter 3). And it suggests as approved reasoning simple induction (as discussed in chapter 4). Other foundationalist theories can suggest other candidates for basic beliefs and approved reasoning, but the important point for our purposes is the strategy that all such theories share of beginning with beliefs which are taken to present a minimal risk of falsity and then to add new beliefs to them by reasoning which increases this risk as little as possible.

In extreme contrast to foundationalist theories are **holist** or **coherentist** theories. ("Holism" is the older term, but "coherentism" is becoming increasingly common as a clearer alternative to it.) According to holism a person is justified in changing their overall pattern of beliefs when the change makes a simple, unified pattern, leaving a minimum of beliefs which contradict or cannot be explained by others. Thus when a person acquires new beliefs by perception they are justified, according to holism, in changing their other beliefs so as to provide explanations of what has been perceived and reject beliefs which the perceptions show to be wrong. Changes in belief should make our beliefs more coherent with one another.

The point to note about holistic theories is that they do not propose any basic beliefs or any particular ways of reasoning from evidence to beliefs that the evidence supports. (Deductive reasoning plays an important role in most holist theories; but they do not propose any specific kinds of non-deductive inference.) Instead, they propose ideals of coherence that we should try to make our beliefs approach. One holist theory might have a simple ideal that there should be no logical contradictions between any beliefs; a more plausible holist theory might have a more complicated ideal that as many beliefs as possible should have explanations, so that there are few mysteries or exceptions. (This more plausible theory has a cost, though; it makes it necessary to say what we mean by "explanation.")

Holist theories are not usually motivated by error-avoidance. They can be taken as attempts to maximize two quantities. The first is the likelihood that any given newly-acquired belief is true *given that* most of the beliefs the person (or society) already holds are true. For holism says "Accept a belief when it coheres with what you already believe." As a result it is biased towards beliefs which are likely to be true if existing beliefs are true. Another result is a conservative attitude to change of belief. That is, when a belief is coherent with other beliefs then, according to holism, we are justified in continuing to believe it even if we do not have specific evidence that that particular belief is true. But many beliefs which we hold for their practical or social consequences are like this: we do not know if other beliefs could work just as well as a basis for technology or medicine or everyday life, but we know that these beliefs taken together with others which we also hold work well enough for these purposes, and so we hold on to them. Both holism and ignorance-avoidance satisfy the slogan "If it ain't broke, don't fix it."

The second quantity holism maximizes is more subtle. It is the approach of the whole body of beliefs in the long term towards the truth. The connection with holism here is that coherence can be taken as a condition truth has to meet. If all of a large body of beliefs is true then they will cohere with one another – there will be no contradictions or exceptions. (Why? Because reality is coherent: incoherence is a result of our thinking.) So if we add more and more beliefs to our overall picture of the world and make adjustments to preserve coherence, we can have some hope that falsehoods are slowly getting weeded out and replaced with truths. There is no guarantee, of course. This argument does not rule out the possibility that we could achieve an enormous comprehensive body of beliefs in which one error can-celled out the effect of another so that we never realized that it was riddled with falsehood. (The nineteenth-century American pragmatist philosopher C. S. Peirce excluded this possibility by defining truth as the limit that our beliefs approach as all possible evidence accumulates. Very few contempo-rary philosophers agree with Peirce, but many have the feeling that some-thing is disturbing about the thought that beliefs could explain all the evidence we could have and yet be largely wrong.) And it positively encour-ages the idea that on the way to large-scale coherence any particular belief may find itself abandoned, in ways that I discuss in the next two sections. Fallibilism remains with us.

3. Fallibilisms

Foundationalism comes from fearing falsehood above all else. Holism accepts the likelihood of falsehood in order to obtain beliefs that will allow us to understand the natural and human world around us. Holist episte-mologies will accept the likelihood of falsehood in another sense too. Since the reasons for accepting or rejecting a belief depend entirely on the way that it coheres with other beliefs, whenever a person comes to acquire a new belief, or loses a belief that they had, their system of beliefs changes. Over time, as new beliefs enter and old ones leave, the whole pattern changes, so that beliefs which were once essential to the coherence of the whole will come to be unnecessary. As a result, holist epistemologies usually claim that any belief could, in time, come to be abandoned. For anything that we now believe, however firmly, we could in the future come to think that it is false. (This is not to say that any belief could *now* be abandoned. The sequence of changes that would be necessary for us to abandon, say, the belief that a million is bigger than ten, or that the parts of the parts of a thing are parts of a thing, might take centuries.)

This claim that any belief could be abandoned raises many questions, though. What kinds of evidence or change of belief would suggest aban-doning beliefs that we now consider certain? How many other beliefs would have to change first? Would beliefs be abandoned as a compulsory or optional matter: that is, is the claim that for any belief there is a situation in which abandoning it is one rational option, or that for any belief there is a situation in which not abandoning it would be irrational? Different answers to these and other questions can determine whether the claim that any belief could be abandoned is a wild and radical suggestion or a harm-less platitude masquerading as a bold idea. Here are arguments defending three possible versions of the claim. Each considers the status of three apparently certain beliefs: the belief that moose are animals, the belief that the earth revolves around the sun, and the belief that $65 + 14$ is greater than 67.

Jungle fallibilism

We might have to abandon any of our beliefs at any time. For we can never know what evidence might appear tomorrow. We might discover that there are tiny radio transmitters buried inside the brains of moose transmitting instructions to them from extra-terrestrial controllers, and also find out that moose calves are not born from mother moose but beamed down from alien spacecraft. (Have you ever seen a moose being born? Do you know anyone who has?) Then we would be forced to conclude that moose are not animals, but machines. Or we might send up a probe into space which collided with a sphere surrounding the earth on which lights move in exactly the patterns they would if there were stars and a sun moving in the way that astronomy claims they do. Or we might discover a new kind of particle in atomic physics such that any apparatus we design to count them gives the result that if you count 33 pairs of them you get the answer 66 but if you count 2 sets of 33 you get the answer 0.

The universe is a jungle in which wild discoveries lie in wait for us. We can never tell what is around the corner or hiding in the trees. All we can do is say: this is what the evidence so far suggests, and tomorrow's evidence might be anything at all.

Boring fallibilism

Any belief could be abandoned, in that for any belief there might arise a situation in which we could reasonably choose to say No to the words which now express that belief. Suppose for example that we find it confusing that "moose" and "mouse" sound alike. (People very often say "mice" when they mean "mooses," moreover the Danish and Latin words for mouse sound like "moose.") So we decide to avoid confusion by calling moose "forest elk." This confusion arose because "moose" and "mouse" both refer to kinds of animals, so it would not be confusing to use the word "moose" to refer, for example, to a kind of knot which has large antler-like bows but gets very tight when one end is pulled. (Be careful, never put your head in a moose.) Then of course people would deny that a moose is an animal. A moose would be a kind of knot. As for the belief that the earth goes round the sun: if by "goes round" we mean that the sun is at a fixed point relative to the other stars in the galaxy and the path of the earth traces a closed loop around this point, then we can deny it since the earth in fact traces a complex path through space, which does not enclose any single solar location. The belief that 65 + 14 is greater than 67 is similarly already false if we understand "=" to mean what it does in some mathematical theories. An example is modular arithmetic, in which two numbers are identical if they leave the same remainder when divided by some "modulus," such as 13. Then 65 + 14 = 1 (since 13 divides into 79 six times leaving a remainder of 1) and 67 = 2 (since 13 divides into 67 five times leaving a remainder of 2). But 1 is not greater than 2 so, understanding equality and greater than in this special way, 65 + 14 is not greater than 67.

Informed fallibilism

We could be forced to abandon any belief, though the route that would take us to this would in some cases be a very long one. Sometimes a rather shorter route would take us to a situation in which abandoning a belief would be a rational option. There are two important ways in which we could come to abandon beliefs which now seem to us obviously true. Call them observation-refining and concept-splitting. Observation-refining occurs when we find ways of making new observations either by observing things that we could not observe before or by classifying our perceptions in new ways. For example, the invention of telescopes and microscopes allowed scientists to observe many things that had been invisible before, and more recently electron microscopes and brain-scan equipment allow completely new observations. (Equipped with these tools, early scientists could come to believe that the planets have moons, or that there are animals that have no blood, beliefs that would have seemed obviously false earlier.) An example of new ways of describing perception is when mathematical analysis of patterns in the output of a microscope or telescope allows us to describe it in completely different terms from the ones that we would naturally use. (An example from the past is the revolutionary idea that some stars are much further away than others. A contemporary example is the description of data in terms of "spatial frequencies.") As our theories of the world become more complex, they open up new ways of making and classifying observations, and thus make available new kinds of evidence, which may, paradoxically, cause problems for the theories that made them possible.

Concept-splitting occurs when we come to accept a belief which shows that we had been running together ideas that are actually different in important ways. An example of this is when we discovered that the animals we had been calling fish were really of several different kinds. There are normal fish which have gills, are cold blooded, and whose young develop from eggs usually outside their bodies; there are whales, which have lungs, are warm blooded, and whose young develop inside their bodies separated from their mothers' bodies by a placenta; and there are squid and also other kinds of water creatures. The fact that these differences are very basic and important only became clear when biological theory developed to a point where it could classify animals in more basic and un-obvious terms than the shapes of their bodies and the way they move.

Both of these processes describe important ways in which we can come to abandon beliefs in which we had felt very confident. Suppose that we discover that the chemical that carries genetic information from an animal to its descendants, DNA, comes in two fundamentally different kinds. Most animals have one of these kinds but a few have the other kind, which shares important features with the DNA of fungi. Among the creatures in this unusual kind are moose. Then it might be reasonable to say that moose are not animals but fungi-like creatures. Or suppose that when we can put telescopes on the moon we manage to relate the movements of the earth and the sun more accurately and learn that they are not quite what we thought they were. We find that the earth is indeed tracing out an elliptical orbit through space but the sun is not at the focus of this ellipse. Instead, the motions of both the earth and the sun are determined by the gravitational field of an invisible massive object, perhaps a black hole.

Lastly, consider how on this account the belief that $65 + 14$ is greater than 67 could be abandoned. Addition of numbers is a feature of the union of sets. To say that $2 + 1$ is 3 is to say that if we have a set A and distinct objects s and t in A, and a set B and an object u in B, and nothing is in both A and B, then there are distinct objects a, b, c in the union of A and B. In other words, adding is counting the objects formed by the union of sets. Now suppose we learn that the union of sets is not the simple thing we naively take it to be. Suppose we learn that there are some kinds of set which do not have unions with other kinds. If there is a set of the first kind and a set of the second kind, then there is no set which is the union of these two sets. Then many basic principles of arithmetic will be challenged. It may no longer be clear that we can say anything in general about $65 + 14$, because sometimes there will be no such thing as the sum of these numbers. (But 65 dogs and 14 cats will still be more dogs-or-cats than 67 dogs-or-cats.)

4. How the Web Changes

Which of these fallibilisms is right? In a way they all are. The processes that each of them describes can and do happen. But there is also a way in which jungle fallibilism and boring fallibilism are very misleading. They suggest that our beliefs change in ways that in general they do not.

Begin with boring fallibilism. Although it is true that we could come to mean something else by "moose," and as a result come to deny the sentence "moose are animals," this would not really mean that our beliefs had changed. We would not have lost the belief that moose are animals. We would still have that belief, and express it with the words "forest elk are animals." Similarly for the beliefs that the earth goes round the sun and that $65 + 14$ is greater than 67. In each case we would not have changed our beliefs, only the words that we used to express them.

Jungle fallibilism is more subtly misleading. It is true that we cannot completely rule out the possibility that, for example, we will discover that moose are machines sent to earth by aliens. But this does not show that this possibility is one that we should take seriously. It is not one that we should prepare for or await. It is not even a kind of possibility that we should expect, although we should expect that there will be really astounding surprises in the future evidence. (Surprises are by definition surprising; but some surprises, even astoundingly surprising surprises, are of kinds that we expect. We expect, for example, that occasionally a tossed coin will land heads 20 times in a row, although it is extremely surprising when one does.) If we know anything about the world, we know that the unexpected refutations of our beliefs will not occur completely at random.

This point can be made in terms of questions about method in the theory of knowledge. Since the theory of knowledge is concerned with understanding and evaluating our reasons for our beliefs, we might think that we should not assume any of these beliefs when trying to gain this understanding. The most we should assume in epistemology is pure logic and an understanding of the meaning of the words we are using. Then perhaps we could add more assumptions when we succeeded in showing that there are doubt-proof reasons for believing them. This would be like Descartes' project in his *Meditations*, and it would commit us to some sort of foundationalist theory of knowledge. The problem with this is that it does not work; we end up with no theory of knowledge at all, because in fact we cannot find enough doubt-proof assumptions to gain any real understanding of how human beings gain knowledge and where their attempts to know the world are likely to succeed or fail. So one result is likely to be jungle fallibilism: we have no assurance that any belief is more secure than any other, or that evidence against our beliefs is more likely to take one form than another.

An alternative approach to understanding our beliefs is to allow us to make the same assumptions as we would in any other kind of investigation. We can use results from psychology, physics, and biology, and of course common sense, in order to describe both human beings and the world around them in ways that help us see the possibilities and limitations of human attempts to understand this world. Of course it makes sense in doing this to take account of the strength of the evidence for the assumptions we are using, to see that there is a lot more evidence for the assumption that, for example, people see with their eyes and hear with their ears than there is for the theory of evolution. Still, you can't do a job without tools, and the tools needed for making a theory of human knowledge have to be put together out of that knowledge itself. (See also the discussion of naturalism in chapter 10 sections 5, 6, and 7.)

If we take this second attitude to epistemological method, we are inclined towards informed fallibilism, or something much like it. For in evaluating the ways in which our beliefs are likely to be wrong, in stating the serious expectations we should have of surprising developments in our understanding of the world, we have to rely on what we know about the way our beliefs have been supported and refuted by evidence in the past, and what we know about the strengths and weaknesses of our capacities for gathering evidence, reasoning, and making theories. And when we combine the history of knowledge with a little psychology in this way, what we learn is that when beliefs that we had thought were certain come to be abandoned it is often either because we have found new ways of obtaining and evaluating evidence or because our theories have given us new concepts which allow us to see that these beliefs were fundamentally ambiguous. And these are the two patterns described by informed fallibilism.

Informed fallibilism can be seen as an aspect of a familiar idea, the web of belief. As chapter 3, sections 4 and 5, explained, Quine and others have argued that our beliefs are connected to each other in a complex structure in which some beliefs have a very central position, so that evidence is relevant to them only very indirectly. Other beliefs are at the outside, affected more directly by evidence and thus changing more readily. The usual candidates for the center are beliefs about mathematics and other apriori beliefs, and the usual candidates for the outside are perceptual beliefs. (See question 18 for relations between this picture and holism.) On this picture, we should not expect beliefs near the center to change very often, and we should expect situations in which we were forced to abandon such a belief (rather than simply having abandoning the belief among our reasonable options) to be extremely rare. We should expect that changes that reach well into the web of belief occur when the structure of the web itself changes, as when beliefs at the edges are augmented with new kinds of perceptual beliefs or when beliefs further in split and are replaced with several new beliefs. But these, again, are the suggestions of informed fallibilism.

Here is an analogy. Our beliefs are like the position and orientation of a leaf blown by the wind. The wind represents experience and observation. The only force leading to change in position and orientation is the wind, but the changes that it produces depend on the initial position and orientation. Two leaves initially near to each other and pointing in similar directions could, when blown by a strong and uniform wind, end up in quite different places pointing in quite different directions, because of the small original differences. So two people or two societies that start with different beliefs about the world could be exposed to all the same evidence and end up with different conclusions. So exposure to true evidence does not automatically produce true beliefs. Thus even though we have been exposed to a large amount of evidence, which we can assume to be reliable, there may still be false beliefs which we will never eradicate and true beliefs that we will never acquire. The body of beliefs we inherit from the past, and which if holism is right we cannot operate without, may make it impossible for the very best evidence to move us to the right destination.

Return to informed fallibilism. It tries to show how the web of belief could change while keeping its power to give us understanding of the world. It describes how as our knowledge grows we may have to discard many of the beliefs with which we began, even though we keep much of the understanding they gave us. We might abandon beliefs like "moose are animals" because of a richer biological classification system that includes the one we use today as a special case; we might abandon the belief that the earth orbits round the sun as a result of observations which rely on the physics we have been building up over centuries; we might abandon the belief that $65 + 14$ is greater than 67 while keeping all the rules for counting animals, money, and so on, that we need in everyday life. Informed fallibilism thus retains some of the optimism about our capacities to increase our understanding that is seen in old foundationalist views. (But with an important difference: unlike foundationalism this view allows that while our understanding may accumulate, our beliefs do not.)

Jungle fallibilism, on the other hand, focuses on cases in which the web of belief disintegrates or shrinks rather than grows. And boring fallibilism focuses on cases in which the web hardly changes at all. The cases described by all three of them occur. But it is informed fallibilism, I am convinced, which points to important facts about the ways in which the structure of our beliefs can change.

Reading Questions

1   Why does the fact that being too easily satisfied with an approximation can mean fewer truths in the long run suggest that it may be impossible to avoid trade-offs between desirable qualities of beliefs?
2   Why would someone who thought they had a method which would give them all and only true beliefs not be concerned about the difference between falsity and ignorance?
3   Why is foundationalism motivated by error-avoidance?
4   Section 2 said that one holist theory might claim that there should be no logical contradictions between beliefs, while another might claim that as many beliefs as possible should have explanations. Which of these is the more demanding ideal, in the sense of being harder to achieve? Can you give an example of a set of beliefs which satisfies the first ideal but not the second?
5   In section 2 it is claimed that the usefulness of beliefs about people's characters and emotions is the same as their coherence. Coherence with what other beliefs?

6   Explain the difference, appealed to in section 3, between a situation in which abandoning a belief is a rational option and a situation in which it would be irrational not to abandon a belief. Give an example.

7   What is the connection between jungle fallibilism, discussed in section 3, and Hume's discovery about induction, discussed in chapter 4 section 2?

8   Here is an old philosophical puzzle. "Suppose that ostriches were called 'horses' and horses were called 'ostriches.' How many legs would a horse have?" What does this have to do with boring fallibilism?

9   Informed fallibilism, discussed in section 3, postulates two processes which underlie the abandonment of well-established beliefs, observation-refining and concept-splitting. Which of these processes is involved in which of the examples of how, from the point of view of informed fallibilism, a well-established belief could be abandoned?

10   In section 4 an objection is made to boring fallibilism's account of how we could come to abandon the belief that moose are animals. Describe similar objections to its account of how the belief that the earth revolves around the sun and the belief that $65 + 14$ is greater than 67 could be abandoned.

11   In section 4 it is said that we expect that a tossed coin will occasionally land heads 20 times in a row, though it is extremely surprising when it does. How can an event be extremely surprising although expected? Explain why this is an analogy for the ways in which evidence against our theories tends to occur.

12   Why might someone think that in order to evaluate our reasons for our beliefs it would be best not to assume any of them?

13   Why, on the "web of belief" picture, should we expect very few situations in which we were forced to abandon a belief near the center of the web?

Thinking Questions

14   In our attempts to understand the world there are virtues and vices, just as there are in our attempts to live with one another. Consider the following virtues: *patience, imagination, tolerance, carefulness, hesitation, enthusiasm*. Which of these are likely to play a role in an error-avoiding approach to knowledge, and which in an ignorance-avoiding approach?

15   Jungle fallibilism may, as argued in the text, suggest a misleading picture of the ways in which evidence against our beliefs is likely to appear, but is it not still *true*?

16   At the beginning of this chapter it was claimed that some forms of fallibilism are "verging on lunacy." The wildest fallibilism discussed in the chapter is jungle fallibilism. But it does not seem to be exactly lunatic. How can it be modified so as to bring out its truly wild possibilities?

17   The criticism of boring fallibilism in section 4 interpreted it as saying that we could abandon any belief simply by deciding to use the words to mean something else. Can the statement of boring fallibilism in section 3 be understood so as to make a less boring claim?

18   The "web of belief" picture is usually thought of as an image of holism. For the threads of the web connect each belief ultimately to every other belief. But holism should allow no basic beliefs, no beliefs which need no support from any

other beliefs. So what about the beliefs at the edge of the web? These are usually thought of as beliefs about evidence from perception. They are at the edge because they respond to factors outside the web itself, namely perception. So are they not in effect basic beliefs, and is this holist picture not really a foundationalist picture in disguise?

19 The analogy of the leaves blown by the wind suggests that holism makes a large chance of error inevitable. Is this not an argument against holism?

Further Reading

Simple expositions of fallibilism are found in chapter 5, section F, of John Cottingham, *Rationalism* (Oxford University Press, 1988); chapter 3 of Martin Hollis, *Invitation to Philosophy* (Blackwell, 1985); and chapter 11 (especially section 6) of Adam Morton, *Philosophy in Practice* (Blackwell, 1995). More advanced treatments are in chapter 15 of Jonathan Dancy, *An Introduction to Contemporary Epistemology* (Blackwell, 1985), and chapter 10 of Donald Gillies, *Philosophy of Science in the 20th Century* (Blackwell, 1993). The crucial distinction between avoiding falsity and avoiding error is made in chapter 1 of Alvin Goldman, *Epistemology and Cognition* (Harvard University Press, 1986). For the contrast between foundationalism and holism (coherentism) see Laurence BonJour, *The Structure of Empirical Knowledge* (Harvard University Press, 1985).

Selections from classic philosophical works relevant to this chapter can be found in John Cottingham, *Western Philosophy: An anthology* (Blackwell, 1996). See part I section 4, René Descartes, "New Foundations for Knowledge," and part II section 1, Plato, "The Allegory of the Cave."

Electronic resources: *Routledge Encyclopedia of Philosophy*: Foundationalism; Knowledge and justification, coherence theory of; Fallibilism; Quine, W. V. *The Stanford Encyclopedia of Philosophy*: justification coherentist theories of; justification contextualist theories of; justification foundationalist theories of.

Chapter 6

DEFINING KNOWLEDGE

1. Top-grade Belief

Consider three cases in which a person does not have knowledge.

A weather forecaster, McA, is preparing to make a radio report on the weather to be expected the next day. He finds, five minutes before he must go on air, that he has lost all the data on which a report was to be based. So he tosses a coin. Heads for rain, tail for dry. Heads for winds under five miles per hour, tails for winds over five miles per hour. And so on. After five minutes he has his report and he goes on air and predicts a hurricane, though the sky is blue, the barometer is steady, and the breezes are gentle.

McA does not *know* that there will be a hurricane the next day. Suppose that by some freak of the weather there is a hurricane the next day. That does not turn his report into knowledge; it was just guesswork and only turned out accurate by chance.

A detective, FitzB, is investigating a murder. Near the victim's body she finds a wallet containing a driver's license in the name of Z. She goes to interview Z and finds that he has left town in a hurry. Z is tracked down and found to have traces of the victim's blood under his fingernails. Moreover his fingerprints are all over the scene of the crime. A little investigation reveals that Z has a long-standing grudge against the victim and stood to gain a lot of money from the victim's death. There are no other suspects. FitzB concludes that she has solved the crime: Z is the killer.

But Z is not the killer. Z was framed by a very clever enemy of the victim who managed to plant all the evidence while leaving no traces of her activities. Z is convicted and executed, and the real killer is never brought to justice. So FitzB did not know that Z was the killer. She thought she knew, and she had very good reasons for so thinking. But in fact her belief was false and so it cannot have been knowledge.

Reflect on these examples. They show that knowledge is a quite complicated business. Not all true beliefs are knowledge (McA), and not all justified beliefs are knowledge (FitzB). That suggests an easy answer: a belief counts as knowledge when it is both true and justified. Think again; another example shows that this is not right either.

A scientist, Dr. O'C, is testing a drug, magicillin, which she thinks may be a good treatment for cancer of the liver. Suppose that her suspicion is right and magicillin does cure liver cancer in a large proportion of human cases. Suppose, moreover, that she performs experiments on both human and animal subjects, designed to measure the rate of recovery when the drug is administered and to rule out alternative explanations. Suppose that her reasoning from these experiments is faultless, so that when she publishes her results in a research paper they do provide very good reasons to believe that magicillin will save the lives of a large proportion of people with cancer of the liver. But suppose also that, although Dr. O'C does not know it, one of her lab assistants has falsified part of an experiment. The assistant replaced one experimental animal, which looked as if it might be diseased, with a healthy animal that had not previously been part of the experiment.

When Dr. O'C finds out she will be furious and dismayed: her experiment has been ruined. After she learns that the experiment has been tampered with she can no longer maintain to her colleagues that she now knows that magicillin cures cancer. She does not know it; she did not know it even before she discovered what her assistant had done, and thereby discovered that what she had thought was knowledge was not. Yet her belief was true, magicillin does cure cancer, and her reasoning is perfect, her belief was justified.

In all three cases we have a belief that fails to be knowledge. But the reasons for this are different. McA does not know that there will be a hurricane the next day because what he passes off as reasoning is so feeble. You cannot predict the weather by tossing coins. So the fault here is in him. FitzB does not know that Z is the killer because her belief is false. As it happens Z is not the killer, although FitzB's reasoning is fine. The fault here is in the relation between her beliefs and the facts. So, as I remarked above, it might seem obvious that to have knowledge you have to have a belief which is both true and justified. Both the facts and your reasoning have to be right. But the O'C case shows that things are not that simple. O'C's belief is true, and her reasoning is fine, but she does not have knowledge. The O'C case is one of many examples (known as **Gettier examples** after Edmund Gettier, who first pointed out their significance) which show that we cannot take "know" to mean simply "true and justified." When we say that someone knows something we are saying more than that they believe it and their belief is true and they are justified in believing it. What more?

This is a controversial question. There is very little agreement about what the right answer to it is, or even whether it is an important question. In this chapter I shall describe several approaches to the question which have been defended by philosophers since the 1970s. The chapter is thus an introduction to a part of the theory of knowledge with a very distinctive flavor of its own. Some people find the questions and approaches here fascinating, others have trouble seeing the point of them. My aim is to make a case for thinking that there are important and central questions here. But before entering this controversy, it is worth stating some simpler and uncontroversial facts about the concept of knowledge, to give us something definite to hold on to.

A belief qualifies as knowledge if, in acquiring it, one has achieved the basic aim in the inquiry that led to it. In other words, we use the term *knowledge* as a kind of stamp of high quality for beliefs: if a belief fails to be knowledge it is because it falls short of some expectation we might reasonably have of it. Thus McA's belief that there would be a hurricane the next day, and the beliefs of the people who believed what he said on the radio, were not knowledge, because we can expect that weather forecasters will pay more attention to the evidence than he did. FitzB's belief that Z is the killer is not knowledge because we want beliefs to be true – that is one of the very most basic aims of having beliefs – and it was not. O'C's belief that magicillin cures cancer is not knowledge partly because we cannot take the evidence and reasoning she presents as grounds for believing it ourselves: once we know that some of the data has been tampered with we know that the experiments are flawed and will have to be re-run and re-analyzed.

This general picture holds in many ordinary cases where we say that someone does know something, too. When we classify a belief as knowledge we are saying that it has the good qualities that a belief should have. When we say that a student knows the answers on a test, we mean that the answers she would give are true and that she is not just guessing. (We mean more than this, but at least this.) When you are asked what the capital of Colombia is and you say "I don't know but I think it's Bogota," you are saying that we should not treat your belief that Bogota is the capital as a completely safe basis for our beliefs. When we say that the police know that a certain person has committed a certain crime, we mean that the police have done their job successfully; they have the right person and they have discovered him by sensible detective work. Moving on to rather different ways of talking, when we say that someone knows about marathon running we are saying that he has beliefs which make him a good source of information for us to base our beliefs about marathons on. And when we say that someone knows which the best restaurants in town are we are saying that she can supply descriptions of the restaurants which can both help us get a good meal and help us find them. Moving on even further, when we say that someone knows how to recognize a good restaurant when she sees it, we mean that in the presence of good restaurants she will form the belief that they are good. Her skills are ones that she and others can base reliable beliefs on.

These are only some of the good qualities that beliefs can have. One way of understanding the definitions of knowledge that are discussed in the rest of the chapter is as ways of classifying and organizing all these desirable features of beliefs. Which are the most fundamental and most important of them?

2. Lehrer's Principle

Dr. O'C's reasoning, though correct, began with a false premise, that the animals with which the experiment ended were those with which it began. Perhaps knowledge is true belief that lies at the end of a chain of reasoning which begins with true premises.

This suggestion is not right either. For suppose that Dr. O'C does other experiments. This time her experiments don't get fouled up. But unfortunately they don't directly indicate that magicillin cures liver cancer; instead, they indicate that it inhibits cell division in a certain complicated way. From this result she infers that it will be effective against cancer. Now as a matter of fact (in this story) magicillin is effective against cancer, but it does not inhibit cell division in the way that the experiments indicated. Again things have gone wrong; again Dr. O'C has not got knowledge, though this time her belief is not only true, and obtained by good reasoning, but also proceeds from true premises.

It seems, then, that for a chain of reasoning to lead to knowledge it must not only start with true premises but also must not have any false steps at any point along the way. It should have no detour through falsity. We have here a fairly simple principle that does seem to correspond to something important about knowledge. Let me call it **Lehrer's principle** and state it more carefully: if a belief is based on reasoning then it qualifies as knowledge if, and only if, it does not depend on any chain of reasoning that has a false step at middle, beginning, or end.

A number of philosophers have accepted Lehrer's principle. Like many valuable philosophical ideas, it contains an enormous fudge. For it says that knowledge cannot *depend on* any reasoning that proceeds through falsity. What does "depend on" mean?

A belief does not necessarily depend on the reasoning by which it was originally acquired. One can first acquire a belief for some reasons (perhaps bad) and later obtain other reasons (perhaps good) for holding it. For example, a person may hold a belief just because someone he dislikes believes the opposite; later he makes some investigations and finds some strong evidence for the belief he already has. Now he may have knowledge, although his first reasons were bad. (Another example is the case of Harvey's belief in the circulation of the blood, mentioned in chapter 1 section 3.)

Nor does a belief depend on just any reasoning which *could* support it, whether or not the person holding the belief uses or is aware of the reasoning. For often something that one clearly knows can be obtained as the conclusion of reasoning which has the fatal characteristics: it is logically correct, one believes each of its steps, but some step is false. This false step should not cause one's belief not to be knowledge if one does not actually use the fatal reasoning to get or support it. For example Dr. O'C may have the false belief that magicillin inhibits cell division; but suppose that although this might be used in a persuasive argument to conclude that it cures cancer she does not base her belief upon this reasoning. She bases her belief instead on a line of reasoning which does not involve any false step. She then knows that magicillin cures cancer; her knowledge is not undermined by the faults of the reasoning she does not use.

We must take "depends on" to mean roughly the following: a person's belief depends on a chain of reasoning when the reasoning is used by the person, publicly or privately, to show why he should hold the belief; if the reasoning is refuted, if the person stops thinking that it is correct or that all its stages are true, then the person will either find some other reasoning to support the belief or cease to consider it as one of his well-supported opinions.

3. Reliability: The Case of the Ancient Mariner

There are problems with Lehrer's principle, cases that it cannot handle. This is not surprising when you consider that although it requires that a belief which counts as knowledge depend on true assumptions, it does not require that it depend on *known* assumptions. So it would seem to count as knowledge a belief that was based on, for example, a hallucination that happened to be true. (You take a drug which makes you hallucinate elephants in the shopping mall, but by amazing coincidence there actually are elephants in the mall, exactly where and when you are hallucinating them.) That kind of problem gives cases where someone does not have knowledge although Lehrer's principle suggests they should. The principle also has problems in the other direction, with cases where someone does seem to have knowledge although the principle suggests they should not. Such cases are given by some beliefs which give reliable predictions although they are in fact partly false. Here is an example. Before the discovery and acceptance of the idea that the earth revolves around the sun, rather than the other way around, sailors used to compute their latitude from the position of the sun and other heavenly bodies by using a theory which falsely assumed that the earth was stationary. As a matter of fact, sailors got the right navigational results this way. Consider now an old sea captain who computes his latitude (how far north or south of the equator he is) from observations of the heavens, and imagine him to have enough astronomical lore to think things through in terms of the old false astronomy. Surely if he gets the right answer, if he makes no mistakes and concludes that his latitude is what it really is, then he knows what his latitude is. But his reasoning involves many false assumptions. Lehrer's principle seems wrong here.

The important thing about this case is that the captain has obtained his result by a method that is reliable – it always works – and that could have been based on true assumptions, though it was not. For the captain's calculations could have been derived from the true astronomical facts, or even on the noncommittal assumption "If the apparent positions of the stars in the sky are such and such then the latitude is the following." It is important that it is a whole method that can be given a true foundation, and not just a single belief. For if the captain had obtained his estimate of his latitude from the horoscopes of the crew, and by pure luck came up with the right answer, then the fact that he could have derived his latitude from sound navigational principles does nothing to confer the status of knowledge on his guess. What is special about the captain's case is that his method is reliable, and it is no accident that it is reliable; given the way things really are, it is inevitable that the method will give true results.

The case of the ancient mariner is important because it leads to another side of the concept of knowledge, as basic as the side expressed by Lehrer's principle. The captain knows where he is because his method of discovery is *reliable*: there is a good reason why it gives the right answers. However rational or irrational he is in using his method, others can rely on his results; seen as a source for other people's reasoning or as part of a larger scientific project, his method is just as it should be. Note that reliability is a clue about what is going on in the other kind of problem with Lehrer's principle, too. If a person is hallucinating elephants in the shopping mall then the way in which she is forming her perceptual beliefs is not reliable, even if they happen to be true. They are true by accident, not as a result of their origins.

The reliability of methods is a subtle business. Another story: Dr. O'C knows that magicillin works against cancer in rats, mice, gerbils and squirrels, and so she concludes that it works against cancer in all rodents, and therefore will be effective in chipmunks. This reasoning is good, and, as it happens, magicillin is effective against cancer in chipmunks. But the way that it cures cancer in most rodents is completely different from the way it works in chipmunks; by some freak of chipmunk metabolism, it is the substance in which the normally active ingredient of magicillin is dissolved rather than that ingredient itself that is effective against cancer in chipmunks. Dr. O'C does not know that the drug works in chipmunks, although her reasoning does not violate Lehrer's principle and is trustworthy, in that it leads and will usually lead to a true conclusion. What is wrong with her belief is that its truth is a sort of accident: the reasons why her roughly inductive reasoning usually works do not explain why it worked this time.

"Reliable" is a word that can be interpreted in several different ways. One way is statistical: a reliable method is one that gives true beliefs a high proportion of the time. (So we could speak of 75 percent or 98 percent reliability.) Statistical reliability is probably not the right way to think about knowledge. For suppose you have a ticket in a lottery and 999,999 other people have also bought tickets. If your method of getting beliefs is to believe everything that has a more than 99 percent chance of being true then you should believe that you will not win the lottery. Suppose you do not win. Although this was the almost certain outcome, it does not seem right to say that you knew in advance that you would not win.

Another way is causal: a belief is reliably acquired if the laws of nature and mind explain why the process that resulted in the belief resulted in a true belief. Reliability thus requires that the ways in which information was transmitted and processed and the influences of various disturbing factors make a firm connection between the fact and the belief. In fact, a process can be reliable, in this way, even if it operates only once and cannot be repeated. For example, I may have been blind since infancy (after a brief sighted period in which my visual system developed somewhat); then, late in life, the injection of a powerful drug allows me to see for a few moments, before it utterly rots away my retinas. During those few moments I know that there are people about me, what their movements are, and the colors of their clothes.

The idea is still vague. A belief is reliably acquired if there is an explanation of why the process that resulted in it resulted in truth. What process? Does Dr. O'C's belief result from thinking, from scientific method, from the particular experimental design she used, or what? Any way of spelling out what the relevant process is will appeal to conditionals, that is, if-statements. Suppose we say that Dr. O'C's belief is reliably acquired if the actual experimental design she used was reliable. That will mean that (given the way human minds and the rest of the world work) if that design had been used in various circumstances the result would have been a true belief. A reliable method is one that when used in the right circumstances will not give a false belief. (Perhaps in many circumstances it gives no belief at all.) So a more precise way of talking about reliability would specify a range of circumstances and of beliefs and then say that if the person were in those circumstances then those beliefs would be true.

One specific form of this idea is the concept of *tracking*. Consider the most basic kind of knowledge: perception. Suppose that you are watching a bird fly across your garden and land in a tree. As the position of the bird changes so does your perception and thus your perceptual belief. If the bird had followed a different path your sequence of beliefs would have been different.

Your beliefs therefore track the position of the bird, much as the eyes of a predator track the position of potential prey, or a blip on a radar screen tracks the position of a plane.

Tracking can be defined in terms of conditionals, if-sentences. If the bird had followed a different course, your beliefs would have been different. And before the bird flew the way it did, it would have been true to say that if it were to fly in the way it did, then you would believe that it was flying that way. Generalizing, we can turn this into a definition:

> A person's belief *tracks* a fact when two conditions are met: (1) if that fact had occurred (perhaps under slightly different circumstances), then the person would have believed that it occurred; (2) if the fact had not occurred, the person would not have had the belief.

(Clause (2) is needed because otherwise we would be allowing a belief to track a fact when it would have been held whether or not the fact had occurred.)

This definition is essentially due to Fred Dretske and Robert Nozick. They suggested that we can define knowledge in terms of tracking: a person's belief counts as knowledge when it tracks the fact that makes it true. So, for example, you know that the bird is halfway to the tree when your belief that it is halfway there tracks the fact that it is halfway there. And this will be so when if the bird had only been a quarter of the way there you would have believed that it was a quarter of the way there, and if it had been three quarters of the way there you would have believed that it was three quarters of the way there.

This approach to knowledge is clearly a version of the reliability approach. Reliability, remember, depends on whether there are good reasons, in the workings of the mind and the routes by which information comes to it, why true beliefs should result. So if a belief is based on a reliable process, then the process should give the belief only when it is true, and should give different beliefs in different situations. In other words, the belief should track the fact that makes it true.

There is something intuitively very right and appealing about this approach. It captures the feeling that when someone knows something then it is no accident that their belief is true: it is true because it tracks the facts. It captures the feeling that a person who has knowledge can be used by others as a reliable source of information: for if you know that the person's beliefs track the facts then you know that if you trust what they say your own beliefs will be true. And it captures the feeling that beliefs based on irrational reasoning or mistakes are not knowledge even if they happen to be true. For such deviations from correct thinking usually introduce factors which make the belief independent of the facts: even if the facts had been different, the person would still have held the belief.

4. Missing Information

But there are still problems, more tricky examples. One family of problem cases involves beliefs that track the facts but do so by accident. Suppose, for example, that you are in a psychological experiment like one of those described in chapter 2. You are given eyeglasses that make everything look upside down. But you do not know that this is what they are; you do not even know you are in a psychology experiment. (Perhaps the experimenters tell you that they are comparing different glasses' frames for comfort.) The glasses are put on you in the dark and when the light comes on you see a scene through a window. By mistake a mirror has been left by the window, which inverts the scene, exactly canceling the effect of the glasses. In the scene a balloon is floating and you are asked if it is rising or falling. You say that it is rising, as it in fact is. Your belief is true, and tracks the facts: if the balloon had been falling you would have said that it was falling, if it was stationary you would have said it was stationary, and so on. But the set-up that allowed your belief to track the fact was a fluke; all the subjects in the experiment before and after you believed that the balloon's motions were the opposite of what they in fact were. Many people when they think about this case will conclude that you do not know that the balloon is rising. Although your belief tracks the fact that it is rising you could too easily have had a false belief. Knowledge should be more secure than this.

One feature of this case is very significant. Suppose that you had been given the true information that you were being fitted with inverting glasses. Then when the balloon appeared to rise you would not have believed that it was rising. You would have thought "I am in an experiment and they are doing weird things to my vision; who knows what may really be happening." So there is true information you do not have which would have prevented your having the belief, even though the belief was true. This fact is closely linked to the accidental way that the belief tracks the truth. For although there is a variety of circumstances in which it is true that if they held you would have true beliefs about them, there is also a slightly larger variety of circumstances in which you would not have true beliefs. In many cases in which tracking is the result of accident, information about the accidental features of the situation can create circumstances in which the person's beliefs would be false.

The failure of a belief to be knowledge is often connected with the fact that it would not have survived exposure to some true information. For example, suppose that you are walking around downtown London thinking about classic rock 'n' roll. Around the corner walks a man you have seen many times in books and on television, though slightly aged from the images you remember. You stare hard and consider whether you might be mistaken, but, no, you still feel sure. You go back to your hotel to tell your friends "Elvis is alive; I just saw him." But there are facts that you do not know. On that day the streets have been flooded with Elvis lookalikes. There are hundreds of them in the area. Moreover this fact has been well publicized; if you had been reading serious newspapers instead of tabloids you would have realized it. Now, as a matter of fact the man you saw was in fact Elvis, who is alive and living a quiet life in London (in this example). But – according to most people who reflect on cases like this – you do not know that it was Elvis. For you could as easily have encountered one of the lookalikes, and then you would have been fooled.

Or consider a more tangled version of the same example. Again you are walking around London and again you see Elvis. But this time there are not hundreds of lookalikes out and about. Instead, there are newspaper headlines visible all over the place saying, falsely, that there are hundreds of Elvis lookalikes wandering the streets. If you had seen any of these headlines you would have not believed that the person you saw was Elvis. And it is a pure accident that you do not see any of these many headlines. In this case too people's reactions are usually that you do not know that the person you are seeing is Elvis. And one explanation of this reaction is that the fact that if you had seen the headlines you would not have believed that the man you saw was Elvis shows that your belief did not rest on a reliable process. Although it gives a true belief in this case there are not very different circumstances in which it does not.

It is interesting to make two contrasts here. One the one hand contrast your situation – seeing Elvis but in the unseen presence of lookalikes or misleading headlines – with that of a close friend of Elvis, who could tell him from all the lookalikes. The friend would know Elvis on sight, even if he knew about the lookalikes or had seen the misleading headlines. On the other hand, contrast your situation with someone who knows Elvis no better, and no worse, than you but just happens to see him coming out of a London shop, when there are no lookalikes about nor misleading headlines to be glimpsed. This person knows that it is Elvis before her, just by using her ordinary powers of perception and recognition and an ordinary level of caution. So the concept of knowledge has a really subtle and interesting combination of strictness and tolerance. It is tolerant in that we can often know things by use of our ordinary capacities to perceive, reason, and remember, even though these capacities sometimes lead to false beliefs. It is strict in that it does not allow that every use of these capacities which leads to a true belief results in knowledge. Sometimes we have to consider a much more specific process operating in a much more specific context, and ask "Is this reliable?"

There are many examples along these lines, in which people's beliefs are not knowledge not because of any false or irrational belief they have but because there are true beliefs they lack. (The facts that they are unaware of, which cause their beliefs not to be knowledge, are called **defeaters**.) Such examples are particularly troublesome for accounts of knowledge based on reliability or tracking. What they show is that if we want to define knowledge in terms of the conditions under which the process behind the belief results in truth, we are going to have a delicate job specifying the right process. If we define it too narrowly, as tracking analyses do, then a belief can fail to be knowledge because there are wider circumstances in which the person would have had a false belief. (For example, we ignore the effect of the lookalikes or misleading headlines in Elvis cases.) If we define it too widely, for example by counting reason or perception as belief-giving processes, then we will run into the problem that these processes often give false beliefs. (So then we wrongly fail to count as knowledge the belief of a normal person under normal circumstances who sees and recognizes Elvis.) We will need a definition narrow enough that the facts of the case can explain why this belief obtained by this process in these circumstances is true, and wide enough that the belief can be seen as a special case of a general truth-producing process. The right balance has not yet been found.

5. Knowledge and Trust

Finding a precise definition of knowledge in terms of suitable clear and more basic concepts may be very difficult. One reason for the difficulty may be that the concept of knowledge plays such a fundamental role in our thinking that it is hard to find clearer and more basic concepts to define it with. (Try defining "thing" or "if.") If we let our standards of clarity slide a little it is not too hard to let a slightly fudge-filled definition emerge from the direction this chapter has taken. A belief counts as knowledge, we might say, when it is derived from information gained by a reliable method by undefeated reasoning (that is, reasoning that has considered all the possible objections that under the circumstances are relevant). Much current work in epistemology accepts that a definition along these lines does capture what is essential to knowledge, and concentrates on thinking out what is meant by "reliable" and "undefeated." (In particular that very fudgy "under the circumstances" has come in for a lot of attention.)

To end this chapter I shall discuss why, assuming that this definition is along the right lines, it might represent a central desirable feature of beliefs, which might be so fundamental that it takes intellectual contortions to define it. The explanation needs some setting up.

People rely on others for information. An isolated individual using the evidence and ways of thinking available to us could know very very little.

There are two ways of using a person as a source of information. The simple way is to trust what they say. If someone says that she saw a moose walking down the street at two in the morning then you believe that at two in the morning a moose walked down the street. The other way is to take what someone says as evidence about their state of mind. You conclude that she believes a moose walked down the street at two in the morning, or perhaps that she believed she could get you to think that a moose had walked down the street. On the first of these ways, you assume that she knows what she is saying. On the second, you simply talk about her beliefs. So one thing we can mean when we say that what someone has is knowledge is: you can trust what they say.

Now consider a rather different use of knowledge. We build our beliefs on other beliefs, using what we already believe as evidence and as background for new beliefs. We do not use all our beliefs in the same way here. We treat some of our beliefs as definite facts about the world, safe to use as guides for future beliefs, and others as conjectures, which we are prepared to revise when more information comes in. (Notice that safety is not the same as certainty or as being apriori. We can treat a scientific theory, for example the theory of evolution, as a basis for evaluating later beliefs, although there will be further evidence to consider, and although we can see possible evidence that could refute it.) The difference between the two kinds of beliefs becomes particularly clear when evidence against a belief appears, and we have to think out how to react. You believe that all mammals have live young and then you discover about the platypus, which has the appearance and metabolism of a mammal but lays eggs. In reconsidering your beliefs you think: perhaps the platypus is not a mammal, or perhaps some mammals lay eggs, but at any rate we know that all mammals in Europe and the Americas have live young, and that the placenta appeared very early in the evolution of the mammals. When you think "at any rate we know," the concept of knowledge is being used to set aside some beliefs which you do not take to be threatened by the evidence at hand. So another thing you can mean by saying that something is knowledge is: we can take this for granted in evaluating the evidence for and against other beliefs.

The most interesting aspect of these two implications of the concept of knowledge is that they are essentially the same. If we treat someone as an authority on a subject matter, taking them as someone who has knowledge about that subject, then we will take what they say on the subject as definite fact rather than conjecture. (You are wondering what to believe about the platypus and so you consult a biologist. If you treat her as a source of knowledge then you revise your beliefs in ways that do not challenge what she says.) And, the other way round, if we treat some of our beliefs as definite facts then we are taking ourselves to be authorities with respect to those facts. (In the morning you seem to remember a moose walking down the street at 2 a.m. If you wonder whether you were dreaming or hallucinating and decide to accept your own memory-beliefs as facts, you are in effect saying: I know what happened to me last night, so I'll trust what I believe.)

I suspect that this is the core of the concept of knowledge. When we classify a belief as knowledge we think it has some of the right properties for using it as an authority in evaluating other beliefs. We are supposing that we can hold it constant as new evidence accumulates and new arguments are considered. We can state it as a background fact or as evidence without having to add qualifications like "according to Sam" or "this is what it looked like, anyway." And if this is what we are doing then it makes sense that knowledge will have the features on which the definition at the beginning of this section depends. Reliability fits into the picture in an obvious way. When we think that someone's belief is based on a reliable process we think that the basis of their belief is one that we judge will often enough accord with the facts. So we can at any rate trust that their belief starts in a way that we can trust. In order for the belief to be fully trustworthy we will need to know more about what has happened to past its basis in some reliable process. We will need to know that the process was not used in some situation in which it was not appropriate. More generally, we will have to know that starting from this basis and reasoning in this way will not in the given circumstances tend to false beliefs. In other words, we will need to know that there are not things that ought to be checked if one was reasoning in that way from that basis. (Are there lookalikes in the neighborhood?) So the defeaters aspect also falls into place.

So we have another formula: to take a belief as knowledge is to take it as something that you can trust when forming other beliefs. But this is not a definition of knowledge. It is much too vague, for one thing. But in addition it is a formula not about what actually *is* knowledge but about which of a person's beliefs that person or another will *treat as* knowledge. The nearest it brings us to a definition is this: it is reasonable for one person, A, to take another person B to know something if from what A knows of B's situation it is reasonable of A to share B's belief. Or, another way of saying the same thing, A should take B to know something when A can take B to be a reliable source of beliefs like the one in question, where what counts as "like" is determined by B's purposes.

Notice that these definitions refer to the purposes of the person who classifies another person's beliefs as knowledge. (Or, very similar, to what it would be reasonable for that person to think.) This element of purpose is often quite clear when we attribute knowledge. Suppose for example one bank robber says to another "The police know it was us who pulled the Chase Manhattan job." The force of "know" here is that the police have information about their identity with a nature and reliability that is relevant to tracking them down. (Compare the examples of special knowledge about police work, restaurants and other topics towards the end of section 1. There is a connection here with contextualism about knowledge, discussed in chapter 11.) When we try to make a general abstract definition of "person P knows fact F," one of the problems we are tackling is that of finding a single core purpose for having beliefs. Is there a unified aim of inquiry in terms of which we can say what counts as a top-quality belief?

Reading Questions

1   The McA case contrasts with the FitzB case. One case shows that truth is required for knowledge and one shows that justification is required. Which is which?

2   The O'C case shows that truth and justification are not enough for knowledge. Why is Dr. O'C's belief justified?

3   Suppose that a person is listening to the radio and hears McA's weather forecast. As a result she prepares for a hurricane. And a hurricane arrives. How does Lehrer's principle apply to her belief?

4   A father believes that his son is wonderful. He defends his belief with good school reports and his son's large number of friends. He also believes that any son of his has to be wonderful. How could we discover what his belief that his son is wonderful really depends on (in the sense described in section 2): the school reports and friendships, his belief that his son must be wonderful, both, or neither?

5   If the old sea captain had derived his estimate of his latitude from the horoscopes of the crew would this method have been more or less reliable than his use of old-fashioned astronomy?

6   Why is my belief that I will not win the lottery (see section 3) statistically reliable? What is the method that is reliable?

7   An officer is using a radar device to measure the speeds of cars on a highway. The device registers the speed of car A as 100 m.p.h. Which of the following are relevant to the question of whether the use of the device tracks the speed of car A?
    (a) If the previous car had gone 60 m.p.h. slower the radar would have registered 100 m.p.h.
    (b) If the car after car A goes 100 m.p.h. the radar will register 100 m.p.h.
    (c) If car A goes 100 m.p.h. the radar will register 100 m.p.h.
    (d) The car is going 100 m.p.h.
    (e) If car A goes 60 m.p.h. the radar will register 60 m.p.h.
    (f) If the car goes 60 m.p.h. the radar will register 100 m.p.h.
    Which of these are relevant to the question of whether the officer knows that car A is going 100 m.p.h?

8   Does McA's belief that there will be a hurricane track the fact that there will be a hurricane?

Thinking Questions

9   Are all desirable features of belief relevant to whether the belief is knowledge? What about: unoffensiveness, simplicity, comfortingness?

10   Newspaper quotation: "The trekkies who follow the voyages of the USS Enterprise have known for years that there are planets of all kinds orbiting practically every star in the galaxy." The author of this clearly does not think that the trekkies' belief is true. But he or she still says that they "know" it. Does this show that knowledge does not have to be true?

11   The definition of knowledge at the beginning of section 5 uses two underdefined terms, "reliable" and "defeater." Are they independent of one another? (In other words, might knowing the extent to which a belief-forming process was reliable determine the kinds of facts that would defeat beliefs based on information given by that process?)

12   Suppose that you look out your open window and see a bird. It is there and you really do see it. What you do not know is that devious psychologists have released clouds of hallucinogenic gas near your house. You have not breathed any of the gas, but if you had you would be hallucinating at this moment. Does this fact mean that though you see the bird you do not know that there is a bird there? Are there implications for the relation between tracking and defeaters?

13   In section 5 it was claimed that to classify a belief as knowledge is to judge that it can be used without qualifications. Is this a feature that a belief can have absolutely, independent of its context or the purpose for which it is going to be used?

14   We might try defining knowledge as belief which is true and justified and would remain justified whatever true beliefs were added to the believer's stock of beliefs. What problems would this definition run into?

Further Reading

Good surveys of work on defining knowledge are Robert K. Shope, *The Analysis of Knowing* (Princeton University Press, 1983), and chapters 2 and 3 of Jonathan Dancy, *An Introduction to Contemporary Epistemology* (Blackwell, 1988). Dancy is probably the simpler of these. See also Linda Zagzebski, "What is knowledge?" in John Greco and Ernest Sosa (eds), *The Blackwell Guide to Epistemology* (Blackwell, 1999).

Part 2 of Robert Nozick's *Philosophical Explanations* (Oxford University Press, 1981) is a standard source for reliability and conditional theories of knowledge. Personal favorites are Fred Dretske, "Conclusive reasons," *Australasian Journal of Philosophy*, 66 (1971), 1–22, and Edward Craig, *Knowledge and the State of Nature* (Oxford University Press, 1990). For an extremely stimulating unorthodox approach to knowledge read Peter Unger, *Ignorance: A Case for Skepticism* (Oxford University Press, 1975). A taste of current work and real insight into the issues can be got from two recent, clearly written, but very demanding papers: David Lewis, "Elusive knowledge," *Australasian Journal of Philosophy*, 74 (1996), 549–67, and Keith DeRose, "Solving the skeptical problem," *The Philosophical Review*, 104 (1995), 1–50.

The philosophical text which started the debates reported in this chapter an be found in part I section 2 of John Cottingham, *Western Philosophy: An anthology* (Blackwell, 1996), Plato, "Knowledge versus Opinion."

Electronic resources: *Routledge Encyclopedia of Philosophy*: Belief and knowledge; Knowledge, causal theory of; Reliabilism. *The Stanford Encyclopedia of Philosophy*: knowledge analysis of; reasons; justification vs. explanation; trust.

Chapter 7

EXTERNALISM AND EPISTEMIC VIRTUES

1. The Escape from Justification

While the search for a definition of "knows" may seem like a small and peculiar part of epistemology, it has had one deep and far-reaching result. It has convinced many philosophers that something is fundamentally wrong with the way that for centuries we have been approaching questions about knowledge, rationality and belief. In terms of the development in this book, the trouble goes right back to chapter 1, where the fundamental issues of epistemology were motivated as a more careful version of the criticisms people make of one another's defenses of their beliefs. That makes it seem as if the most important idea in epistemology is that of justification: some beliefs can be justified, and it is reasonable to hold them, while other beliefs are not justified and should be abandoned. If this is our point of view then it comes as a nasty surprise that, as we found out in the previous chapter, knowledge is not justified true belief. Something more seems to be required. Many philosophers have searched around looking for a way of supplying the missing ingredient that preserves the idea that what we are most of all looking for are beliefs that we can defend with rational arguments and evidence.

Other philosophers, though, suspect that the difficulty of defining knowledge in terms of justified belief suggests that knowledge represents a very different ideal from justification. Some of the fundamental qualities we want our beliefs to have, they suspect, have nothing to do with justifying or defending them or supporting them with reasons. To see the basic idea behind the suspicion, consider perception. A person opens her eyes and sees a bird on the window ledge. She knows that there is a bird there. Does she have any good evidence for what she knows, any other beliefs that justify it? Well, she has her eyes open and her vision is normal. If her claim that there is a bird on the ledge was challenged she might say that it certainly looked to her like there was a bird there. But this belief about how things looked to her was not one she had until she was challenged, and she surely knew the bird was there even before she reflected on how things looked. Moreover the reliability of her visual perception – the fact that nearly always what she learns when she looks is right – may not be something that she knows enough about to be able to use it to justify her belief. The fact is, her perception just is reliable, whether or not she knows it, and it is safe for her to rely on it. A small child or a cat can know that there is a bird on the ledge by seeing it, even though they do not have the resources for providing a rational justification of what they learn.

(Do not confuse a belief's being justified with its being justifiable to use it as a ground for another belief. If our person uses her belief that there is a bird on the ledge as evidence that the ledge is not covered with a layer of acid then the latter belief may be justified. But we must be careful before assuming that a justifier must be justified. Perhaps it is enough for a justifier to be known.)

Perception might be a special case. But once we begin to doubt that everything that can be known can be justified we begin to see many other possible examples. Each one is controversial, but together they add up to a striking thought. Consider some stories.

Someone you know slightly is telling you a long story about his recent troubles, which you can see is leading up to a request. You have the sudden thought "He's lying; there's a trap in here somewhere." You can't identify any obvious flaws in his story or any give-away signs in his manner; but you find the conviction that he is not being straight with you persists and even grows. So you make an excuse to get away, feeling somewhat irrational and guilty. Later it turns out that he was indeed lying and was planning to lure you into a scheme that would be to his but not your advantage. Suppose now that very often your feelings about things like this are right, in fact that it is not just by good luck that they match features of the situation. (You may not know how often you are right; you may not often get a chance to check.) Then if we say that you often know when people are lying to you, we can be taken to be attributing an important skill to you. But it is not the skill of explicitly considering the force of evidence for your beliefs about people.

Another example. An art dealer has a sense of who painted a picture. She has an eye for fakes and misattributed paintings. She can see a cobweb-covered canvas taken from someone's attic and declare, "This might be a Rembrandt," and sometimes as she passes a painting labelled "Cezanne" in a museum she will quietly mutter "Fake." She is always right. She has no idea how she does it. She just says "I have a feeling and then I feel sure."

A different kind of example, raising many issues: Consider someone who has grown up in a society in which there is slavery and in which women are treated as the property of their fathers or husbands. Suppose that this person has the strong conviction that these things are unjust and morally wrong. But suppose that he is naive and badly educated and cannot defend his conviction against sophisticated people who have all sorts of clever arguments for defending their way of life. Suppose that in the face of all these clever arguments he changes his mind, and decides that it was silly to have supposed that slavery was wrong. It is very tempting to describe this by saying that he realized the wrongness of slavery until he was overcome by reasoning. He had a kind of knowledge which could not survive the impact of argument and evidence.

We do have skills like these. Different people have different skills, but there are some skills that we all have. We may not know the full range of accurate belief-acquiring skills that people possess. We certainly do not in most cases know how we do it. As we learn more about human psychology it becomes less and less likely that the processes in our minds that give us reliable beliefs resemble the reasoning by which we would show that they are reliable. Instead, we have a large number of special-purpose patterns of thinking ("mental modules" as they are sometimes called) which give accurate beliefs on specific topics under specific circumstances. The beliefs that they produce are true often enough that we can often rely on them. That is, a person can trust her own beliefs, and other people can trust that person's beliefs, when they are formed by such a process and when the conditions are right. (It is often not easy to know if the conditions are right, though. More on this in section 4 below.) To that extent we have many beliefs which we cannot easily justify – or to put it more carefully, to justify them requires more information than is usually needed to acquire them – and which play important responsible roles among our beliefs.

There are many ways of linking reflections such as these to standard positions in the theory of knowledge. One link is provided by the not really controversial conclusion that we should aim not only for critical reflection on our own beliefs, but also for the kind of understanding of how people form beliefs that can guide us in evaluating the claims that others make. A much more controversial conclusion, which is certainly not forced on us, would be that the concept of knowledge is independent of that of justification: much of what we know is not justified and what is valuable about knowledge is not a matter of evidence and good reasoning.

2. Externalism

The controversial conclusion just described is an extreme instance of a general attitude to epistemology called **externalism**. Externalism is as general an attitude as skepticism or empiricism; it comes in many forms. An externalist approach to an epistemological issue will insist that many of the important factors to be taken into account may be unknown to the people whose beliefs are in question. **Internalism**, in contrast, requires that important concepts such as knowledge and justification should be defined, as far as possible, in terms that people can apply to themselves on the basis of their own self-knowledge. The broad general motivations are clear. Internalism is driven by an aim of managing one's own beliefs so as to make them as true and rational as possible, and we cannot manage our beliefs if important features of them are unknown to us. (After all, if we are trying to reassure ourselves that some skeptical scare story is not true, we won't get any comfort from facts that we are not even aware of.) Externalism is driven by an aim of understanding human information-gathering capacities, and in doing this it does not want to be hampered by arbitrary restrictions on the kind of considerations it can consider. (After all, if we were investigating human capacities to see things, we would not consider only parts of a person's eyes that that person can see.)

There are stronger and weaker externalist positions. The controversial conclusion of section 1 would be a very strong externalism. A much weaker externalism could be derived from the considerations about "defeaters" in the previous chapter. Remember the example: your claim to know that you have seen Elvis in London is undermined by the fact that there are many Elvis-imitators in the neighborhood, even though you have no reason to believe that they are there. Or, to put it differently, your claim to knowledge is undermined by your failure to have checked whether there are Elvis imitators around. The externalist element here is the fact that the relevance of your failure to have checked for Elvis imitators may depend on factors that you cannot know just by thinking about what you believe and how you have been reasoning. Suppose, for example, that there is an annual Elvis lookalike contest in London. Then it is plausible that checking that it wasn't a lookalike is required before someone can claim to know that it was Elvis they saw. And if such contests are banned – Elvis lookalikes are thrown into the tower of London on sight – then checking is not required. If this is right, then whether a fact undermines a belief – prevents it counting as knowledge – depends on factors outside a person's awareness.

It is "plausible" that checking is required if there is an annual context and not required if there is not. But it is not more than just plausible: one could try to explain the conditions under which a failure to rule out a possibility defeats a knowledge claim entirely in terms of the structure of the person's beliefs. That would be an internalist approach to the question. (And the fact that most philosophers grappling with the issue do not take this tack shows that they are, to that extent, accepting a mild externalism. But they could be wrong.) A more daring variation on the idea would be to make it part of an account of justification. This variation would begin by assuming that justification was necessary for knowledge, but would continue by building non-defeatedness into the definition of justification. That is, knowledge would be defined as (or conjectured to be) belief which is true and justified and possibly satisfies some other conditions, and a belief would be justified only if there was no known or unknown factor that undermined it. If an account along these lines were accepted, then not only knowledge but also justification would depend on factors outside a person's awareness. You would often not have the information to know if your beliefs were justified.

3. Cousins of Knowledge

When philosophers think about knowledge they usually think of "knowing that": knowing that $2 + 2 = 4$, knowing that you exist, knowing that the earth goes round the sun. But we also speak of knowing how: knowing how to find your way home, knowing how to bake a cake, knowing how to persuade someone to buy a worthless car. We speak also of knowing where, which, and who: knowing where there is a good Chinese restaurant in Oklahoma City, knowing which Chinese restaurants in Oklahoma City are good, and knowing who took you to the best Chinese meal you have ever had.

Knowing how is the most different from knowing that. For if you know, say, where there is a good Chinese restaurant you know that there is a good Chinese restaurant at some particular location. But if you know how to ride a bicycle there need be no fact that you know to be true. (But note also that if you know where there is a good restaurant, you know how to find it. Knowing where or who can be squeezed into the pattern of knowing that or of knowing how.) Knowing how seems very different from knowing that, if we think in internalist terms. For in order to know how to, say, ride a bicycle, there does not have to be any chain of correct reasoning or inference leading to a bicycle-riding conclusion. But seen from an externalist point of view there are basic similarities. To know how to ride a bicycle one has to possess a mental process that reliably produces acts of bike-riding. The attempts at riding must not succeed by accident. (If I claim to know how to ride a bike and then when I try I don't fall off only because my wheels are stuck in tramline tracks while a strong wind pushes me along, my claim has not been confirmed.) Some quite subtle features of knowing that have analogs with knowing how. Consider defeaters again. Just as you do not know that it really is Elvis if you have not ruled out various ways in which what seems to be Elvis is not, so too you do not know how to ride a bicycle if there are easy problems which you could not counteract, even if they do not actually arise. If the combination of a small stick in the road and a side-wind would have made you fall off, you do not know how to ride, whether or not you ever meet such a combination. The same goes for knowing how to do anything: you don't have the practical knowledge unless you have the capacity to counteract the effects of various dangers, whether or not they actually threaten. (Imagine someone claiming she knows how to fly a 747 when she could not handle a landing in a crosswind.) And, to deepen the resemblance, you may be quite unaware of some of these potential disqualifiers. If many of the streets in your neighborhood cross rail-road tracks then being able to ride a bicycle means being able to handle the bumps as the road meets the rails, even if you have no way of anticipating that this will be required.

The point of making analogies between knowledge-how and knowledge-that is the same as the point of the examples of reliable belief-acquiring capacities skills. Both are meant to bring out reactions that might counteract your exposure to over-intellectualized descriptions of knowledge. In much of your education you will have met the ideal of knowledge that is based on evidence and good reasons. Scientific knowledge is better than ignorant superstition because there is carefully obtained and assessed evidence behind it. In order to convict an accused person a jury must know beyond a reasonable doubt that he or she is guilty, evaluating the evidence produced by prosecution and defense rather than relying on hunches and intuitions. Influenced by such ideals, you are likely to undervalue beliefs that are not the result of good reasoning from carefully considered evidence. So it is worth emphasizing the opposite side of things – that very many of our beliefs are the result of processes which work well, and sustain essential aspects of our lives, but which do not consist in evidence and reasoning. Moreover we apply labels of approval, such as "know," to such beliefs in systematic ways that are at least as much concerned with reliability as with rationality.

4. Skepticism and Knowing that You Know

Suppose that an externalist, who we will call Xavier, and an internalist, who will call Inta, discuss the extent of human knowledge. Their discussion might go as follows.

Inta: I see the point that there are many good qualities of beliefs besides their being reasonable. After all, truth is such a quality, and truth is a matter of whether the world agrees with your thoughts, not of how well you are reasoning. The theory of knowledge, as I see it, is all about the relationship between reasoning and truth. The central question is how safe a grasp on truth we can have by being rational.

Xavier: And suppose the answer was that reason alone will not get us many of the true beliefs we want or need? Suppose that human social life depends on our having true beliefs about one another's moods, and that we can have these, as long as we trust our natural sense of these things, and don't try to think everything out. That's just one example among many.

Inta: If that were true then skepticism would have achieved a small victory. We would have discovered that although many of our beliefs about one another's moods are true, we cannot justify them.

Xavier: That's a particular kind of skepticism, which focuses on justification. I prefer to focus on knowledge. We would still *know* about one another's moods, even if this knowledge is not based on the kind of thinking scientists and lawyers go for.

Inta: I'm not sure we would, if the knowledge is based on the reliable processes you like so much. Each such process is reliable only under specific conditions, and a person usually doesn't know if those conditions hold. So imagine you just feel sure that the person you are talking to is lying to you, but can produce no good reasons for it. You have no way of knowing that your liar-detection processes are working well or that this is the kind of situation in which they are reliable. So you don't really know if your belief is true.

Xavier: No, there's a mistake there. In the case you just described I have no way of being sure that what I have is knowledge. But that doesn't stop it being knowledge all the same. Very often I know something, but don't know that I know it. In general, a lot of situations where you internalists think skepticism may win because we don't know something are really cases where we don't know whether we know it. But people often know things without knowing that they know them.

Inta: I find the idea of knowing without knowing that you know really weird. After all, suppose you have good enough reasons for believing something, good enough that they make it knowledge if it is true. And suppose it is true. Then you can tell, just by thinking about them, that they are good enough.

Xavier: But knowledge isn't a matter of good enough reasons. Not always, anyway. And even when it is you may not have this apriori grasp of them. So it's likely that quite often we are nearer to, or further away from, knowledge than we think.

Inta: That seems like giving in to skepticism, without admitting it. Where I honestly say we may not know something, you say we may know it, but not know that we know. Same conclusion in different words.

Xavier: Well, actually, I'd say sometimes that we don't know whether we know, sometimes we know but don't have a justified belief that we know, and sometimes just plain don't know. These are all different.

Inta: I don't think I want philosophy to be as complicated as that. The point of thinking about these questions is to understand how we believe in a way that helps us to have better beliefs; but the way you're taking them seems to me to provide nothing that we can actually use.

5. Virtues

Inta is right in one way, at least. Things are more complicated for an externalist. (Richer, truer to the facts, an externalist might say.) In particular, the externalist substitute for the concept of rationality is significantly more complicated. For an internalist epistemologist the central feature of human beings is that they can think rationally. When they think rationally on the basis of well-collected evidence the result is justified belief. So in looking for justified beliefs we are exercising our capacity to be rational. For an externalist there is a more complex story to tell about human capacities. These capacities are very varied and many of them do not connect closely with rationality. They vary from the capacity to see well to a good memory to the skill of telling when someone is trustworthy. The externalist does not have to assume that when we do reason successfully there is a single quality of rationality that we are exhibiting. Rationality itself may be a bundle of overlapping and competing capacities. (For example, there is the capacity to follow a complex line of reasoning, and there is the capacity to know when reasoning is too complex for one to handle without getting confused. These complement one another but also sometimes pull in opposite directions.)

Externalists believe that there are many independent and irreducible capacities that we employ when we try to know. They call these capacities **epistemic virtues**. The term fits well, for emphasizing the variety of our knowledge-gathering skills is like emphasizing the variety of the ways we can live a moral life. Moral virtues such as courage, honesty, and self-control vary greatly in the ways they help people to live good lives and in the psychological demands they make. A person can be honest but lack self-control, or brave but dishonest, and then we will find it hard to sum up the person's moral character as good or bad. Similarly, a person can be very good at drawing conclusions from evidence, but very bad at noticing evidence that undermines her beliefs. Then we will find it hard to sum up the person's knowledge-gathering capacities as rational or irrational.

It would be good to have a survey of epistemic virtues, a comprehensive classification of the characteristics that help us expand our knowledge. No one has ever come near to producing such a classification. The epistemic virtues are too varied. Many of them are versions of moral virtues. There is intellectual courage, for example, as shown by someone who defends a position others find implausible. There is intellectual honesty and intellectual self-control too. Many epistemic virtues are general virtues of intelligent activity, and will apply to making decisions or playing games as well as to acquiring knowledge. For example, there is attention to detail and its complement the ability to see through the detail to the larger picture.

Some epistemic virtues are purely epistemic. For example, there is respect for evidence, already mentioned. Like most virtues it has to be balanced with a complementary opposite, in this case the capacity to allow that an interesting idea might be true even though there is not yet enough evidence to accept it. (This latter virtue is interesting for being contrary in spirit to traditional epistemology: it is the virtue of knowing when lack of evidence does not mean that an idea should be rejected.) There is also the capacity to amass a body of evidence and keep it in an organized manner, the capacity to assess the relevance of evidence to hypothesis, and so on. There are also purely epistemic virtues that fit less neatly into traditional epistemology. There is the capacity to think up experiments that will indicate whether one hypothesis rather than another is more likely. There is also the capacity to know when one is likely to be deceiving oneself about the force of the evidence for a claim one does not want to accept. And there are many others. It seems overwhelmingly likely, though, that none of these virtues are self-contained psychological capacities: each of them is most likely the application of a more general mental ability to the special activity of belief-acquisition.

Epistemic virtues can serve as a substitute for the concept of justification. One reason for wanting such a substitute would arise if we adopted the externalist definition of justification sketched at the end of section 2. If we did that we would not call a belief "justified" simply because it is linked by good reasoning to good evidence. For a person could have such beliefs which were defeated by factors she was not aware of. We would then need some other term for beliefs that are securely based on evidence. We would still want to praise people whose beliefs had this quality and we would still want to strive to make our own beliefs have it. We could apply any label we wanted. But in so doing we would be defining an epistemic virtue of reasonableness, respect for evidence. So then on the occasions where we used to ask whether a belief was justified, we would instead ask whether the person acquired or held it by exercising such epistemic virtues. We could ask this question even if we did not adopt the externalist conception of justification; we could ask it as a way of getting something like the internalist conception of justification from an externalist point of view. The answer to the question is likely to be more complex, though, since in exercising one virtue a person can be violating another. For example, a person may exhibit intellectual courage while disregarding intellectual caution or attention to detail. This could happen if the person believes an interesting new hypothesis which is consistent with most but not all of the available data, trusting that explanations will be found for the few facts that seem not to fit. Then the person is exhibiting the kind of bold, far-seeing attitude that leads us to radical changes in our knowledge, while also exhibiting the kind of haste that sometimes leads to big mistakes. Is the belief justified; is the person rational? It is hard to say, but it is much easier to say which epistemic virtues were exhibited and which were neglected.

6. The Externalist Attitude

Externalism is a set of questions rather than a set of answers. It suggests that we ask what capacities we must have in order to know what we do, given that the world around us is as it is, rather than ask how we can find patterns of reasoning leading from plausible evidence to beliefs that need justification. The externalist questions do not need to exclude the internalist ones: we can ask both. We may find answers to questions of both kinds, or we may fail.

But to represent internalism and externalism as simply different but compatible programs is to miss the deep difference in attitude between them. If either program could completely succeed then the other would have to fit into it in a subsidiary role. If we could explain how to achieve our aims in acquiring beliefs entirely in terms of the use of reasoning from prior beliefs and sensory input, then the only reasons for thinking about reliability or respect for evidence would be to explain why we value justified true beliefs (or beliefs that are true, justified, and have some other internalist quality), or what the obstacles to acquiring them are. Externalism would have to be a back-up to internalism or be a waste of time. Suppose on the other hand we could explain what those belief-acquiring aims are, in terms of our need for beliefs that meet a set of basic requirements, such as reliability, usefulness, and manageability by limited intelligence. Then although good reasoning from good evidence would still be important, it would become a means, perhaps one means among many, to achieving reliable. useful, and manageable beliefs.

Again an analogy with ethics might help. If we could find a set of rules such that if everyone followed them then human life would go as well as it possibly could, then we would not need to talk of courage or moral insight except as shortcut ways of describing some of the rules or as part of a further account of the psychological traits needed to follow the rules. And if on the other hand the good human life consisted of essentially opposed characteristics such as courage and caution, generosity and self-respect, then any rules we could formulate would just be approximate formulas which would serve as rules of thumb to guide us around the space defined by these basic values.

These are very deep issues and will color the discussion of the remaining chapters of this book, especially chapter 8 on knowledge of minds and chapter 9 on moral knowledge. (Chapter 10 on Bayesian epistemology is largely an exposition of the purest and most detailed internalist theory yet to appear.) There will generally be three competing voices: a skeptical voice that suggests that we may not know what we seem to on some topic, an optimistic internalist voice that suggests ways in which beliefs on that topic can be supported by reasoning and evidence, and an externalist voice that suggests that while we may have knowledge about the topic we do not do so by virtue of our rationality.

Reading Questions

1   Why does the fact that knowledge is not justified true belief suggest that knowledge and justification may have very little relation to one another? Why does it merely suggest it?

2   Why does the fact that children and animals can know many facts by perception suggest that reasoning and evidence are not essential to knowledge? Why does it merely suggest it?

3   Why would the London Elvis-imitation context suggest that a person could not know whether she had checked all the relevant possibilities that might defeat her claim to know that Elvis was alive in London?

4   Why does the emphasis on reasoning in internalism make it hard for an internalist to see knowledge-how and knowledge-that as similar phenomena?

5   When Xavier distinguishes knowing whether you know from having a justified belief about whether you know, how is this a reply to what Inta has just said?

6   Why does the fact that in exercising one virtue a person can be violating another suggest problems for defining justification in terms of the exercise of epistemic virtue?

Thinking Questions

7   Externalism has been presented in terms of defeaters and in terms of reliability. What connections are there between these two ideas?

8   Knowledge-how was presented as having a lot in common with knowledge-that, and it was hinted that knowledge-who (-where, -what, . . .) was similar. But can the hint be turned into an argument?

9   Find an example where someone knows something and knows that they know it, but does not have a justified belief that they know it. (An example, that is, which an externalist would argue has these features.)

10   Was Inta right at the end of the dialogue to claim that externalism gives no ways of criticizing and improving our beliefs?

11   Does externalism have to involve a variety of basic incomparable epistemic virtues? Why could there not be just one fundamental virtue, that of having beliefs that are reliably linked to facts?

Further Reading

A thorough treatment of the main questions of this chapter is given by Ernest Sosa, "Skepticism and the Internal/External Divide" in John Greco and Ernest Sosa (eds), *The Blackwell Guide to Epistemology* (Blackwell, 1999). For a discussion of internalism versus externalism see Laurence Bonjour, "Internalism/externalism." For a discussion of virtue epistemology see

John Greco, "Virtue epistemology" in Jonathan Dancy and Ernest Sosa (eds), *A Companion to Epistemology* (Blackwell, 1993). Linda Zagzebski, *Virtues of the Mind* (Cambridge University Press, 1996) puts virtue epistemology in a very general setting.

Electronic resources: *Routledge Encyclopedia of Philosophy*: Internalism and externalism in epistemology; Knowledge, tacit; Virtue epistemology. *The Stanford Encyclopedia of Philosophy*: justification, internalist vs. externalist conceptions of.

Chapter 8

KNOWLEDGE OF MINDS

1. Psychological Beliefs

Many of our beliefs are about our thoughts, characters, and feelings. These beliefs are central to our social and practical lives: without beliefs about what we and other people want and think we could not co-operate with one another in any sort of practical, scientific, or social activity. These are **psychological beliefs**, they include beliefs about what we think, know, hope, want, love, hate, remember, and all the other activities of our minds. Human beings could not live human social lives if they did not attribute belief, desire, emotion, and other states of mind to one another.

Psychological beliefs are needed for almost all other beliefs. Scientific beliefs, for example, are based on evidence and reasoning that is shared between many people. Some people do experiments and gather data by observation. Other people search for theories to explain the data. Still other people organize the data and theories and write textbooks making sense of them for students and other scientists. None of this could happen if scientists were not operating socially, using their beliefs about one another's minds to transmit, criticize, modify, and organize information which eventually emerges as scientific knowledge. One-person science would not be science as we know it. So here too our psychological beliefs are an essential background to the way we get and justify other beliefs.

Because psychological beliefs are so central to our lives, we rarely even notice them. Most of the time we take it for granted that what people tell us, and what we read in books and newspapers, is true. So we accept without realizing it the belief that other people have beliefs and that most of these beliefs are true. Similarly we accept without realizing it the belief that most people's actions are motivated by desires, and that most of these desires are for things we can sympathize with. We believe that other people have beliefs and desires and that we understand what they are. Because this is so central to our lives, we feel very confident about many of our psychological beliefs. We act as if they were certain.

Yet it is not so obvious that this confidence is justified. We are sometimes very mistaken about one another's minds. (We are sometimes mistaken about our own minds.) When someone lies to you, or tricks you, or acts in a way that you do not expect, you realize that your beliefs about that person's mind were not true. You had misunderstood their beliefs or desires or feelings. If this happens often enough, or if you simply begin to notice how often you are wrong in your beliefs about other people's minds, you may begin to suspect that the confidence we have in our beliefs about one another may be a mass delusion. You may become a skeptic about our psychological beliefs, thinking that however useful to us they are, we do not have good reasons for thinking that they are true.

There are deep philosophical issues here. One of them is known as the **other minds problem**. That is the problem of finding good reasons to believe that the other people around you have minds like yours, with similar beliefs, desires, and feelings. Might not other people be robots, or have mental states completely unlike yours? This is much more far-reaching than the doubt that is possible every time that you assume that you know what someone is thinking or feeling, but on reflection realize that your reasons for assuming this are not very convincing.

There are many connections between these issues and general positions in the theory of knowledge. One important connection is with the contrast between foundationalist and holist (or coherentist) theories of knowledge, described in chapter 5, section 2. As we shall see, on foundationalist accounts the other minds problem is much harder to solve than on holist accounts. Another important connection is with the contrast between error and ignorance, described in chapter 5, section 1. If we choose to minimize error, and take very few risks of having false beliefs, then we will be very suspicious of our psychological beliefs. But if we choose to minimize ignorance, and take few risks of not having beliefs that we need to understand the world and live our lives, then we will be more willing to accept them even at the risk that some of them may be false.

Very intuitive and very abstract issues are closely linked here. On the one hand, the possibility that beliefs about ourselves and about other people on which we rely in everyday life may not be certain, in fact that some of them may not be true, is a disturbing one. And on the other, the philosophical project of giving reasons to separating the reasonable beliefs from those which we believe only because they are familiar or convenient is deeply threatened by problems about psychological beliefs. If we cannot give a good account of our beliefs in our own and other people's minds then an enormous hole appears in our account of all our other beliefs.

Philosophers have often reacted to this situation by simplifying. They try to show that large classes of psychological beliefs are certain, and that we can base the less certain ones on them. In this chapter we will see three such attempts: self-centered, behavioral, and materialist. The conclusion of the chapter will be that the truth about psychological beliefs cannot be simplified. Each of the simplifying theories makes some important points, but in the end there remain deep and difficult questions which we should not pretend to have simple answers to.

2. Self-centered Theories

There is a tradition in philosophy, dating back at least to Descartes, which divides a person's psychological beliefs into three kinds. The first kind are that person's beliefs about their own experience, that is, their beliefs about what they are perceiving and feeling, and about the thoughts, desires, and memories that pass through their consciousness. It is assumed that a person has very little difficulty knowing what they are feeling or thinking, so these beliefs are taken to be certain. The second kind of psychological beliefs are beliefs about action, that is, beliefs about what behavior this person and others perform under various circumstances. This too is taken to be fairly easy to know: to know whether someone is, for example, tying their shoelaces you just have to look and see what they are doing with their hands. The third kind of psychological beliefs are beliefs about other people's experience, that is, about the perceptions, feelings, beliefs, desires, and memories of others. These beliefs are much less certain, according to this tradition. They present us with the other minds problem, which is understood as the problem of justifying the third kind of belief in terms of beliefs of the first two kinds.

One attempt at solving the problem, found in empiricist philosophers such as Locke and John Stuart Mill, is the **argument from analogy**. The idea is to use inductive reasoning (as described in chapter 4) to get from beliefs of the first two kinds (about your own experiences and about behavior to beliefs of the third kind (about other people's experiences). The argument runs as follows. You know what experiences you have, and you can observe your own behavior. As a result you can notice correlations between your own behavior and your own experiences. For example, you can notice a pattern of bringing a hammer down on your thumb, followed by the sensation of pain, followed by waving the thumb in the air and producing interesting language. So you can reason by simple induction to the conclusion that whenever you bring a hammer down on your thumb the first result is pain and the second result is a waving of the thumb and violent language. Then you can observe that other people sometimes hit their thumbs with hammers and then wave their thumbs in the air while cursing. So you extend your inductive generalization to conclude that in all people the pattern is: hammer-on-thumb, pain, cursing. So you have reason to believe that other people feel pain just as you do.

This is not a very convincing argument. If someone *really* believed that other people did not have experiences like their own they would not find their belief seriously challenged by it. Think first of the two stages of inductive reasoning. Each of them has problems. To get to the first conclusion, that simple patterns connecting behavior and sensation are found in your own experience, you have to be able to find such patterns, without exceptions, in your own experience. But in fact such simple patterns are pretty rare. Sometimes the hammer hurts a lot and sometimes hardly at all. Sometimes you jump up and down and curse and sometimes you just hit the next nail extra hard. The second bit of inductive reasoning – from a generalization about your own experience to one about other people – is just as bad. It too is affected by the variability of behavior. And in addition it involves an enormous leap from one small class of events – your own behavior and sensations – to another very different class – those of someone else. What reason is there for believing that the same generalizations hold among these different events? It is like discovering, say, how much iron expands when heated, and then concluding that copper will expand by the same amount. Or like discovering that all fish can swim and concluding that all animals can.

3. Behavioral Theories

Some twentieth-century philosophers have responded to the inadequacies of the argument from analogy by reasoning in the opposite direction, starting with beliefs about people's behavior and ending with conclusions about their experiences. The basic thought of these theories is that in order to have beliefs about people's experiences we have to learn words for those experiences. To believe that someone is in pain you have to know what pain is; to know that someone wants to hunt moose you have to know not only what moose are but what wanting is. We learn what pain is or what wanting is when we are children and adults describe other people or ourselves as being in pain or wanting things. So we learn to use words like "pain" and "wants" to describe people, on the basis of their behavior. If someone is holding their finger tightly while moving in an agonized way and moaning we think that their finger hurts, and if someone is trying with force and persistence to get a coin into a drink-dispenser we think that she wants a drink.

Assume for the moment that these considerations show that we can be reasonably certain in our beliefs about other people's states of mind (their beliefs, desires, feelings, and so on). Assume, that is, that by observing what people do and then applying what we have been taught about how people behave in various states we can often enough give a correct description of their minds. Then, according to behavioral theories, we can reason to conclusions about *our own* minds. A person can reason: when other people exhibit this behavior they are in pain (or angry, or sad, etc.), so since I am exhibiting this behavior I must be in pain (or angry, or sad).

At first sight, this reasoning may seem completely pointless. Why should anyone need to consider their own behavior to know what they are feeling or thinking? If you are angry or sad do you not know it immediately, with no need to observe your actions? These reactions show the hold that the self-centered view of psychological beliefs has on us. But if we reflect, we can find many cases where this behavioral reasoning makes a lot of sense. Consider three.

A person, A, finds that he feels very strange in the presence of another person, B. He speaks much less than usual when B is around and when he starts to speak he often stops because he finds what he was going to say stupid or embarrassing. He often finds himself acting in a way that might suggest anger, resentment, or sullenness after meeting B. This puzzles A until he is reading a love story and finds the behavior of a character falling in love described in exactly these terms. He thinks: perhaps I love B, though that is not the kind of person I ever expected to be attracted to.

Another person, C, has recently been widowed. She had given up her career as a painter to support her husband's life's work of writing books about Mexican history, and then to nurse him through his illness. But there is still work to do; his last book needs to be edited and published, and there are always letters from younger scholars about his work that need answering. C finds herself often tired and depressed, and sometimes reacts very irritably when people make perfectly reasonable requests. She is discussing with a friend the depression of a mutual friend who has been abandoned by her no-good husband. C thinks "I'm behaving in just the same way. I think I'm angry at my husband, first because I abandoned my painting for the sake of his books, and then because he died and left me with all this work to do alone."

A third person, D, is stung on the back by a wasp. "Does that hurt?" asks a friend. "No," says D "stings never affect me much." An hour later D is driving home and twice narrowly avoids an accident. Wondering why this happened, D realizes that he has been frequently taking his hand off the wheel to reach around and rub his back. "That must hurt more than I admitted," he concludes.

These three cases are typical of many everyday situations where people learn important facts or possibilities about themselves by observing their own behavior and thinking what states of mind it indicates. One important conclusion to draw is that this is something that actually does happen: we do reason from our behavior to our minds. Another conclusion is that sometimes a good way to understand yourself is to consider your behavior in the way you would someone else's and ask yourself what conclusions you would draw. A third conclusion is that sometimes people have false beliefs about their own minds, when they are relying just on their convictions about themselves and not paying attention to their behavior, seen objectively.

The behavioral point of view is not as absurd as it might at first seem, then. It points out that people can have mistaken beliefs about themselves, and that the assumption built into self-centered theories that people can be certain in their beliefs about their own minds is not obviously true. In fact, it makes us ask difficult questions about a person's beliefs about their own mind. To what extent are these beliefs based on a capacity to "look into" our own minds and to what extent on beliefs about our own behavior?

Although the behavioral point of view is not absurd, serious problems arise if we try to use it to give a simple theory of psychological beliefs. The simplest such theory is *crude behaviorism* Crude behaviorism assumes that each person can observe their own behavior and that of others and then classify it into a number of simple categories, such as "angry behavior," "frustrated behavior," "pain behavior," and so on. Then in terms of these categories each person can define the words for states of mind. "Pain," for example, might be "producing pain behavior and not producing faking-pain behavior," and "seeing" might be "having open eyes pointed in the direction of an object and reacting to changes in that object." People can then use these words to describe their states of mind to one another, and they do not understand anything more complicated than the behavior associated with each word in order to communicate. (There is no room for doubts like: does she mean by "love" what I mean by it.) As a result, people can form beliefs about one another's minds which are supported by what they say and by simple observation of what people are doing. So, for example, if you want to know if someone is in pain you have to see if they are producing pain behavior and whether there is also evidence that they are producing behavior typical of someone who is faking pain. Faking behavior may be harder to observe than pain behavior, but there is nothing mysterious or invisible about it. So when you have observed the person's behavior enough you should be able to conclude with some probability either that they are in pain or that they are not.

The most basic problem of crude behaviorism is the assumption that for each state of mind there is a kind of behavior which indicates it. This does not seem to be true even of simple states of mind like being in pain. A person may be in severe pain but not wince or groan or writhe, for example, because he does not want some other person to think that he is ill. And one person's responses to pain may be very different from another's: one person may scream when another would grit their teeth or even joke.

Another problem with crude behaviorism is the assumption that all states of mind reveal themselves in behavior at all. This is a much more subtle and controversial issue. Suppose that two people are tasting an expensive wine. One of them knows nothing about wine and the other is an expert wine-taster. They both sake a sip and think about the taste and smell. Does the wine taste the same to both of them? Suppose it does not. Then each one is in a different state of mind: the states of tasting something which has the taste and smell qualities it does to each of them. (They have different "qualia" as contemporary philosophers of mind say.) But the two people may behave in exactly the same way. Both may say "Yess, that's the best one yet," or "Good lord, how did this rotgut get onto the list?" Both may smile or wince.

More subtle theories which take beliefs about behavior to be certain and define states of mind in terms of behavior face similar problems. The problems they face can be compared to those facing a radical empiricism. They want to base our beliefs about things that cannot be observed on our beliefs about what we can observe, and they run into difficulties when we describe unobservables in terms which are hard to translate into the language of observations. How do you define "atom" or "justice" without referring to anything you cannot see or touch or hear? How do you define "pain" or "love" or "believing that there is life on Mars"?

4. Folk Psychology

Neither self-centered nor behavioral theories give adequate accounts of our psychological beliefs. Both give over-simplified pictures of how to distinguish the sure from the unsure among our beliefs about our own and other people's minds. In fact, the consensus among contemporary philosophers and psychologists is that no theory as simple as either of these can be right. We are often wrong about our own minds, and often right about others. Yet some of our beliefs about our own minds are very reliable. And there are patterns in this, useful things to say about which of a person's beliefs about themselves and about others tend to be reliable, and which not. This section and the next explain some recent work by philosophers and psychologists, in terms of which some of this pattern can be described.

To begin, accept that not only are many of the facts about our own and other people's minds uncertain, but that many of them are mysterious. It is clear that other people's behavior is often mysterious: you often have no idea why some other person did what they did. Moreover your own behavior and your own thoughts and feelings may be in some ways as puzzling to you as those of others: very often you may ask "Why did I do (or think, or feel) that?"

The basic fact is that all human behavior can be pretty mysterious. And trying to understand why people do things is a basic human aim, partly because we need to know what people are likely to do next, and partly because we need to know people's character and trustworthiness. (And partly just because otherwise we would be so puzzled by each other.) People's behavior is often mysterious to themselves, too. We lessen the mystery by learning to explain what people do. As children learn how to get along with others they learn a lot of rules, principles, and theories about how people work. They learn when people are likely to get angry, what kinds of things people are likely to notice or overlook, what kinds of things people try very hard to get, and so on. You wouldn't survive in kindergarten without knowing a lot of this. And as children learn these things, they find that they understand some of their own feelings and behavior.

An example. You are walking across the room with a coin in your hand, approaching a coffee machine. A friend is watching you; someone asks her "Why is that person walking across the room?" Your friend says "To get a coffee." This prediction is based partly on knowing what people usually do and partly on knowing that you like coffee. If this explanation is doubted they may ask you "Why are you going over there?" And your reply is "I wanted a cup of coffee and I'm going to get it from the machine."

What your friend says about you in this example is the same as what you say about yourself. And the reasons you have for what you say are very similar to the reasons your friend has. You too know that the most likely reason why you are walking in the direction of the coffee machine, digging a coin out of your pocket, is that you want a cup of coffee. You too have noticed that you often want a cup of coffee at that time of day. So when you are asked why you are walking across the room you may answer so quickly that you do not even notice what your reasons are. It is true that you may have some information that your friend does not. You may be aware of sensations of thirst and caffeine withdrawal. But your friend may have some information that you do not have. Your regular craving for coffee at that time of day may be something which is obvious to your friends but something that you find it hard to acknowledge, perhaps because you do not want to admit how much coffee you drink.

What examples like this suggest, together with facts about how children and adults ascribe states of mind to themselves and others, is that we make sense of what people do by comparing their actions to standard patterns we have learned. These standard patterns are like outlines of stories, for example stories about how someone gets angry when they don't get what they want and then works off their anger on someone else. And they are also like rough theories, for example the theory that people deceive themselves about many of their motives. Philosophers call this mixture of stories, theories, and rules **folk psychology**. People use folk psychology in everyday life to explain why other people do things. They also use it to explain why they themselves do things. In both cases we often do not notice that we are using folk psychology. We just say "He is angry at me because I took his parking space," or "I am upset because I didn't get the job I applied for," as if these things were perfectly obvious.

The folk psychology account of psychological beliefs includes aspects of both self-centered and behavioral theories. It is like self-centered theories in that it allows that people often have to go through complex reasoning to discover what other people's thoughts and feelings are. It is unlike self-centered theories, though, in that the reasoning it describes is not inductive reasoning but instead a variety of more complex uses of the theories and rules of folk psychology. (Central here is the reasoning called "inference to the best explanation." See chapter 4, section 8.)

The folk psychology account is like behavioral theories in that it allows a person to reason from their own behavior to conclusions about their own mind. But it is unlike behavioral theories in that it does not base all of a person's beliefs about their mind on observations of their behavior. Another basic difference with behavioral theories is that, instead of using a few fixed connections between states of mind and behavior, the folk psychology approach allows an infinite variety of behavior to correspond to any state of mind. For instead of assuming that we understand states of mind by defining them in terms of behavior, it assumes that we understand them by the way they explain behavior. So we can reasonably attribute any states of mind at all to a person, as long as we can use them to explain why the person acts as they do.

The most important difference between the folk psychology approach and both these previous approaches, though, consists in the account it gives of why it is reasonable to attribute states of mind to people. Both self-centered and behavioral approaches try to base our beliefs about other people's minds on evidence we can get from our senses, and that means our observations of their behavior plus our sensations of our own minds. But it turns out that it is very hard to justify these beliefs in terms of just this evidence. It isn't enough. The folk psychology approach accepts that it is not enough, and suggests that in everyday life we observe a person's behavior, interpret it in terms of folk psychology plus our own experience, and then use folk psychology to find the best explanation of the behavior.

When we use folk psychology we explain people's actions in terms of their beliefs, desires, emotions, and other states of mind. We suppose that people really do have all these states of mind because we have no other way of explaining what they do. If we did not think that they cry because they are sad, get angry because they are frustrated, make friends because they want co-operation and affection, and so on, we would find their behavior completely mystifying. But this obviously does not prove that the states of mind we ascribe to people are always, or even often, correct. It does not even prove that the whole business of describing people in terms of beliefs, desires, memories, fears, pains, and all the rest, must capture the way we really are. It just says: if you want to understand what people do and feel, and if you are living in our time in our culture, then these are the beliefs you have to have. We do not have any better way of explaining human actions so, for all its faults, folk psychology is what we have to assume if we want to be able to predict and explain our actions.

Note the ifs. The folk psychology line is definitely based on avoiding ignorance rather than falsity. If you want to take absolutely no risk that any of
your beliefs are false then the conclusion to draw, from the problems of self-
centered and behavioral theories and the advantages of the folk psychology
approach, is that you should keep your beliefs about both other people's
minds and your own mind to a minimum. Since nearly all your beliefs
depend to some extent on trusting your own and other people's memories,
and on relating your beliefs to those of others, the result will be that you
will have very few beliefs. So considerations about psychological beliefs
suggest that extreme falsity-avoidance might be a crippling strategy.

5. Materialist Theories

One of the big ifs in the justification of folk psychology was "if you are living
in our time in our culture." We do not now have any better ways of understanding one another than in terms of beliefs, desires, sensations, emotions,
and other psychological concepts. But this may change. We may find other,
perhaps better, ways. Since the mind and the brain are very closely related
it is natural to wonder whether when we learn more about the human brain
we may discover facts and create concepts which can replace some or even
all of our present psychological concepts. The most extreme such position
is that of *eliminative materialism.*

According to eliminative materialism, folk psychology is a fairly useful
account of human action, with a long history and some success. But it is
false. It supposes that there are such things as beliefs and desires which
cause people to do what they do. But when we investigate the human brain
we find no evidence of such things. In fact, we find evidence that the
aspects of mind that folk psychology groups together as "belief," "desire,"
"memory," and the like have no real unity. There are a large number of
brain functions which correspond loosely to "memory" for example, and
they work in very different ways: it is misleading to think of them as being
all of the same kind. As a result, folk psychology leaves us unable to explain
how children develop, how learning occurs, what happens in mental breakdown, and other equally fundamental aspects of human life. Our best attitude to folk psychology, according to eliminative materialism, is to think of
it as a temporary but very inadequate crutch, which we must depend on
until we understand the brain well enough to find a more adequate substitute for it.

Eliminative materialism is a program rather than an analysis. It does not
tell us how to understand our present psychological beliefs, and how to separate the reasonable ones from the unreasonable. Instead it tells us to wait
for something better. One reaction is to agree: wait and see if something
better than folk psychology emerges. But don't hold your breath! There are

important points to make even in the absence of a concrete suggestion about what might replace folk psychology, though.

One very important point is that eliminative materialism assumes that folk psychology is a theory, basically like a theory in physics or biology or any other science. Like any theory it should be accepted if it does a good job of explaining the available evidence, and rejected otherwise. Critics of eliminative materialism argue that this assumption is quite dubious. Unlike a scientific theory, no one ever created folk psychology; the reasons we believe it are not because we have evaluated the evidence for it but because it is deeply embedded in our everyday lives. And we do not use folk psychology simply to explain people's behavior in an objective scientific manner: instead we use it as part of our attempts to love, co-operate, deceive, and judge one another. Its uses are as rich and varied as human social life. So, some critics argue, we should ask about folk psychology and any proposed substitute for it not just "Is it true?" or "How strong is the evidence for it?" but also "What kind of a social and emotional life could it be part of?" Perhaps in deciding whether we should believe something these latter questions are at least as important.

A second basic point to make about eliminative materialism is more positive. The problem of other minds is often presented as if we had to find evidence against beliefs that no one could actually hold: that all human beings are mindless robots, or that human behavior is caused by mysterious factors that we can never understand. Eliminative materialism provides instead a much more concrete skeptical possibility, with some basis in scientific theory. Perhaps, it suggests, human life forces on us an attitude to one another which, when we consider the evidence objectively, we can see to be flawed and, in fact, inferior to a conceivable alternative.

6. Errors of Self-attribution

Behavioral theories and materialist theories both suggest that our beliefs about our own minds may be less accurate than we suppose. On behavioral theories this is because we can make as many mistakes reasoning from our own behavior as from that of others. And on materialist theories this is because the real facts lie in our own brains, which are no more available to us than the brains of others. However much or little truth there is to either of these positions, they are in the spirit of much of the philosophy and psychology of the twentieth century, which have eroded our confidence in our ability to know ourselves.

The work of Sigmund Freud, the founder of psychoanalysis, is the most famous example of this. Although few people believe everything that psychoanalysis claims, almost everyone accepts that repression and self-deception are real. We believe, now, that people often hide their real desires and beliefs and feelings, even from themselves, so that they do not act on them directly and are not aware that they have them. For example, a parent may believe that their child is a little angel, in spite of the evidence that the child bullies other children and tortures animals. Philosophers studying self-deception try to understand what sounds impossible, that a person can believe something (for example that their child is sweet and good) while having what seems like a deliberate strategy to avoid evidence against it (finding reasons to ignore what other parents say, thinking that the neighbor's cat must have brought in all those dead birds). How can a person have a strategy to avoid evidence that they believe does not exist? One answer is that the person is subconsciously aware of strong evidence against something that they consciously believe.

Another example of how we have come to doubt self-knowledge is provided by recent cognitive and social psychology. A large number of experiments show pretty clearly that even when people are aware of their beliefs and desires, they are often wrong about which ones are causing their actions. Even when people are accurate about what they think and want, they are mistaken about why they think and want them. A typical (but imaginary) experiment of this kind might divide a sample of teenagers into two groups, Group A is simply asked to arrange a list of rock bands in order of desirability (which band would you go 100 miles to hear, which ones would you go 1 mile to hear, and so on.) People in group B are first given CDs by bands on the list, and only then asked to rank the bands in order of desirability. Then people in both groups are asked why they ranked the bands the way they did, and in addition people in group B are asked whether their rankings were affected by the fact that they had been given CDs of some bands. The result is that the two groups have very different rankings of the bands but very similar explanations of their reasons. For people in group B deny that being given the tapes affected their judgments, though it is clear by comparing them with group A that it did affect them. (So a person is given a CD by the Depraved Moose but not given one by the Perfect Crystals, and rates the Depraved Moose high and the Perfect Crystals low, though people who have not been given a CD rate them in the reverse order.)

There are many such studies, and they point to systematic errors in our beliefs about our own minds. They show in particular that people are very often wrong about their reasons for believing and wanting things, and wrong in their predictions about what they will believe or want in future circumstances. There is a connection with folk psychology here. People base their explanations and predictions of their choices on folk psychology, and folk psychology does not give true explanations and predictions in these cases. Moreover psychologists studying how children learn folk psychology find that at some stages they make mistakes about what they are thinking which seem very strange to adults. So learning to use folk psychology in a way that gives accurate predictions of our actions is not an easy task.

7. Dispositions, Occurrences, and Reliability

We have a confusing mass of facts and possibilities here. It certainly does not seem that we can find large simple classes of psychological beliefs which we can be sure are true. Nor are there large simple classes which we can be sure are false. But the considerations of the preceding three sections simplify the confusion in one particular way. They allow us to see a pattern in the psychological beliefs which are most relevant to the theory of knowledge, that is, the ones that we have to assume when we are acquiring or evaluating all our other beliefs.

One clear conclusion about the unreliability of our psychological beliefs is that we are often wrong about the causes of our actions and states of mind. Some states of mind are by their nature causes of actions and other states. These are known as *dispositions*. Dispositions are causes of general patterns of behavior. For example, states of character like being cruel or being generous are dispositions. So are moods like depression and elation. So are unconscious beliefs like information a self-deceived person has but will not admit to having. All of these are states of a person's mind over a period of time – from a few minutes to years – which are revealed in their effects on a person's actions during that time.

We show both remarkable insight and remarkable fallibility about one another's dispositions. For example, people sometimes have intuitive convictions that other people have dangerous character dispositions ("I can't put my finger on it, but I just have a feeling that he is not to be trusted"), and sometimes these convictions are true. But sometimes they are false, too. And people are often deeply mistaken about their own moods and character. There is no clean separation here between the states we can attribute reliably to ourselves and the states about which we are more fallible.

Contrast dispositions with *occurrences*. A mental occurrence – sometimes called a mental event or an occurrent mental state – is something that happens in your mind at a particular moment in time. If it causes actions or other states of mind they also will have to occur at that particular moment. Two important examples of mental occurrences are perceptions and conscious thoughts. Suppose you look out the window and see a ginger cat climbing a pine tree. Then you have visual sensations of orange, brown, and green, and you perceive the cat in the tree. You also have the thought that there is a cat in the tree. At that moment these sensations, the state of perception, and the thought, are occurrences. The perception that there is a cat in the tree and the thought that there is in a cat in the tree are different occurrences, since someone could have the thought without having the perception. But they have the same *content*, they both describe the world the same way. (Similarly a sensation of red, brown, and orange, and a dream-image of red, brown, and orange would have the same content.) An ocurrent thought can have the same content as a disposition: the belief that Ottawa is the capital of Canada is usually just a disposition to speak and behave in certain ways, but when someone asks "What is the capital of Canada?" the thought comes into my mind for a few moments, even if it leads to no actions.

A person usually does not have more accurate beliefs about another person's mental occurrences than about their dispositions. Someone watching you looking out the window may not know what you see and that you are thinking that there is a cat in the tree, even if they also see it. But a person usually has accurate beliefs about their own mental occurrences.

They are accurate in a very special way. First, if a person believes that they are in a certain occurrent state then that belief is usually true. Second, if a person's belief that they are in a certain occurrent state is false, then the reason is more often that the person is wrong about what kind of a state it is than that they are wrong about the content of the state. A person can think that she is perceiving a green and orange scene when actually she is dreaming about a green and orange scene, but it will still be true that she is having green and orange sensations. A person can think that he is thinking that the cat is going to fall out of the tree when actually he is just hoping that the cat will fall, but it will still be true that he had the thought that the cat was about to fall, whether the thought was a belief or a hope. (People often deceive themselves about what state they are in, while having a correct understanding of the content of the state. For example, someone can think he fears that the plane carrying his wife will crash, while in fact he hopes that it will crash. Or a person can think she believes in reincarnation, when actually her attitude is one of wanting reincarnation to be true.)

The knowledge people have of the content of their ocurrent states is really rather amazing and mysterious. How do I know such a lot about myself? Sometimes it feels as if I were almost observing a movie screen on which my thoughts are appearing. But that cannot be literally right. Some of our skill in knowing our ocurrent states can be explained in terms of a process called an **ascent routine**. To see how an ascent routine works, suppose that you are looking out the window where there may be a ginger cat climbing a pine tree. (A moment ago you saw something that may have been the cat, but it might also have been a shadow.) Someone asks you if you think there is a cat in the tree. To answer this question you do not have to search your mind to find your beliefs about cats and trees. You look out, not in: you take another look out the window and if you think there is a cat in the tree you say that you think there is a cat in the tree. Or, to put the point differently, in order to answer the question "Do you think (believe) that there is a cat in the tree?" you first answer the question "Is there a cat in the tree?" If the answer to this question is Yes then you say Yes also to the question about your belief, otherwise you answer it No.

Ascent routines will nearly always allow a person to know the contents of their own beliefs. If you are trying to find out whether you believe something you first ask yourself whether that something is true. If your answer is that it is, then you conclude that you do. Otherwise you conclude that you do not. There are limitations, however. Ascent routines are less effective at giving a person answers to questions like "Do you have any beliefs which are inconsistent with this idea?" or "What do you believe about moose that could be relevant in this situation?" And they are not completely reliable for distinguishing belief from hope or conjecture or other similar states. To tell belief from hope or conjecture you might try asking yourself, for example, "Is there a cat in the tree?" and then seeing whether your answer seemed to you to be a straightforward statement or wishful or suspicious. The trouble with this is that you might just not know whether your answer was wishful or suspicious. Or you might be wrong about this.

Ascent routines will therefore allow people to know whether a particular thought is passing through their mind at a particular moment. They will not allow people the same access to all the dispositions that lie behind the thoughts of the moment. But knowledge of the thoughts of the moment is a more substantial kind of knowledge than it might at first seem. If you think that you believe something then you know two things for sure: that *that* is what you believe and that *you* are the person who believes it. You can be confident of the content and of your identity. Both these factors apply to a wide range of states of mind. People's knowledge of their own states of mind is fairly immune to error from misidentifying either the content or their own identity. So when you perceive an orange, green, and black scene you can be sure that, however deluded you are, it is you that is having some perceptual experience involving orange, green, and black.

When we move beyond knowing who you are and the content of your thoughts, reliability suffers. People do have a variety of powerful ways of attributing states of mind to themselves and to others, though these ways are far from infallible. Some of them are part of human nature, some learned as part of the socialization into a particular society. And some are individual tricks which individual people find to work for them. For example, I have found that my own judgments of my day-to-day moods are based in part on how hard I find it to think about philosophical issues. (Melancholy stills the philosophical imagination, excitement makes it irresponsible.) These are surely improvisations of my own rather than a universal means of self-knowledge. I imagine that such improvisation is widespread, and that each person has a collection of thoroughly idiosyncratic methods for keeping in touch with the dispositions of his mind and for intuiting the dispositions of others.

8. Conclusion: The Indispensability of Psychology

We have beliefs about minds, our own and others', because of the lives we lead. We are psychological beings, and the adaptation each one of us makes to living with others equips us with skills and beliefs which we can use to attribute mental states to ourselves and to others, sometimes with considerable certainty. We can augment these with psychological theories, if we have the knowledge and the patience. Both the skills and the beliefs that we use in ascribing mental states can result in truths and in falsehoods. In some circumstances we are justified in trusting them, because in some circumstances they work.

Roughly, they work in those circumstances for which the processes that developed them, in the species or the individual, have prepared them. Thus people are pretty good at telling what thoughts are running through their minds as they prepare to speak, for the co-ordination of speech and thought is a primary function of consciousness. And people can tell fairly well when others are angry or affectionate toward them, as one of the basic purposes of being able to read another's face is to know whether to approach or to flee. For similar reasons people are not very good at judging their own characters or telling what thoughts are running through other people's minds. (You usually know what you are thinking and whether someone else is evincing hostility; you often don't know what the other is thinking, and whether you are showing hostility.)

In the theory of knowledge one particular use of psychological beliefs is most important. That is the attribution of beliefs and knowledge to one another when information is passed from one person to another. We think that we know what beliefs other people have and (to a lesser extent) what kinds of reasons they have for their beliefs. As a result we are able to draw on the experience of previous generations and the discoveries of others in the present. Without this capacity human knowledge would be a much feebler thing. To have this kind of knowledge of one another, on which almost all of our other knowledge relies, we do not have to make the full range of attributions that are found in everyday life. In fact, some of the less reliable kinds of psychological beliefs, such as those concerning people's moods and characters and the reasons for their actions, do not play a large role here. That is not to say that the assumptions about our minds that we make in transmitting information from one person to another are beyond doubt. We have to trust that human memory is largely correct, that humans make only limited errors in reasoning, and that people generally believe what they assert. These beliefs could be false. But if we do not assume them we find that we have reasons for very few of our other beliefs. This gives beliefs in the general reliability of human testimony a kind of apriori status: if we were forced to revise these beliefs we would be forced to doubt almost everything else we believe.

Reading Questions

1   Which of the following are psychological beliefs? Your belief that you are looking at a book. Romeo's belief that he loves Juliet. Romeo's belief that Juliet loves him. Romeo's belief that Juliet is a woman. Romeo's belief that Juliet has a brain. Romeo's belief that Romeo has a brain. Romeo's belief that Juliet wants him to love her. Romeo's desire that Juliet believe he loves her.

2   Could you doubt whether someone else has the beliefs, desires, and feelings they seem to, without doubting that they have a mind?

3   Why is the second stage of the argument from analogy, described in section 2, an inductive argument? Why is it, like the first stage, affected by the variability of behavior?

4   An advantage claimed for the behavioral point of view in section 3 is that it shows how we can have false beliefs about ourselves which can be corrected by looking at our behavior objectively. In the three examples of that section, what are the false beliefs that A, C, and D have?

5   In section 4 there is an example in which one person says "He is angry at me because I took his parking space." How could this be an application of folk psychology? (What behavior might be explained, and what common-sense principle might be being used to explain it?)

6   What is it in the behavior of a self-deceived person that makes it possible to describe them as acting as if they were subconsciously aware of the evidence against their conscious belief?

7   Why in the example of the Depraved Moose and the Perfect Crystals do the subjects have false beliefs about the causes of their desires?

8   Describe how by using an ascent routine you can tell whether you believe that $35 + 76 = 116$.

9   If a person believes that they are in a certain occurrent state then that belief is usually true. Consider the reverse claim, that if a person is in a certain occurrent state then they usually have a true belief that they are in that state. Is this claim true?

10   Why cannot an ascent routine answer the question "What do you believe about moose that is relevant to this situation?"

Thinking Questions

11   In section 1 it is claimed that one-person science would not be science as we know it. Does this mean that one-person science would be impossible? Consider how much of our science – physics, chemistry, and biology in particular – one intelligent but uneducated person alone on a desert island would be able to develop in a normal lifetime. What about a super-intelligent being with a life span of several centuries?

12   The inductive reasoning in the argument from analogy, discussed in section 2, is implausible partly because it assumes that the causes of other people's behavior must be similar to the causes of your behavior. Could there be more

plausible inductive arguments to the conclusion that all people have similar experiences based on the similarity of all human nervous systems?

13 Do the examples in section 3 show that people can know facts about themselves on the basis of considering *only* their behavior?

14 In section 4 one advantage claimed for the folk psychology approach over the behavioral approach is that it allows us to attribute any states of mind that will explain a person's behavior. But given perfectly ordinary behavior, such as drinking a cup of coffee, we can think up completely bizarre explanations. For example, we can explain it by saying he thinks that drinking coffee is a signal to aliens that one has a polluted body and thus is not worth kidnapping. How could a folk psychology approach find a difference between our everyday explanations of what people do and these bizarre explanations?

15 Experiments such as the imaginary one in section 6 with the teenagers and the rock groups are sometimes interpreted as showing that people interpret their choices as being more rational than in fact they are. Why might this example be interpreted in that way?

16 Are beliefs dispositions or occurrences? Consider: your belief that the sky is above the earth, your belief that you are reading a book, your belief that $2 + 9 = 11$.

17 What might ascent routines for knowing what your desires are be like?

18 Rewrite section 8 from the point of view of deep skepticism. (See chapter 1 section 5.)

Further Reading

Basic distinctions in the philosophy of mind are explained in Peter Smith and O. R. Jones, *The Philosophy of Mind: An Introduction* (Cambridge University Press, 1986), and Peter Carruthers, *Introducing Persons* (Croom Helm, 1986). More advanced, but still readable, philosophical papers on self-knowledge and its problems are in Quassim Cassam (ed.), *Self-knowledge* (Oxford University Press, 1994). For a very clear and interesting discussion of psychological work on failures of self-knowledge see Richard Nisbett and Lee Ross, *Human Inference: Strategies and Shortcomings of Social Judgement* (Prentice Hall, 1980).

Ideas about self-deception are developed by the papers in Amelie Rorty (ed.), *Perspectives on Self-Deception* (University of California Press, 1988) and in David Pears, *Motivated Irrationality* (Oxford University Press, 1984). Personal favorites are Paul Ziff, "The simplicity of other minds," *Journal of Philosophy*, 62 (1965), 57584 (reprinted in his *Philosophic Turnings*, Cornell University Press, 1966), and Hilary Putnam, "Other minds," *Philosophical Investigations*, 2 (1979), 71–2 (reprinted in his *Mind, Language, and Reality*, Cambridge University Press 1975). The best exposition and defence of eliminative materialism is chapter 4 of Paul Churchland, *Scientific Realism and the Plasticity of Mind* (Cambridge University Press, 1979). Further more experimental ideas are found in Paul Churchland's "Reduction, qualia, and the direct intro-spection of brain states," *Journal of Philosophy*, 81 (1985), 8–27. For criticisms of eliminative materialism see Patricia Kitcher, "In defence of intentional psychology," *Journal of Philosophy*, 81 89–106 (1984).

Selections from classic philosophical works relevant to this chapter can be found in John Cottingham, *Western Philosophy: An anthology* (Blackwell, 1996). See part III, section 4, René Descartes, "The Incorporeal Mind"; part II, section 8, John Stuart Mill, "The Problem of Other Minds"; part II, section 10, Gilbert Ryle, "The Myth of the 'Ghost in the Machine'"; and part IV, section 4, Sigmund Freud, "The Partly Hidden Self."

Electronic resources: *Routledge Encyclopedia of Philosophy*: Introspection, epistemology of; Testimony; Solipsism. *The Stanford Encyclopedia of Philosophy*: behaviorism; folk psychology as mental simulation; folk psychology as a theory; materialism, eliminative; other minds; testimony, epistemological problems of.

Chapter 9

MORAL KNOWLEDGE

1. Knowing Right from Wrong

Children are sometimes said to be responsible for their actions when they are old enough to know the difference between right and wrong. But studying philosophy can make you uncertain that anyone of any age knows the difference between right and wrong. Moral philosophy is a confusing subject, and anyone exposed to it might conclude that no one knows the difference between right and wrong. After all, so many philosophers, religious thinkers, and political theorists have come up with such a zoo of contradictory ideas about right and wrong. If these brilliant thinkers cannot agree on what the difference is, how can the rest of us have a hope of knowing it?

In recent years philosophers have produced a number of interesting ideas about our moral beliefs: beliefs about right and wrong, justice and injustice, kindness and cruelty. One effect of these ideas is to make it much easier to see how a simple common-sense idea about moral knowledge could be right. In spite of all the clever confusions of the philosophers, and in spite of the fact that we may not know which philosophical view of morality is right, we may be capable of knowing that acts are right and wrong, that societies are just and unjust, that people are kind, brave, and horrible. The aim of this chapter is to explain these ideas, and to connect them with general themes in the theory of knowledge, in particular with the externalist ideas explored in chapter 7.

2. Thick and Thin Moral Beliefs

It is not necessary to have a general philosophical theory about morality to know that a particular act is wrong or that a particular person is morally admirable. There are two reasons for this. First, throughout our experience we find that we can often make reliable judgements without being able to give an intellectual description of what we are distinguishing and what criteria we are using. Almost everyone can tell the sound of a flute from the sound of a saxophone, but very few people can say what the difference between the sounds is. Almost everyone can recognize the faces of famous people, but no one can say precisely what it is about a particular person's face that distinguishes it from all others. We are sure that we know that the instrument we hear is a saxophone and not a flute, or that the face we see is one person rather than another. So why should we not consider ourselves to know that, for example, rape is wrong, or that a society without slavery is more just than one with slavery, even if we cannot give clear and uncontroversial explanations of why these are so?

These beliefs could not be knowledge if they were not true. According to one philosophical theory of morality, **emotivism**, assertions about morality are not true or false sentences, but just expressive noise. According to emotivism, to say that rape is wrong is something like saying "rape: ugh." According to another theory, assertions of morality are not statements but commands, so that to say that rape is wrong is to say "Do not rape." Few philosophers now believe any such crude theories of morality. Yet more sophisticated theories can have similar consequences. The error theory of morality, due to John Mackie and refined by others, holds that our beliefs about morality are a kind of a myth. We find it useful to act as if there were a real difference between right and wrong and so we invent words for moral qualities and use them to make complex judgments, while in reality these words do not describe any objective facts. According to the error theory, saying that rape is wrong is like saying that Hamlet killed Polonius or that the wolf ate Little Red Riding Hood's grandmother: we all agree to these and think of them as the "right" thing to say, but there is nothing in the world that makes them true.

Even if an error theory of morality were right, many moral beliefs could still count as knowledge. Consider, for example, beliefs about people's character. Suppose someone borrows money from you to pay for an operation for his sick cat, and tells you with apparent sincerity that he will repay you next week. When paying-up time comes, he has no money, and gives as an excuse that he has had to buy a plane ticket to go to his mother's funeral. You learn later that he spent the money at a casino, boasting to friends that he could always get more money by telling you a sad story. You know then that he is a liar, and untrustworthy. That is something about his moral character that you have plenty of evidence for, and which no subtle moral theory could undermine.

Consider a very different kind of example. Suppose that a political candidate proposes to abolish all the laws against fraud. The idea is that if companies do not have to worry about avoiding lawsuits they will be able to carry out their business more efficiently and the economy will thrive.

After thinking about the proposal for a while you see the problems with it. Unscrupulous companies would be able to make false claims to their customers without being discovered until after money had been paid. The main victims would be individual members of the public, especially poor people, without the resources to check the claims made on behalf of goods and services. But companies would also suffer, and since they would often be doubtful that their suppliers' descriptions were true or that contracts would be honored, they would be very reluctant to do business with any company that they had not been long associated with. So the trust which commerce requires would be eroded. Summing this all up you say "It would be a disaster. The result would be exploitation and mistrust. And injustice: the poor and ignorant would be victims of the rich and well-informed."

When you say that the person in the first example is an unreliable liar, and when you say that the proposal in the second example would result in exploitation and injustice, you are making definite claims for which you have strong evidence. If the evidence is not misleading – and other knowledge-defeating factors are not present – then your claim is knowledge. You know that the person is a liar; you know that the proposal would result in injustice. These are moral beliefs and they are knowledge: they are moral beliefs because they are about the way that we think that people and societies should be, and they are knowledge because they are related in the right way to the facts.

It is not always so straightforward. If you tell the liar that he is a liar he will probably be offended and try to defend himself against your description of him. For he will probably agree with you that it is not a good thing to be a liar. But suppose that instead he grins and says "Sure, I'm a liar; and you're a sucker, but you've realized it a bit too late." Then he shares your belief about his character, but for him it does not have the same moral force. It may be that he has very few moral convictions, and does not care whether or not he is a liar. Or it may be that he has different moral convictions to you and will go on to say "I admire a good liar; I don't respect anyone who has to stick to the feeble truth. A good person can tell a good lie." This suggests that the kinds of moral beliefs for which there can be such straightforward evidence are also kinds which do not have direct consequences for what a person ought to do.

Two somewhat opposite conclusions emerge. First, that many moral beliefs can be known in the same ways that other beliefs about the world around us can be. Second, that not all moral beliefs can be known in these ways. Beliefs such as that someone is a liar or that a social measure would lead to exploitation of poor people are sometime known as "thick" moral beliefs. So now we have to ask in what ways non-thick moral beliefs can be known. One way to answer that question would be to run through the standard theories in ethics: what is the answer according to utilitarianism, what is the answer according to Kantian ethics, and so on. But that is a potentially misleading way, since it gives the impression that we have to decide which of these theories is right before we can say anything about how basic moral beliefs can be known. A different tactic is to describe some other kinds of beliefs that can be compared to thick and thin moral beliefs. This is the purpose of the next section. Then we will be ready for a return of the main question, and the appearance of some standard moral theories.

3. Analogies: Color, Humor, and Witches

Some other kinds of beliefs resemble moral beliefs in interesting ways. There are resemblances to beliefs about humor, beliefs about colors, and superstitious beliefs, which bring out important aspects of our moral beliefs and allow us a perspective on philosophical theories about them.

Humor may seem very different from morality. After all, morality is a serious business. But consider some similarities.

You cannot explain a joke. If someone does not see why something is funny then putting the humor into explicit terms may make the person understand why others laugh, but it will not make her join in herself. Imagine someone who is completely immune to humor, who never finds anything even mildly amusing, and who is puzzled when other people laugh at stories and pictures. (I think I know a couple of people like this; but perhaps they are playing a very straight-faced joke on me.) It might be possible to explain to such a person the psychology of humor, so that they could predict what kinds of things people will laugh at. (Perhaps, although the best laughs are the ones that take you completely by surprise.) But all the explanation in the world would not produce a chuckle. If you don't get it you don't get it.

Now imagine someone who had no sense of morality. Such a person need not be a monster: they might treat others decently, keep promises, and cooperate reliably in social activities. They might do this in order to get others to treat them well and co-operate with them, or out of a fear of punishment. But the person would not feel revulsion at examples of evil and would not feel admiration at examples of heroism or self-sacrifice. Most fundamentally, if the person was considering an action and came to see how it would be dishonest or cruel, the person would not feel a shiver of realization that what they were considering was wrong. Explaining that most people feel guilt, remorse, and moral admiration, and explaining when they feel these things, might help such a person to understand how normal human beings act. But it would not enable the person to experience these emotions. If you don't feel it you don't feel it.

For the next example consider our beliefs about colors. Human beings can judge fairly reliably when objects are red, green, blue, and so on. Under similar conditions of illumination most people describe objects using the same color words. (Except for a few well-known cases. The boundary between blue and green is a mess, which no two people seem to see in exactly the same way.) As a result people have long tended to suppose that colors are simple properties of objects, like their masses or shapes or locations. But physics and physiology teach us that this is not so. We call things green, for example, when they reflect several different patterns of wavelengths to our eyes. It is hard to describe these patterns so that they seem like basic features of objects. Instead we find ourselves saying something like: an object is green when normal human beings seeing it in normal illumination call it green.

Color is therefore in some ways like humor. It is hard, perhaps impossible, to specify what all green things have in common without referring to the ways human beings will react to them. And a color-blind person could know a lot of physics and psychology, understanding how light works and how the eye works, and still be unable to say what objects other people will call red, green, purple. So when a person knows what color an object is, their knowledge is in part about what reactions other people will have to it.

Now a third and last example. This example is semi-imaginary, though. Imagine a culture in which there is a concept of a "witch." These people often call a woman a witch and then burn her at the stake. The process that results in being called a witch begins with rumors. Perhaps a child fell ill or perhaps a farmer's crops were blighted. Someone must be blamed and it is suggested that a witch may be involved, so gossips wonder who the witch may be. If a woman's name is mentioned often enough in such gossip it is said publicly that she is a witch. She is then tried, for example by being tied up and thrown into the river. (If she floats she is a witch, since the river has rejected her; if she sinks she is acquitted, lucky woman.) If the trial "proves" that she is a witch she is burned.

Do people in this culture know that the people they have burned are witches? Do they know that there are witches? In a sense they do. They know that particular women have been convicted of witchcraft. They know that there are women who if tested will turn out to qualify as witches. And in a sense they do not. They do not know that there is any real or objective difference between the women they have burned and anyone else. They do not know that there are people who have a special property which will cause them to fail the witch tests. Their lack of knowledge turns on their misunderstanding of their concept of a witch. They do not know that being a witch consists almost entirely in other people deciding that the person is a witch.

The three examples – humor, color, and witches – are different in many ways. What they have in common is that in all of them people have beliefs which concern their own and other people's reactions. They all concern beliefs which have more of a human-specific content than people may realize. In all three cases a skeptical person can find grounds for saying that the beliefs are not objectively true. They can seem just made up, true because we decide that they are to be. The last example, witches, is the most extreme. In it people have beliefs which, unbeknownst to them, are almost entirely about what judgments other people will make. The least extreme is the second, colors. For although the limits of what gets called "green" are determined by the way human beings react to light, at least the light is real, and objects that are called by different color names do reflect different wavelengths of light. In terms of objectivity, humor lies between witches and color. Humor is very human, and it might be argued that if there were no humans nothing would be funny. But on the other hand some jokes are funny and some are not, and some people have definitely false beliefs about which jokes (particularly their own) are funny. So we do not simply make up the facts about humor.

Are moral beliefs more like beliefs about witches, humor, or color? Different philosophies of morals will give different answers. Some philosophies make morality a completely objective matter, more objective than beliefs about color. For example, if you think that what is right is what God commands then you will think that an action's being right is as objective a feature of it as its location or date. So will you if you think, as utilitarians do, that right actions are those which produce the maximum amount of happiness among all people. On the other hand if you think, as emotivists do, that to say that something is wrong is just to express an emotion of disapproval of it, then you will think that calling something wrong is a lot like calling someone a witch. It is more an expression of subjective attitude than of objective fact.

The most important fact here is that we do not have to choose between these extremes. Morality does not have to be either as objective as the mass and shape of an object or as subjective as the quality of being a witch (as described in the third example above). There are many positions in between. Morality may be like humor or like color.

A strong case can be made for beliefs about morality being rather like beliefs about color or humor. Beliefs about the moral character of individual people or about the fairness of particular institutions are much like beliefs about color, in that they describe aspects of the world which a person lacking certain basic capacities might be incapable of understanding, but which are caused by real psychological features of people and real structural facts of institutions. Some people really are difficult to co-operate with, or in other ways do not fit well into the attempts of others to live satisfactory lives together. And although the exact ways in which, for example, being untrustworthy differs from being a cheat may not be possible to describe except by using moral concepts, the fact that someone is untrustworthy or a cheat is a fact about something very real, namely the ways in which that person will fit into co-operative activities with others.

Beliefs about "thin" moral topics, such as what a person ought to do, or whether a given act is wrong, may also be like beliefs about color. Or they may be like beliefs about humor, rather less objective, rather more closely tied to human reactions, but still capable of being true and false in ways that are independent of our judgments. Different moral beliefs may be at different places on this spectrum. (For example, beliefs about what kinds of acts are right or wrong may be different from beliefs about what people should do in particular real-life moral dilemmas.) To get a general picture of the precise degrees of objectivity of moral beliefs we need a general theory of morality. And here the standard philosophical theories are relevant. For example, a moral theory based on God's commands will give some moral beliefs a very high degree of objectivity, as high as any fact about the natural world. And the effect of utilitarianism (the view that the right action is the one that produces the most satisfaction to the most people) will be similar. In spite of the radical differences between a morality based on God and a morality based on bringing happiness to other people, in both cases there is a completely objective answer to questions about what a person should do. On the other hand, on theories according to which morality is a matter of social convention or, as in existentialism, arbitrary choice, moral beliefs have a much lesser degree of objectivity, more like beliefs about humor than like beliefs about the solar system.

The important point here is not that some moral theories make morality very objective and others much less so. Instead, the point is that nearly all moral theories make morality at least as objective as humor, and most of them make it as objective as colors. And these are fairly objective domains. We do not hesitate to say that one person knows what color his socks are, or that another knows that the joke she has told is really not very funny. We have no problems in saying that there is no evidence that red roses turn green when nobody is looking at them, or that there are good reasons for thinking that racist jokes will not often be extremely funny. Beliefs about humor and about color often qualify as knowledge; there can be evidence for and against them; they can be supported or undermined by other beliefs. And this should make us more willing to accept the obvious interpretation of the fact that we say exactly similar things about moral beliefs. We certainly use the language of knowledge, justification, and reasons about moral beliefs. We say that one person knows that she really should confess that she was the one who put the dent in the car, or that there are good reasons for doubting that eating apples is wrong. If someone wants to argue that all these things we say are mistaken, she had better have some pretty strong arguments.

4. Cognitivism

One argument for thinking that moral beliefs cannot be known or justified comes from the moral theory called non-cognitivism. This claims that what we call moral beliefs are not really beliefs at all. For they cannot be true or false. The best-known version of this theory is emotivism, referred to at the beginning of this chapter, the theory that when people say things like "slavery is wrong" they are not making statements but expressing feelings. If emotivism or some other non-cognitivist theory were right then one could no more know that slavery was wrong than one could know a scream.

Non-cognitivists have to find ways around some powerful objections. The main arguments against non-cognitivism depend on the fact that we use our moral beliefs in all the ways we use our other beliefs. We can deny them: one person says "slavery is wrong," and the other says "No, slavery is not wrong." We can deduce consequences from them: we can reason "If slavery is wrong and working for no wage is slavery, then working for no wage is wrong." We can worry about consistency between moral and non-moral beliefs: for example we can worry whether the moral belief that individuals should be judged as good or bad in terms of the acts they perform is consistent with the scientific belief that events have causes and many of the actions of human beings are caused by facts over which they have no control. And we can make distinctions between different moral concepts: one person can say "Slavery is wrong" and another can reply "Slavery is unjust, as an institution, but people who live in slave-owning societies are not all evil." These are all ways of using moral beliefs that are hard to explain except by saying that moral beliefs are real beliefs, like any others, involving a rich body of concepts and building on our capacity for logic and reasoning.

The problem for non-cognitivists here is that they have to explain what moral beliefs are if they are not real beliefs. And most of the explanations they give suggest falsely that we cannot reason with moral beliefs or argue about them. (This is not to say that non-cognitivism is a hopeless position: but this is the central challenge it has to meet.) The challenge to non-cognitivism is most explicitly developed in theories of ethics which use the idea of what John Rawls calls **reflective equilibrium**.

Central to this idea is the contrast between moral beliefs about particular situations and general moral principles. For example, you may have beliefs about certain situations in which someone did the right thing in not telling the whole truth to someone else (perhaps to spare that person pain, or even to save their life) and, contrasted with this, you have beliefs about when, in general, telling or withholding the truth is right. And these two kinds of beliefs may be hard to reconcile with one another. So we defend or criticize beliefs of each kind by comparison with the other, changing a general principle if it conflicts with many judgments about particular cases and changing a judgment about a particular case if it conflicts with general principles.

For example, if you believe the general principle that it is wrong ever to tell less than the whole truth, you may find that this principle conflicts with your reaction to a situation in which if information is not withheld from someone they may become suicidally depressed. And enough conflicts like this can make you modify the general principle. In the same way, your judgment that, for example, some person is paid a fair wage may conflict with your general principle that people should be paid the same wage for the same work. And then you may change your judgment on the particular case. Eventually, Rawls hopes, by adjusting both judgments and principles we will get a set of beliefs about justice (or other moral concepts) which is in harmony with itself. This is reflective equilibrium.

Rawls' idea of reflective equilibrium makes most sense in terms of a holist rather than a foundationalist picture of knowledge. For according to this idea a moral belief is justified when it fits well with the rest of our beliefs. It brings out, though, the basic fact that our beliefs usually do not fit well together, and that getting our beliefs into a coherent whole is nearly always a long struggle. There are many versions of the main idea, and related ideas are found in other modern ethical theories. (And also in modern versions of traditional theories such as Kantian ethics.)

One very basic fact about morality that Rawls' idea captures is that moral ideas are always open to debate. People argue about what to do in particular situations, and about what a good society would be like. These arguments go on, for generations, and change our moral beliefs. Among the strands in the pattern of moral debate there is an important role for skeptical arguments. Mild moral skepticism suggests that many of our firm moral beliefs may be mistaken (perhaps there is nothing inherently wrong with telling lies). More fundamental moral skepticism suggests that the belief in morality itself may be an illusion (perhaps it is just out of sentimentality that we think there are constraints on how people can treat other people). The ultimate moral equilibrium would have answers to skeptical arguments as well as to differing moral views. We obviously are not there yet; the vital thing is that the argument goes on.

Cognitivism makes clear how much our use of our moral belief resembles our use of our beliefs about colors, humor, or for that matter the solar system. On all these topics we debate, produce evidence and arguments, make distinctions, and occasionally try a radical line to sweep away large chunks of belief. Seen in this way, morality and science look remarkably similar. Looking simply at the behavior of people engaging in science and engaging in moral debate an observer might say: these both look like knowledge-gathering activities.

5. Knowing What You Know

This chapter has not gone deeply into philosophical ethics. Its aim has been to say some of the things that can be said about moral knowledge without arguing for any particular moral philosophy. We only really need two conclusions from moral philosophy: (1) The idea that there are no moral facts can be defended. If a clever philosopher wants to argue that beliefs about right and wrong are not true and false in the way that beliefs about the physical nature of the world are, then she can get away with it, though she may need some clever moves. (2) There are plausible and defensible philosophies according to which there are moral facts, whether they concern the balance of pleasure and pain produced by an act, God's commands, or social conventions that are in everyone's interest. Most such moral philosophies will also describe ways in which people can know what is right. That is, they will describe ways in which a moral fact will shape people's beliefs about right and wrong.

Very few people can decide which philosophy of ethics they agree with. Most people have never even heard of any moral philosophy. So most people have no way of deciding what kinds of fact they are dealing with when they talk about right and wrong, good and bad, fair and unfair, decent and villainous. Indeed, when pushed even a little way with tricky philosopher-style questions about morality, most people run out of answers. They become inarticulate and bad-tempered. (You only have to push a little further on these topics to make philosophers inarticulate and bad-tempered.)

Does this mean that most people have no knowledge of right and wrong, only habitual opinions? Colors and humor again. Most people have never considered whether something's being red is a different kind of fact to its being square, or weighing 35 grams. They have never compared weighing 35 grams to being red to being hilarious. And if you sprang these comparisons on most people and asked their opinions, what they would say would be confused and uninformed. (The philosophers can do better?!) Does this mean that people do not know what color socks they are wearing, or whether their parents' jokes are feeble? Of course not.

A well-known episode in Mark Twain's *Huckleberry Finn* illustrates the point. Huck is helping Jim to escape from slavery. He has been brought up to believe that the act he is committing is theft, or aiding theft (for Jim is stealing himself from his legal owner). But Huck concludes that, right or wrong, if he doesn't help Jim he will not be able to live with himself. In fact, he says that since he is clearly committed to doing wrong he might as well be a thorough wrong-doer and help Jim as much as he can. ("And for a starter, I would go and steal Jim out of slavery again; and if I could think up anything worse, I would do that, too: because as long as I was in, and in for good, I might as well go the whole hog.") Huck does not know that it is his conscience – or whatever you want to call his way of telling in particular cases what he should do – that is giving him the belief that he must help Jim. He knows what he ought to do, but he does not know that what he has is moral knowledge.

But what about witches? In a culture which believes in witches people will confidently say that some people are witches and that others are not. They think they know these things. But they do not know, not only because there are no witches but because the concept of a witch is confused and illusory. It describes fantasy rather than reality and the evidence these people cite for calling someone a witch points in fact just to the their own self-fulfilling beliefs. If these people applied some philosophy and some science to their beliefs they might find out quite how hollow their supposed facts were. But might not our moral beliefs be like this?

There is a point here. The information available to most people is not enough to show that their moral beliefs are more like beliefs about colors than beliefs about witches. And while a bit of philosophy combined with a bit of science allows you to be better informed about such questions, the more you learn the harder the issues seem. The choice between type 1 moral philosophies and type 2 moral philosophies remains open. So perhaps no one has a completely trustworthy opinion here. If this is so then no one knows whether we have moral knowledge. But this does not show that no one has moral knowledge. It is easy to get confused on this point. Knowing something and knowing that you know it are very different. You probably know the answers to all the questions in an average primary school arithmetic test. But you may lack confidence in your arithmetic skills and so be uncertain whether you know the answers to any of them. In that case you know a lot more about basic arithmetic than you know you know. This is a common situation. And moral knowledge may be the same. Suppose that in addition to the lack of confidence many people have in their knowledge of arithmetic there were also skeptical philosophers who went around trying to persuade people that numbers may be mythical or that when we calculate we may really be guessing. And other philosophers with elaborate philosophies of mathematics, which most people cannot choose between. (Actually, both of these exist.) Then the situation would be like with our moral beliefs. We would know far more than we know we know.

This does not show that moral skepticism is false. (Nor does it refute emotivism and other non-cognitivist philosophies.) Instead it suggests that we do not have to refute moral skepticism in order for some of our beliefs about right and wrong to be knowledge. It is enough that we can find evidence for them and defend them when challenged, and that this process links them with the facts, whatever they are, about which actions are right and wrong. If there are no such facts then of course we cannot be linked with them, but if there are such facts we can link with them whether or not we know that we do.

Similar issues arise with other kinds of belief. A skeptic about belief in the physical world may challenge you to show that you are not a brain in a vat of nutrient fluid being fed false information by a supercomputer (or some even harder to imagine source of consciousness being misled by some even more mysterious source of virtual reality). You may find that you cannot answer this skepticism. Does that mean that you do not know that you have existed more than a year, or that you have a nose and a mouth, or that you are on the planet earth? One question here is whether the evidence you have that you are on the planet earth can be good evidence if it cannot show that you are not a brain in a vat (where the vat is not on earth). On many ways of understanding "good evidence" this can be so. For if we reject foundationalism (see chapter 5, section 2) we can use evidence which is not itself completely certain. The evidence that you are on earth, although sufficient to make it reasonable to hold this belief, can itself be challenged, for example by the possibility that you are a brain in a vat. (Bayesian approaches, discussed in chapter 10, give a similar diagnosis.) So you can have good evidence for a belief without having evidence that proves that your evidence can never mislead you. You can know without knowing that you know.

Reading Questions

1 Section 2 argues that since we can tell saxophones from flutes without being able to say how they differ, so might we be able to tell right from wrong. Which of the following is the important similarity here?
   (a) Some people cannot tell saxophones from flutes just as some people cannot tell right from wrong.
   (b) You can sometimes know when something is of one kind rather than another although you cannot put the difference into words.
   (c) Only expert musicians and psychologists know how flute-sounds and saxophone-sounds differ just as only philosophers and wise people know how right is different from wrong.

2 Why can you know that someone is a liar even if the error theory of right and wrong is correct?

3 Why would someone with no sense of right and wrong not necessarily act in evil ways?

4 Specify more fully than the text why knowing the color of an object is in part knowing how other people will react to it.

5 How can people in the witch-punishing culture know that a particular woman is a witch when "really" there are no witches?

6 Why does the fact that we can deny and argue about moral beliefs make a problem for emotivism (or other non-cognitivist theories)?

7 Which of the following is suggested in section 5?
   (a) We know which philosophy of morals is correct but we do not know that we know it.
   (b) We know that we do not know which philosophy of morals is correct.

(c) We know that many particular acts are right and many wrong, but do not know which are which.

(d) We know of many particular actions that they are right and we know of many particular actions that they are wrong, but we do not know that we know these particular actions are right and wrong.

8   Why did the previous question say "suggest" rather than "assert"?

Thinking Questions

9   Suppose that you tell the liar that you have found him out and he replies "Sure, I'm a liar, but I don't want not to be." He seems to know that he is a liar, but can this be moral knowledge for him?

10   Are there any properties that are not to some extent relative to the way humans apply them? Is there such a sharp contrast between "green" and "weighs 35 grams"?

11   Section 3 claimed that "some people have false beliefs about which jokes are funny. So we do not simply make up the facts about humor." How widespread could this be? For example, could a whole culture have a mistaken idea about what is funny?

12   Section 3 classifies "witch" as less objective than "funny" which was less objective than "green." Why should they be ranked in this order?

13   Suppose that you think that what is right is what God commands. Could God have commanded differently? If he could have, would different acts have been right? If he could not have, is there some deeper source of morality than what God commands?

14   Is it true that if utilitarianism is right then we can know what acts are right? Consider the fact that utilitarianism takes account of the effects of an act on all people during all future time.

15   Section 5 suggests that people with naive moral beliefs may be confused by exposure to moral skeptics and questioning philosophers. Perhaps this is like the situation studied in section 5 of chapter 6, where people do not have knowledge if there is confusing information that they could have encountered. If this is so, really naive people might have moral knowledge but this would be destroyed by the presence of philosophers, even if they are not exposed to their views. Could this be right?

16   The end of the chapter can be taken as arguing that we have moral knowledge but do not know that we have it, or that we do not know whether we have moral knowledge. What is the difference between these?

Further Reading

There is no really simple introduction to these issues. J. L. Mackie, *Ethics: Inventing Right and Wrong* (Penguin, 1977) is a good place to start. A book of stimulating contemporary essays on the topic is Walter Simmott-Armstrong and Mark Timmons (eds), *Moral Knowledge? New Readings in Moral Epistemology* (Oxford University Press, 1996), especially the pieces by Sinnot-Armstrong, Blackburn, Morris, and Railton. Also relevant are the essays in Geoffrey Sayre-

McCord (ed.), *Essays in Moral Realism* (Cornell University Press, 1988). Recent work is described in Stephen Darwall, Allan Gibbard, and Peter Railton, "Towards *fin de siecle* ethics: Some trends," *Philosophical Review*, 101 (1992), 115–90, and in Robedrt Audi, "Moral knowledge and ethical pluralism" in John Greco and Ernest Sosa (eds), *The Blackwell Guide to Epistemology* (Blackwell, 1999).

The source for reflective equilibrium is chapters 1, 2, and 3 of John Rawls, *A Theory of Justice* (Harvard University Press, 1971). Reflective equilibrium is related to ideas about knowledge in chapter 11 of Adam Morton, *Philosophy in Practice* (Blackwell, 1995), chapter 14 of which discusses issues about color. The philosophy and psychology of color is explored in great depth in C. L. Hardin, *Color for Philosophers* (Hackett, 1988). A deep reflection on the way that intellectual reflection can erode moral certainty (see question 15) is found in Bernard Williams, *Ethics and the Limits of Philosophy* (Fontana, 1985), especially chapters 1, 2, 6, 9, and 10.

Selections from classic philosophical works relevant to this chapter can be found in John Cottingham, *Western Philosophy: An Anthology* (Blackwell. 1996). See part VII section 7, Henry Sidgwick, "Utility and Common-sense Morality"; part VII section 8, Friedrich Nietzsche, "Against Conventional Morality"; and part VII section 10, John Rawls, "Rational Choice and Fairness."

Electronic resources: *The Stanford Encyclopedia of Philosophy*: moral epistemology; religion, epistemology of.

Chapter 10

BAYESIAN AND NATURALIST THEORIES

1. Why Probability?

Many questions in the theory of knowledge are questions about how strong our reasons for various beliefs are. Are our reasons for believing that other people are happy or sad as strong as our reasons for believing that the earth is round? Are our reasons for believing in science stronger or weaker than our reasons for believing in religion? Philosophers' answers to these questions give broad general pictures of what counts as a reason for a belief (empiricism, rationalism, foundationalism, holism). But they do not often supply the details which would allow one to decide how strongly particular reasons support a particular belief. How strong is the evidence for the theory of evolution? Is it stronger or weaker than the evidence that the earth is a sphere, or the evidence that influenza is caused by a virus?

Some brave philosophers have tried to describe the relation between beliefs and evidence with enough precision that strength of evidence can actually be measured. The obvious advantage of trying to do this is that it would help to give answers to questions about what we should believe. A less obvious, but important, advantage is that an epistemological theory that actually comes out and says which beliefs are more and which less justified is itself testable. If the theory says that beliefs which are clearly very uncertain are strongly supported, or if it says that there is only weak evidence for many beliefs which are intuitively very well supported, then we should consider the possibility that there is something wrong with the theory. So, by making precise versions of vague and general theories of knowledge, we can begin to get an idea of whether these theories could possibly be correct.

Rudolf Carnap (working on these issues between 1940 and 1960) was one of the first philosophers to see these points clearly. He wanted to construct definite rules which, given a belief and a statement of the evidence relevant to it, would determine how strongly the evidence supports the belief. In trying to do this, he came to some conclusions which have influenced all later attempts. One feature of Carnap's approach that has been retained by most later attempts to construct a precise epistemology is the centrality it assigns to probability.

This is a very plausible idea. There are good reasons why we might try to describe the strength of evidence for beliefs in terms of probability. In the next section some very basic probability theory is explained. For now, just consider the similarities between evaluating evidence and comparing chance events.

Assume that when there is evidence for two different beliefs we can compare their strength. We can say at least in a rough way which evidence supports which belief more strongly. Now suppose you have a bag with 50 green balls and 50 red balls in it. You reach inside and grab one at random, and before you can see it, you have to say what the probability is that it is a red one. You will say that the probability is 50 percent, or 0.5. If instead there had been 10 green balls and 90 red ones, you would have said that the probability was 90 percent, or 0.9. The important point is that probability can be taken as saying two things. On the one hand, as the probability of getting a red ball increases, so does the number of red balls you will on average get if you pick them at random over and over. (If the probability is 0.5, you will get a red one on average five times out of ten; if it is 0.9, you will get a red one on average nine times out of ten.) On the other hand, as the probability of getting a red ball increases, so does the strength of the confidence you should have that the next ball you will pick will be red. If your evidence about the proportion of red and green balls leads you to give a 0.5 probability to getting a red ball, then you should be less confident of getting one than if it gives a 0.9 probability. So probability can measure two things here: how often something will happen on average, and how strong the evidence for a belief is.

Probability is usually like this: the probability of an event can usually be taken as measuring the strength of evidence for a belief. Now remember our assumption that the strength of evidence for different beliefs can be compared. This means that if probabilities can measure the strength of evidence for beliefs about balls and bags, or roulette wheels, or tosses of coins, then they can measure the strength of evidence for anything. We can ask, for example, whether the evidence for the theory of evolution supports it more or less strongly than the evidence that a bag had 80 red balls and 20 green ones would support the belief that an arbitrarily chosen ball drawn from it would be red. So we can hope to measure strength of evidence in terms of probability.

Looking at strength of evidence in terms of probability brings a subtle shift of perspective. Familiar themes in the theory of knowledge begin to look rather different. In particular, issues about the role of background beliefs in reasoning become different and clearer. There are connections between this probability-based perspective on background belief and a different perspective, naturalism, which will be discussed in the final sections of the chapter.

Note: It is impossible to explain Bayesian epistemology without explaining some probability theory. For some readers this may be welcome. And this really is a very simple exposition. But if you want to avoid anything at all mathematical, you should read only sections 3, 5, 6 and 7.

2. A Guide through the Theory of Probability

Probability can measure both how likely it is that an event will occur and how strong the evidence is that a belief is true. These are closely connected. Suppose that a belief concerns a possible event: for example, a coin's landing heads when tossed. If the event is very likely, then the facts that make it likely should be strong evidence for the belief. And if there is strong evidence for the belief, then someone who knows this evidence and knows no other relevant evidence should think that it is very likely that the event will occur. For example, if the coin has been tossed a hundred times and landed heads each time, then this is strong evidence that the coin is biased; so the probability that it will land heads the next time is very high, and the belief that it will land heads next time is strongly supported by the evidence of the previous tosses. So it is no accident that the likelihood of events and the strength of evidence for beliefs can both be measured by probability.

The basic fact about probability is that there is a limited amount of it: when one belief becomes more probable, then others become less probable. If you come to think it more likely that the coin is biased to heads, you should think it less likely that the coin will land tails next time. This can be visualized diagramatically with "stretchy Venn diagrams." The familiar Venn diagram represents the relations between properties, so that, for example, the relations between "cat," "carnivore," and "mammal" can be represented as in figure 2.

When thinking about probability, it helps to use Venn diagrams where the areas represent not properties but propositions, possible beliefs or

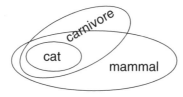

Figure 2. Venn diagram showing relations between three classes.

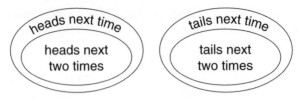

Figure 3. Relations between four chance propositions.

heads, heads	tails, heads
heads, tails	tails, tails

Figure 4. The area enclosed by the heavy line corresponds to the probability that a coin will come down heads at least once. Given that the coin has landed heads once, (tails, tails) is ruled out, so the conditional probability of (heads, heads) is 1/3.

events. So, for example, we might make a diagram with the four propositions "Heads next time," "Tails next time," "Heads the next two times," and "Tails the next two times." We would then get figure 3. Think of the regions in this diagram as representing ways or scenarios in which the propositions could come to be true. You can see from this diagram that there is no way in which the coin can land both heads and tails, and that all scenarios in which it lands heads (or tails) twice are also scenarios in which it lands heads (or tails) once.

Figure 3 does not yet have probability in it. To visualize probability, think of the sizes of the regions in figure 3 as representing probabilities: the larger a region is, the higher the probability of the proposition it represents. In some cases you can think of this as there being more ways in which the proposition can come to be true. This is illustrated in figure 4. As you can see, the probability that the coin comes down heads once (either on the first or the second toss) is the same as the probability that it comes down heads on the first and not the second toss plus the probability that it comes down heads on the second and not the first toss plus the probability that it comes down heads on both tosses. (Look at the diagram and see that the area must be the same.) This will always be true; that is, for any two propositions A and B, if we write "Prob" for "the probability that," we have:

$$\text{Prob}(A \text{ or } B) = \text{Prob}(A \& \text{not } B) + \text{Prob}(\text{not } A \& B)$$
$$+ \text{Prob}(A \& B)$$

Since there is a fixed area to the diagram, the total amount of probability is limited. To simplify things, it is standard to take the total amount of probability as 1. So, since for any proposition A, any point in the diagram is either in the area associated with A or in the area associated with not A (since A is either true or false), another basic principle of probability is

Prob (A) + Prob (not A) = 1.

These two principles can be used as a basis for all of probability theory. If you understand them, you really can understand everything about probability. In fact, if you can think in terms of stretchy Venn diagrams, you can understand all of probability theory. But one more basic concept is also needed. For analyzing the relation between a belief and the evidence for it, the most important notion used by probability theory is that of of **conditional probability**.

Conditional probability states how probable a proposition would be if some evidence were accepted. Suppose that you know how likely you think some propositions are, and then you discover that something you thought very unlikely is in fact true. You see a moose riding a motorcycle, or a coin landing heads 20 times in a row. One very simple way of adjusting your beliefs to the discovery goes as follows. Call the new discovery E (E for evidence). Step 1: give all propositions probabilities in accordance with how compatible they are with E, according to your previous probabilities. (This will mean giving probability 0 to all those beliefs which are now shown to be false: that is, to the denial of E and other propositions inconsistent with E.) Step 2: adjust the values so that E is the new standard of certainty, with probability 1, and all other propositions have probability in proportion to it.

This is called **conditionalization**. In terms of stretchy Venn diagrams, conditionalization is very simple. It means removing *not E* from the diagram and leaving everything else unchanged (step 1), except that the region that was previously just E now has to be considered the new diagram, with area 1 (step 2). So we wipe out part of the old diagram, the *not E* part, and stretch the rest so that it covers the whole area. (Consider, for example, how to get the conditional probability of a coin's landing heads twice in two throws, given that it has landed heads on the first throw. In figure 4, remove the area that corresponds to tails on the first throw, and notice that of the three remaining areas only one has two successive heads. So although if the coin is fair, the probability of two heads in a row is 1/4, given that it has landed heads the first time, the conditional probability that both tosses are heads is 1/3.)

The standard notation for the conditional probability of a proposition B given evidence E is "Prob (B, E)." (This says how much you should believe B given evidence E.) Prob (B, E) is obtained by considering just the probability of B & E (as in steps 1 and 2 above), and then adjusting the values so that the probability of E becomes 1 (step 3). This means taking the probability of B & E and dividing it by the probability of E. That is:

Prob $(B, E) = $ Prob $(B \& E) / $ Prob (E).

This formula corresponds exactly to the stretchy Venn diagram description of conditionalization. The new probability of B (after discovering E) is the probability of what is left of the proposition P after removing the refuted proposition not E – that is, Prob (P & E) – which is then rescaled in accordance with its relative proportion among the non-refuted propositions: that is, divided by E. Part of the diagram is thrown away, and the rest is stretched to size. Suppose, for example, you see a coin land heads 20 times in a row – take this as E – and you had originally thought that the coin was fair – take this as B. Then your new probability for the belief that the coin is fair is the (old) probability for the proposition that it was fair and lands 20 times in a row divided by the old probability of the coin landing 20 times in a row. Unless the old probability for the coin's being fair is almost 1, the new probability, conditional on E, will be very small.

3. The Bayesian Picture of Evidence

An influential school of philosophers and statisticians believe that conditionalization, and other rules closely related to it, gives a model of how we ought to change our beliefs when we learn new evidence. These thinkers are called *Bayesian*. They use this label because their central idea about the force of evidence depends on a consequence of the definition of conditional probability first pointed out by Thomas Bayes in the eighteenth century. Bayes' theorem describes the probability of B given E in terms of the probability of E given B. More precisely,

Prob $(B, E) = $ Prob $(E, B) \times $ Prob $(B) / $ Prob (E).

This formula gives us a way of measuring how much support evidence gives a belief. It tells us to look first at how likely the evidence would be, given the belief. Then, the more likely the evidence would be if the belief were true, the more likely it is that the belief is true given that the evidence is true (with the ratio of Prob (B) / Prob (E) determining exactly how much). This is a simple and powerful idea, and it does capture many features of how we often understand the force of evidence. This can be made clear by describing three consequences of the theorem.

Less likely evidence gives stronger support. If a theory predicts that cats eat mice, then observing that cats eat mice does not give very strong evidence for the theory. On the other hand, if a theory predicts that stones subject to some novel influence will rise into the air, then observing that they do rise under those conditions gives strong evidence for the theory. If you think that a coin is fair, then you should not be very shaken in your belief by a series of 8 heads and 7 tails. But a series of 14 heads and one tail should make you reconsider your belief. (Notice that as Prob (E) gets smaller in the formula, Prob (B, E) gets larger.)

Evidence supports beliefs that make it more probable. Suppose a geologist defends a theory which predicts an earthquake somewhere on the Pacific coast of North America sometime in the next two years. Then if an earthquake occurs at a particular place and a particular time, the theory is somewhat supported. Suppose, on the other hand, that another geologist defends a theory which predicts an earthquake of force 5 on the Richter scale with its epicentre on the UCLA campus on September 14 (the anniversary of Carnap's death, incidentally) in the year 2020. If this were to occur, it would be very strong evidence for the theory. Or consider the hypotheses that a coin is fair and that it is biased. Suppose that the coin is tossed and lands heads 14 times and tails once. This evidence is consistent with both hypotheses, but it has very low probability on the hypothesis that the coin is fair and much higher probability on the hypothesis that the coin is biased. So it gives much stronger evidence for the hypothesis that the coin is biased. (Notice that as Prob (E, B) gets larger, so does Prob (B, E).)

It takes very strong evidence to support beliefs with very low probability. Suppose that a bright light is seen moving at high speed through the night sky. Consider the reactions to this observation of two people. One of them thinks that it is possible that the earth is occasionally visited by alien spacecraft, and the other one thinks that this is very unlikely, almost impossible. For the first person the evidence will increase the probability of the alien visit hypothesis, while the second person will dismiss this possibility and provide other explanations for the evidence. Or consider two people, one of whom believes that a coin may be biased, estimating the probability of bias at around $1/2$. The other completely rules out the probability that the coin is biased, estimating the probability of bias at around 0. They both observe a series of 14 heads and 1 tail. For the first person this will move the probability that the coin is biased upwards, perhaps making it fairly high, while the second person will just point out that a fair coin can come down heads many times in a row, and leave the probability of bias near 0. (Note that if Prob (B) = 0, then Prob (B, E) = 0 for all E.)

These three consequences are relevant to issues about induction. In a way, they give answers to basic questions about the justification of inductive reasoning. To see this, consider more coin-tossing examples. You see a coin tossed five times, and each time it lands heads. You know nothing about the coin or where it came from. You are asked how likely you think it is that it will land heads the next time. The rule of simple induction, taken very simply and literally, says that since you have seen five instances of the coin landing heads and no instances of its landing tails, you should believe that it will always land heads. This seems a very rash conclusion. Of course, a less naive application of induction will remind you that you have often seen coins land heads for several times in a row and then land tails. Coins in general are usually fair, and when they are biased, it is as often to tails as to heads, so that, given a new coin, you should believe it as being as likely to land tails as heads. So you either treat this coin as a completely isolated case, in which case, if forced to decide, you say that the coin will come down heads, or you treat it as a coin among the zillions of coins in the world, in which case you say that heads and tails are equally likely. Both of these reactions seem wrong.

Contrast this with the Bayesian approach. Take it that the problem is that of determining what the bias of the coin is. Simplify the situation by supposing only three possibilities. Is it a fair coin, or a coin that always comes down heads (as naive induction might suggest), or a coin that always comes down tails? Call these three possibilities H-bias, Fair and T-bias. Suppose that before seeing the evidence you think that the coin is most likely fair, but it just might have one of the extreme biases. To be specific, suppose that your prior probability for Fair is 0.99, and for each of H-bias and T-bias it is 0.005. Then we can calculate the probability of each of them using Bayes' theorem. The probability of Fair, given the evidence, call it E, that it has landed heads five times in a row, is, according to Bayes' theorem, Prob (E, Fair) × Prob (Fair) / Prob (E). This is 0.861. Similarly, the probability of H-bias, given the evidence, is 0.139, and the probability of T-bias, given the evidence, is 0. So the hypothesis that the coin is fair remains the most likely one, but its probability has dropped considerably, and the probability that the coin has an extreme bias to heads is more than 20 times as likely as it was. The hypothesis that it has an extreme bias to tails has been refuted. In a more realistic case, with a large number of hypotheses covering many different degrees of bias, the result would be that a hypothesis of some smaller bias towards heads would have the greatest probability on the evidence.

(These figures are obtained as follows, if you really want to know. Prob (Fair) and Prob (E) are the probabilities *before* seeing the evidence, and Prob (E, Fair) is calculated in terms of them. Prob (E, Fair) is 1/32 = 0.0312. Prob (E, H-bias) is 1; Prob (E, T-bias) is 0; Prob (Fair) is 0.99; Prob (H-bias) = Prob (T-bias) = 0.005, as we assumed. And Prob (E) is the average of Prob (E, H-bias), Prob (E, Fair) and Prob (E, T-bias), where the average is weighted by the probability of each; that is, 0.005 × Prob (E, H-bias) + 0.99 × Prob (E, Fair); + 0.005 × Prob (E, T-bias) = 0.0359. So:

Prob (Fair, E) = Prob (E, Fair) × Prob (Fair)/Prob (E)

$$= 0.0312 \times 0.99/0.0359 = 0.861.$$

Prob (H-bias, E) = Prob (E, H-bias) × Prob (H-bias)/Prob (E)

$$= 1 \times 0.005/0.0359 = 0.139.$$

Prob (T-bias, E) = Prob (E, T-bias) × Prob (T-bias)/Prob (E)

$$= 1 \times 0.005/0.0359 = 0.)$$

There are several striking contrasts between the Bayesian solution to the problem and the solution based on simple induction. The most important is that Bayesian thinking does not attempt to tackle the problem unless it first has some probabilities. Then it looks at the evidence and considers how the probabilities are changed by it. So you never reason from a completely blank mind; you start with some ideas and see how they are affected by what you discover. Another basic contrast is that the conclusions of Bayesian thinking do not tell you *what* you should believe. Instead, they tell you how you should spread your probabilities among the propositions you are considering, and therefore *how much* you should believe them. Both these contrasts are clear in the example above. We get no answers unless we assume some probabilities that the coin is biased, which we can then change when we see the evidence. And we do not in the end get told whether or not to believe that on the next toss the coin will land heads. Instead, we are told how the probability of its landing heads has changed.

So in a way Bayesianism gives a solution to the problem of induction, and in a way it does not. It solves the problem in that, given prior probabilities and evidence, it provides a clear and reasonable way to revise the probabilities in the face of the evidence. And in doing this it neither depends on any assumptions about the regularity of nature nor pretends that the world may not have sharp surprises in store for us. It does not solve the problem in so far as it assumes that we can start with prior probabilities; nor does it tell us where to get them from. (Some prior probabilities will be versions of assumptions about what kinds of patterns we can expect to find in the world: see section 5 of chapter 4.) And the conclusions it gives are not beliefs, but probabilities. It does not solve the problem as much as it transforms it. The question we must ask is whether the transformed, and solved, problem is a satisfactory substitute for the original.

4. Objections to Bayesianism

For all its advantages – its smooth scientific appearance and the clear thinking it brings – Bayesian epistemology has some problems. There is a lively debate in contemporary philosophy about whether the theory of knowledge can be shaped around conditional probability, and there are debates among Bayesian thinkers about the form their theory should take. Some of this discussion is very subtle and very technical. This section describes some very simple objections to the Bayesian point of view, and indicates how Bayesians might try to reply.

Beliefs cannot be measured in numbers.   Often we do not know whether we are more sure of one belief than another. Can you say whether you are more confident that Washington is the capital of the United States than that dogs have legs? You know neither whether you are more confident of one than the other or whether they are both equally sure for you. Yet, if Bayesianism were right, you would have a probability for each of them which would be an exact number, so either one would be greater, or they would be the same.

   This problem is particularly sharp when the beliefs are very uncertain. For according to Bayesianism, evidence cannot support a proposition with probability zero. So if we think that there is any chance that there might be evidence for a proposition, however small, we should not give it a probability of zero. So consider the following propositions: the cube root of 1,728 is not 12; Nelson Mandela was not the first non-white president of South Africa; hydrogen is not a gas; brown is not a color. Since there could conceivably be evidence for any of these, as any skeptical philosopher will tell you, you should hesitate before giving any of them probability zero. Instead you should give them very small probabilities, just marginally above zero. But can you really see such a fine structure in your beliefs, discriminating those a hair's breadth above probability zero from those which can safely be relegated to permanent disbelief? And among the almost-but-not-quite-zero propositions, can you really say which ones are more and which ones less certain?

Conditionalization gives the wrong answers.   Consider the following example (adapted from Alvin Plantinga). Your probability for "Maureen is tone-deaf" (M) is 0.3, and your probability for "90 percent of people who go to heavy metal concerts are tone-deaf and Maureen goes to heavy metal concerts" (E) is also 0.3. But your probability for M & E, "Maureen is tone-deaf and she goes to heavy metal concerts and 90 percent of people who do that are tone-deaf," is only 0.001. Then, when we do the calculations, we find that Prob (M, E) is pretty low, lower than Prob (E). (In fact it is 0.0003.) So on Bayesian principles E is not evidence for M. But this seems wrong, since if you learn that Maureen goes to heavy metal concerts, and that 90 percent of people who go to heavy metal concerts are tone-deaf, you should consider this to be evidence for the belief that Maureen is tone-deaf.

Bayesianism does not define the strength of evidence. The example above assumed that evidence supports a belief when the probability of the belief conditional on the evidence is higher than the probability of the belief on its own. But as the example suggests, this may not be the best way to understand evidence in terms of probability. And it does not fulfil one of the promises of Bayesianism, to give a measure of how much support a given piece of evidence, E, gives to a given proposition, P. Should this be measured simply by Prob (P, E), or by Prob (P, E) − Prob (E), or by Prob (P, E) / Prob (E)? (Some Bayesians choose to measure it by log (Prob (E, P) / Prob (E, not P)) !) But until they decide among themselves, we cannot evaluate their theory. And the fact that all these thinkers cannot agree about the right measure might suggest that there is something fundamentally wrong here.

Bayesianism needs a fixed body of propositions. Much scientific progress occurs when someone finds a new concept. Space-time, genes, kinetic energy and even matter were concepts that had to be discovered. This process of concept creation continues, so we are always having to consider propositions that are completely novel to us. But we cannot have a prior probability for a novel proposition: when the proposition is first formulated and understood. So Bayesianism will have to say either that there can be no evidence for novel propositions or that their degree of support given any evidence is zero. Both are ridiculous responses, and prevent Bayesianism from connecting with the most interesting questions in epistemology and the philosophy of science, which arise when someone creates a completely new theory and we have to decide whether to believe it.

Bayesians have replies to all these objections. Very briefly, here are the outlines of what a Bayesian might say to each of the four points.

The objection that the sureness of our beliefs cannot be measured in numbers represents, according to Bayesians, a misunderstanding of their aims. They are not trying to describe how our minds actually work. In fact, when we consider what to believe, our minds are filled with illogicality and fuzziness. But we can keep before us an image of what a perfectly logical person would be like. Such a person would have definite numerical probabilities for all the propositions she considered, which she would change by conditionalization in the presence of new evidence. We finite and confused people can approach rationality even if we cannot achieve it, and we can see how near or far from rationality we are by comparing ourselves to this ideal.

The Bayesian answer to the objection that conditionalization gives the wrong answers is that it doesn't. Consider the example again. It assumes that the discovery that Maureen goes to heavy metal concerts and that 90 percent of people who do this are tone-deaf is evidence that Maureen is tone-deaf. But suppose you believed that 99 percent of all people are tone-deaf. Then the discovery that only 90 percent of people who go to heavy metal concerts are tone-deaf would suggest that Maureen's going to such concerts is evidence that she is *not* tone-deaf.

The third objection was that Bayesians do not give us a single definition of how much a proposition is supported by evidence. A Bayesian would admit that this is right, and express the hope that Bayesian philosophers will reach more agreement on the matter soon. (In reaching agreement, they might discover that they did not all mean exactly the same thing by the support that evidence gives a proposition.) Then the Bayesian might go on to say that strength of evidence is in practical terms a side-issue. What we want to know is how much we should believe the propositions we are considering. And Bayesianism gives us a definite answer to this: we should believe a proposition in accordance with its probability, conditional on the available evidence.

The last and most serious objection concerned the difficulty of knowing what probabilities to give novel propositions. There are several Bayesian responses to this problem. One is to argue that we can rationally give a completely novel proposition any probability we like. Some probabilities may be more convenient or more normal, but if the proposition is really novel, then no probability is forbidden. Then we can consider evidence and use it, via Bayes' theorem, to change these probabilities. Given enough evidence, many differences in the probabilities that are first assigned will disappear, as the evidence forces them to a common value.

These replies raise important issues to which we will return: issues about rationality, evidence and the nature of belief. They are issues that are hotly contested in contemporary epistemology. It is more important to think through the tensions between the objections and the replies than to settle on a simple adjudication between them.

5. Background Beliefs

Bayesian epistemology can be understood so that it is not a rival to other accounts of how we should change our beliefs. Instead, it can be thought of as a way of making a model of belief and evidence in terms such that they can be easily understood and tested. (This is certainly not how all Bayesians understand their project. Many of them intend something much more threatening.) Bayesian ideas are easiest to apply when we are dealing with beliefs about tossed coins, dice, lotteries and other probabilistic processes. By making a link between the theory of probability and statistics that applies to these, and traditional issues in the theory of knowledge, Bayesianism can allow us to test our theories about belief and evidence on cases where there are definite numerical answers.

Seen in this way, Bayesian considerations support a mild holism with a very limited bias towards ignorance-avoidance rather than error-avoidance. (For both holism and ignorance versus error, see chapter 5, sections 1 and 2.) To see this, we can translate some Bayesian conclusions out of the language of probability into the language of *background beliefs*.

Background beliefs are beliefs which must be assumed in order for evidence for a proposition to have force as evidence. Suppose that we have a belief and some evidence. We might be considering whether some newly found evidence is evidence for or against the belief. Or we might be wondering whether some fact that we have known for a long time can provide a good reason for the belief. In either case, when we think about how the evidence might give a reason for holding the belief, we often find that it would give a reason for the belief only if we also assume some other belief.

For example, in the previous section we considered whether the proposition "Maureen goes to heavy metal concerts and 90 percent of people who go to heavy metal concerts are tone-deaf" is evidence for the proposition "Maureen is tone-deaf." The background belief then was: "Less than 90 percent of the general population are tone-deaf." If we deny this belief – for example, by supposing that 99 percent of the general population are tone-deaf – then the evidence no longer supports the proposition. The belief that less than 90 percent of the population are tone-deaf is a typical *background belief*. That is, it is a belief which affects the force which other beliefs have as evidence. Background beliefs are often, as in this case, beliefs which are considered to be obviously true. This makes it easier for them to function invisibly, since it will at first seem unnecessary to cite them among the reasons for holding a belief.

Three basic facts about background beliefs can be illustrated with Bayesian reasoning.

Background beliefs influence the force of evidence. You have a coin and you are considering the proposition that heads and tails are equally likely the next time it is tossed. Your evidence is the number of times the coin has landed heads in a series of preceding tosses. If you believe that the coin could not be biased – if you give it a probability of zero – then after seeing the coin land heads a hundred times in a row, you should still take heads and tails to be equally likely on the next toss. After all, a fair coin can come down heads a million times in a row; unlikely things happen. But if you give the proposition that the coin is biased a probability greater than zero, even only slightly greater than zero, then after a series of heads you will consider it more likely that the coin will land heads than tails the next time. So the probability of the coin's being biased functions as a background belief: it is essential for the evidence of a succession of heads to affect the probability you assign to heads and tails on the next toss.

Background beliefs are changed by evidence. Although background beliefs influence the way evidence supports or refutes other beliefs, they are themselves changed by evidence. As long as you think it is possible that the coin could be biased, by giving it a probability greater than zero, then as more and more heads appear, you will think it is more and more likely that it actually is biased, until eventually you think that it is more likely than not to be biased.

Some background beliefs make evidence powerless. If you think that the coin could not possibly be biased, then a hundred heads will not convince you. In fact, no number of heads will convince you. So the belief that the coin could not possibly be biased makes it impossible for this kind of evidence to change your beliefs about how likely another head is. But as long as you think there is even a very small possibility, enough evidence will eventually change your mind. So in a way it is better to leave open a very small possibility that the coin might be biased. If we can have beliefs about which of the things that we do not think true could be true, and which are more likely than others, then we have a better chance that, as more evidence comes in, it will direct our beliefs towards the truth.

These conclusions about background beliefs suggest a mild holism. Whether a person is justified in believing a particular proposition depends not just on the evidence that person might cite for the belief, but on a wide range of other beliefs, whose relevance the person may be completely ignorant of. This opens up an interesting function for the theory of knowledge: discovering these background beliefs and making it clear how our beliefs depend on many assumptions besides the ones we might suppose.

They also suggest a holism that is linked to mild ignorance-avoidance. The Bayesian-inspired attitude to background beliefs just sketched is based on the idea that the combined effect of evidence and background beliefs is to tell us not what propositions are certainly true, but how much confidence we should have in them. (And crucial in this is not the list of background beliefs that we think certainly true, but the exact degrees of confidence we have in different background beliefs.) This already shifts the emphasis away from error-avoidance, since it forces us to think in terms of less than perfect certainty. The shift becomes more definite when we consider that propositions with probability considerably less than 1 can still be used to guide actions – think of weather forecasts, or a doctor's guess of a patient's life expectancy – so that part of the aim in using evidence to revise our beliefs must be to get probabilities which can guide us in everyday practical life.

The most profound realization about background beliefs is that they can change in response to evidence. We need a rich background of beliefs in place before we can interpret evidence (see chapter 2, section 5), and before we can evaluate the support our evidence gives to propositions (see this section and the previous one). But this does not mean that we are stuck with the background beliefs we start with. They too change. So we can hope that we can use whatever background beliefs we have to find and evaluate evidence which will change all of our beliefs, leading to new interpretations of new evidence, so that false beliefs are, in the fullness of time, filtered out.

We may hope for this. But it is a hope, not a certainty. Some background beliefs, as we have seen, do not respond to evidence. (If you are absolutely certain a coin is fair, a run of a million heads will not change your mind.) In fact, it is a very hard problem to say which background beliefs will respond to evidence. In special cases we can prove, for example, that some assignments of probabilities will converge on the true values, given enough evidence; but the general situation is very hard to understand. This is another important task for epistemology: to find ways of describing those combinations of belief which will respond flexibly to evidence, and separate them from others whose unresponsiveness makes of them traps from which evidence cannot rescue us.

6. Rationality Naturalized

The last section suggested that we can rely on the evidence as it emerges to determine the shape of our beliefs. This attitude can have far-reaching consequences. Pushing it a little further, it suggests that the job of deciding what is to count as evidence and reasonable belief can also develop with our evolving system of belief as it grows and changes. We would then expect epistemology not to stand outside the rest of our beliefs judging whether they live up to its standards, but to be a set of beliefs like any others, changing as we make new discoveries. The natural fear about such a suggestion is that it would result in an epistemology that simply rubber-stamped our existing beliefs, judging them by no standard outside themselves. This fear is partly countered by the point about the changeability of background beliefs. The standards we apply to our beliefs can change, just as the rest of our beliefs do.

This is an intriguing – indeed, an exciting – suggestion. It is the suggestion that epistemology is part of natural science, the part that studies the information-gathering capacities of the human animal. It is thus a *naturalistic* suggestion, in that it takes human beings and their knowledge to be part of the natural world. But it is not obvious how to make it work. Since W. V. Quine made the first suggestion along these lines, there have been many attempts to push the idea further. The result has been a lot of interesting work; but the overall impact on the theory of knowledge is hard to assess. The greatest potential impact is on the way we think about rationality.

The theory of knowledge centres on ideas about rationality. For example, evidence supports a belief when a rational person who accepts the evidence would come nearer to holding the belief. (An irrational person might ignore the evidence, or take it as grounds for thinking that the belief was false.) And the theory of knowledge aims at discovering which of our beliefs we can hold rationally, and which we hold because of habit, prejudice or misunderstanding. But its attempts to give a clear picture of rational belief have not been very successful. We have a fairly clear understanding of logical reasoning, given by deductive logic. Though we do not know much about what happens in a human person's mind when conclusions are deduced from premisses, we do have a definite idea of what the relation between premisses and conclusion is when an argument is deductively valid. We know what standards we are applying. Inductive reasoning, on the other hand, is a much murkier business. We do not know how to describe the patterns of inductive reasoning that we find plausible, in a way that distinguishes them from the ones that seem ridiculous to us. (That is a conclusion of Goodman's problem, described in chapter 4, sections 3 and 5.) Most importantly, we do not have a clear statement of what we mean when we say that some inductive reasoning is good or valid, reasoning that a rational person ought to find persuasive. Should it be reasoning that will more often than not give a true conclusion? Or reasoning that will give a true conclusion in 99 percent of similar cases? Or reasoning that most people with normal intelligence will find persuasive? All these answers have problems.

Other aspects of the theory of knowledge show the same tendency to leave rationality unexplained. Holist (or coherentist) theories do not say why it is rational to have coherent beliefs. (Are they more likely to be true? Are they easier to remember?) Empiricist and foundationalist theories do not give us clear reasons why it is rational to make perception the basic source of our beliefs. (At any rate, we do not have clear reasons when we no longer think that perceptual beliefs are never false or that people can know with certainty what is in their own minds.)

Naturalism can enter here. Instead of taking the concept of rationality for granted, we can try to approach it in terms of what we believe and can discover about human reasoning. We can see deductive reasoning, inductive reasoning, the search for coherence and the use of perception as some among the many ways in which people interest with their environment and arrive at beliefs about it. There are surely very many different belief-acquiring processes. For example, the ways in which people form opinions about one another's moods and characters on first meeting them are most likely not formed through step-by-step deduction but by some innate human social capacities.

When we focus on actual human information gathering, rather than on ideals of rationality, we are much less likely to think that many of our beliefs are the result of careful explicit reasoning which can be put into words and defended in the way that scientific theories or philosophical positions can be. At any rate, we want not to assume anything like this unless we can discover more about how human information gathering actually does work. Psychologists and philosophers are hard at work now, trying to put together a picture of psychological belief-acquisition processes, a picture that will link up with traditional philosophical questions about knowledge and rationality. There are two basic questions they face: what are the fundamental human capacities that are involved in belief acquisition, and what probability of producing true beliefs do they have under various conditions? And, given a particular belief, what processes (what applications of what capacities) can it result from, and what conditions are required for these processes to deliver true beliefs?

One example of this fits right into the themes of this chapter: our beliefs about probability. In everyday life people frequently have to think about how likely events are and how much they ought to believe that they might occur. So without studying probability theory, people have ways of thinking through problems that are really problems about probability. We can study these ways, and when we do, we find that they differ from "correct" probability theory as described by philosophers and statisticians in several respects. Three of them are framing effects, base-rate fallacies, and persistent illusions.

Framing effects

Framing effects are found in situations like the following. A group of subjects is divided into two subgroups. Subgroup 1 is given question 1 below.

> *Question 1.* Imagine that the country is preparing for the outbreak of an unusual disease, which is expected to kill 600 people. Two alternative programs to combat the disease have been proposed. Assume that the exact scientific estimate of the consequences of the programs is as follows:
>
> If Program A is adopted, 200 people will be saved.
> If Program B is adopted, there is a 1/3 probability that 600 people will be saved, and a 2/3 probability that no people will be saved.
> Which of the two programs would you favor?

At the same time subgroup 2 is given question 2 below.

> *Question 2.* Imagine that the country is preparing for the outbreak of an unusual disease, which is expected to kill 600 people. Two alternative programs to combat the disease have been proposed. Assume that the exact scientific estimate of the consequences of the programs is as follows:
>
> If Program C is adopted, 400 people will die.

> If Program D is adopted, there is a 1/3 probability that nobody will die, and 2/3 probability that 600 people will die.
> Which of the two programs would you favor?

The usual result is that most people is subgroup 1 prefer program A, and most people in subgroup 2 prefer program D. But program A is the same as program C, and program B is the same as program D. They are just described in different words, differing in whether they emphasize numbers dead or numbers saved. But most people prefer A when they read the first question and D when they read the second. Probability theory, by contrast, says that if you prefer A, you should prefer C, and if you prefer B, you should prefer D. This is called a framing effect, because it shows that when people think about probabilities, they are influenced not just by the simple probabilities, but also by the way the probabilities are framed by a story. Tell the story differently, and the same numbers produce the opposite reaction.

Base-rate fallacies

Base-rate fallacies are a way in which people often give too much weight to the evidence at hand rather than to their background beliefs. For example, consider your answer to the following question:

> George weighs 300 pounds and has very strong legs. He is either a sumo wrestler or a swimmer. Which is he more likely to be?

Your answer may be that George is a sumo wrestler. For he seems to fit that profile more than that of a swimmer. But this answer is wrong. There are more 300 pound swimmers with strong legs in the world than there are 300 pound sumo wrestlers with strong legs. That is because there are so few sumo wrestlers compared to swimmers, even though there is a much greater proportion of 300 pounders among them than there is among swimmers.

The mistake here may be a confusion of proportions with absolute numbers. Or it may be a more subtle confusion about conditional probabilities. Whatever it is, everyone is susceptible to it. It is in a way a framing effect, since it is sensitive to the way in which a problem is described. And it is in a way a *persistent illusion* – that is, a situation in which people can be relied upon to give what probability theory describes as the wrong answers.

Persistent illusions

Another class of such persistent illusions concerns risk. Given two situations, in one of which there is very little risk of a big loss and in the other of which there is a serious risk of a big loss counter-balanced with a corresponding possibility of a big gain, people will very often choose the "no loss" option, even when the "possible loss" option gives just the same average probability of loss or gain. (See question 19.) But the most striking case is the so-called *gambler's fallacy*. Suppose that you see a coin tossed ten times. It comes down heads every time. It is about to be tossed again. Which way do you expect it to come down? Inductive reasoning and probability theory suggest that you should either think that the coin is biased and so expect another heads, or put the run of heads down to chance and expect that heads and tails are equally likely. Yet some people will expect the coin to come down tails next time. They think: a run of eleven heads in a row is even more unlikely than a run of ten heads, so the coin will probably come down tails on the eleventh throw. But this is a mistake. (See question 13 below for more on why it is a mistake.) Reasoning like this, people sometimes shelter from thunderstorms under lightning-struck trees, thinking that lightning rarely strikes the same place twice. And in bombardments people sometimes sit in bomb craters, thinking that the probability of a bomb hitting the same place twice is very low.

The most remarkable feature of the gambler's fallacy is how universal it is. Psychological studies of probabilistic reasoning suggest that everyone, whatever their familiarity with probability theory, falls into the fallacy if it is sufficiently disguised. Most people fall for fairly simple versions, whereas professors of statistics fall for more subtle versions. It seems to result from some deep tendency in the way we process information about uncertain outcomes.

Framing effects, base-rate fallacies, and persistent illusions all point to a single conclusion: that when people reason with probabilities – or about the kinds of questions concerning risk and uncertainty to which probability applies – they tend to do so in ways that diverge from probability theory as understood by philosophers and statisticians. It seems that thinking probabilistically is not something that we do naturally or accurately.

7. Bayesianism versus Naturalism

The Bayesian approach and the naturalistic approach have important similarities. Both emphasize the importance of background beliefs and the futility of trying to find evidence for our beliefs from a completely neutral standpoint. There are also important differences between them. The most basic concerns the concept of rationality.

For Bayesian epistemology it is rational for a person to believe a proposition to a certain degree when she accepts some evidence, if that is the degree of belief that she gets when she begins with the probabilities (degrees of belief) she had before accepting the evidence and then conditionalizes on the evidence. It is the change of beliefs, rather than the degrees of belief at the beginning or end of the process, that is the focus of the theory. But the theory requires that both the beginning and the end beliefs must fit probability theory, and that the end beliefs must be obtained from the beginning beliefs by conditionalization. In this way probability theory supplies the definition of rational belief that Bayesianism uses. And that definition is not negotiable; it is the most basic assumption of the theory.

Naturalism challenges this definition. It does so in both a broad and a narrow way. The broad way is by suggesting that instead of defining rationality by an unchangeable *apriori* definition, we should study the way human reasoning actually proceeds, to discover when it is more and when it is less reliable. The narrow way is by suggesting that reasoning about probability is not something that humans do very well. So the ideal of beliefs which model perfect probability and which change in accordance with conditional probability may not be a suitable one for human beings. It may not be an ideal which we are capable of following; it may not be an ideal which we ought even to try to follow, if we want to get true and usable beliefs.

Naturalism challenges standard ideas in epistemology in other ways too. One important dimension is the realization of the finiteness of human intelligence and memory. As psychologists study the ways in which we process, store and access information, it becomes clear that the ways of thinking that might be best for perfectly rational, intelligent beings are often not ways that human beings can handle. We are just too limited. So, for example, when we want to know what explanation of a phenomenon to accept, we cannot go through all the propositions we can conceive, comparing how well each one explains the phenomenon or how probable it is on the evidence. This would be too great a challenge for our powers of reasoning and memory. Instead, we have to consider the few possible explanations that our habits or our scientific traditions suggest are plausible. We can then carefully compare the advantages and disadvantages of each of these. Even that is often at the limit of our capacities.

Moreover, when we accept a new belief, we cannot check to see whether it is consistent with all the beliefs we already hold. A perfectly rational creature would do this before accepting a new belief, for otherwise, as beliefs accumulate, so may inconsistencies. But real human beings do not have the time, memory or reasoning power to do this. So we make only quick, superficial checks of this kind. Before accepting a new theory in geology, scientists do not check to see if there are un-obvious, complicated deductions showing that it contradicts theories in economics or medicine or history. They accept it if it seems consistent in the domains where trouble might be expected to arise, leaving it for future thinkers to iron out any surprising conflicts. As a result, inconsistencies are always being created in our beliefs. (A result of this is that there is always more work for philosophers.)

Another challenge derives from the inherently social dimension of human knowledge. Standard epistemology does discuss testimony, asking when it is reasonable for one person to believe what someone else says, and when this can give knowledge. But the emphasis is still on when an individual person knows a particular proposition. Social scientists, on the other hand, study the ways in which scientific traditions develop and interact, and the ways in which circles of co-operating and competing researchers find their way to new discoveries. Many of the relevant factors do not fit with the traditional image of rational individuals impartially considering what they should believe. For example, there is a division of labour between people who create theories and people who devise experiments to test them. Each of these tribes has knowledge and skills not shared by the other, and often the reasons for taking a theory or some evidence seriously lie more in the reputation of the scientist and the relation of one circle of researchers to another than in matters of intellectual content. It depends more on who knows who and who takes whose ideas seriously than on the objective force of evidence. Relating these factors to issues of justification, rationality and knowledge is not going to be easy.

Naturalism challenges epistemic ideals that do not take account of our actual capacities and limitations. It suggests that some of these ideals may be inappropriate for human beings to aspire to. These doubts are still only suggestive, though. We do not yet know enough to see how serious they are. More important is the very fact that doubts about the appropriate epistemic ideals can be based on facts about human information processing. Epistemology cannot stop with considering how the beliefs of perfectly intelligent creatures might develop. We also want to understand how real human beings, with human limitations and human resources, can succeed or fail in their search for usable true beliefs.

Reading Questions

1 Suppose you want to know whether you should believe the theory of evolution. How would it help to have a precise measure of the strength of the evidence for it?

2 Below are four assertions of probability. Describe each in terms of how often some kind of event happens, and also in terms of how strongly it would be reasonable to believe something? Are some easier to describe one way than the other?
   (a) The probability of rain is 0.8.
   (b) The probability of living to 80 at your age is 0.4.
   (c) The probability of this coin landing heads three times in a row is 1/8.
   (d) The probability that the terrorists will kill their hostages is 0.3.

3 Make diagrams like figures 3 and 4 for the propositions "Speedy wins the race," "Frontrunner wins the race," and "Frontrunner drops dead." Assume that it is very probable that Frontrunner will win the race and very very improbable that Frontrunner will drop dead. (Speedy and Frontrunner are race-horses, needless to say.)

Find the areas of the diagrams corresponding to "Speedy wins the race & Frontrunner drops dead" and "Speedy wins the race & Frontrunner does not drop dead." What area corresponds to "Speedy wins the race & Frontrunner wins the race"?

Find the areas of the diagram that represent the probability of Speedy wining the race conditional on Frontrunner dropping dead.

4   Suppose that the probability that Speedy will win the race and that Frontrunner will drop dead is 0.1, and the probability that Frontrunner will drop dead is 0.001, what is the probability that Speedy will win the race conditional on Frontrunner dropping dead?

5   Show how Bayes' theorem follows from the definition of conditional probability. (Hint: write out the definition of Prob (B, E) and the definition of Prob (E, B), getting the latter just by reversing the letters in the former. Then find a factor common to both of them so that you can solve an equation.)

6   How does the example about earthquake predictions fit the slogan "Evidence supports beliefs that make it more probable"?

7   Consider the theory that everything in the world is affected by the actions of tiny invisible gremlins, whose actions are completely whimsical and unpredictable. Using the three statements in section 3, describe how strongly each of the following pieces of evidence supports the theory by comparison with the support they give to standard scientific theories.
   (a) A rocket which had been thoroughly checked before launch explodes shortly after blast-off.
   (b) A person wins the lottery against 10 million to 1 odds.
   (c) A teacher drops a heavy and a light ball before a class to demonstrate the laws of gravity. They pause in mid-air and hover for two seconds, then the light ball falls before the heavy one does.

8   Do the probability calculations in the example in section 3, assuming instead that Prob (Fair) = Prob (H-bias) = Prob (T-bias) = 1/3. Compare the conditional probabilities to those in the example. What conclusions are suggested?

9   The first objection to Bayesianism in section 4 mentions the denials of the beliefs that (a) Washington is the capital of the United States, (b) dogs have legs, (c) the cube root of 1,728 is 12, (d) Nelson Mandela was the first non-white president of South Africa, (e) hydrogen is a gas, (f) brown is a color. All these are beliefs that you might want to give probability 1. If you had to rank them in order of certainty, what would the ranking be? Does this suggest that not all of them should have probability 1?

10   Make an exact calculation to back up the Bayesian reply to the example about Maureen and heavy metal concerts.

11   Use the calculations in the biased coin case of section 3 and question 8 to support the statements of section 5 that "Background beliefs influence the force of evidence" and "Background beliefs are changed by evidence." Find some prior probabilities for this example that support the third slogan, "Some background beliefs make evidence powerless."

12   In the example illustrating framing effects, why will probability theory say that if you prefer A, you should prefer C, and if you prefer B, you should prefer D? (You do not need to appeal to anything deep about probability to answer this. Why, when you see questions 1 and 2 side by side, is it clear that these should be the preferences?)

13   You have a box with 90 coins in it. You know that 30 are fair coins, 30 strongly biased to heads, and 30 strongly biased to tails. You reach into the box and bring out a coin at random. You toss it, and it lands heads ten times in a row. Is the coin more likely to be a fair coin, biased to heads, or biased to tails? How is this relevant to the gambler's fallacy?

14   why can geologists considering a new theory not check to see that it is consistent with all their other beliefs? Can they not go through a limited number of other beliefs that are likely to be relevant, and quickly find any possible contradictions?

Thinking Questions

15   At the end of section 1 there is an argument as to why the strength of evidence can be measured with probability involving, on the one hand, hypotheses about random events and, on the other hand, scientific theories such as the theory of evolution. How is this argument affected if we deny that when some evidence supports one belief and other evidence supports another belief, the evidence for the one belief must always be either stronger, weaker or the same as the evidence for the other belief? Can we deny this and still say that some evidence is strong and some is weak?

16   Go back to the ravens paradox described in chapter 4, section 3. What might a Bayesian solution to the paradox look like?

17   In the biased coin example in section 3 the probability that the coin has an extreme bias to tails, conditional on the evidence, is zero. It would be zero if the evidence were only one toss in which the coin landed heads. If we now change our probabilities by conditionalization on the evidence, we will find that the probability of an extreme bias to tails remains zero whatever the evidence. Is this an undesirable feature of the Bayesian approach?

18   The Bayesian response to the fourth argument against it was: "We can rationally give a completely novel proposition any probability we like. Some probabilities may be more convenient or more normal, but if the proposition is really novel, then no probability is forbidden." Suppose that a scientist comes up with a novel explanation of some phenomenon, and other scientists assign it a probability of zero, so that no evidence whatsoever will support it. Is this reasonable?

19   Suppose that you have to make both of the decisions below. Which choice would you make in each case?
(i)   Choose either (a) a sure gain of $60 or (b) an 80 percent chance to gain $90.
(ii)   Choose either (c) a 25 percent chance to win $60 or (d) a 20 percent chance to win $90.
    Many people will prefer (a) to (b) and (d) to (c). But if the average gain of (a) is greater than that of (b), then the average gain of (c) is greater than that of (d). (Average gain, or expected value, is the gain averaged over all possible situations weighted by how probable they are. Thus since (b) represents two situations one with probability 0.2 in which you gain nothing and one with probability 0.8 in which you gain $90, its average gain in money is $0.2 \times 0 + 0.8 \times 90 = \$72$. The gains do not have to be measured in money.) Some econ-

omists and psychologists use this as evidence that there is a persistent illusion in human decision making. Is this persuasive?

20   Issues of human finiteness and of the different roles that different people play in science link to the difference between rational and justified belief, discussed in chapter 1 (see questions 16 and 17 of chapter 1). Suppose that a geologist accepts a theory because there is a lot of geological evidence for it, no geological evidence against it, and she can see no reason in chemistry, physics or biology why it should not be true. However, it turns out that a basic law of physics combined with the new geological theory contradicts some well-known fact. (Perhaps it entails that the Sahara desert should have more rain than it does.) Showing this needs a lot of advanced mathematics which the geologist had no reason to consider relevant, and which had not been part of her training. Was she justified in believing the new theory (before learning about the problem)? What would Bayesianism say? What distinctions might a naturalist approach suggest?

21   Two naturalistic challenges to traditional epistemology, the challenge from human finiteness and the challenge from the social nature of knowledge, were described in section 7 as challenging much of epistemology. But they present particular problems for a Bayesian approach. Why?

Further Reading

Simple introductions to probability theory and the Bayesian approach to evidence are found in Brian Skyrms, *Choice and Chance* (Dickenson, 1966), and Richard Jeffrey, *The Logic of Decision* (2nd edn, Chicago, 1985). Good books giving Bayesian approaches to scientific method are Colin Howson and Peter Urbach, *Scientific Reasoning: The Bayesian Approach* (Open Court, 1989), and Mark Kaplan, *Decision Theory as Philosophy* (Cambridge University Press, 1996). A classic source is Rudolf Carnap, *Logical Foundations of Probability* (University of Chicago Press, 1962).

A middle-level survey of issues about naturalism in epistemology is Philip Kitcher, "The naturalist's return," *Philosophical Review*, 101 (1992), 53–114. Issues of human finiteness and the psychology of probabilistic reasoning are discussed in Alvin Goldman, *Epistemology and Cognition* (Harvard University Press, 1986), and Edward Stein, *Without Good Reason* (Oxford University Press, 1996). Criticisms of the Bayesian approach are found in chapter 7 of Alvin Plantinga, *Warrant: The Current Debate* (Oxford University Press, 1993), and chapter 8 of his *Warrant and Proper Function* (Oxford University Press, 1993). The transmission of knowledge is discussed in Michael Welbourne, *The Transmission of Knowledge* (Aberdeen University Press, 1980). See also chapter 5 of W. V. Quine and Joseph Ullian, *The Web of Belief* (Random House, 1978).

Electronic resources: *Routledge Encyclopedia of Philosophy:* Probability theory and epistemology. *The Stanford Encyclopedia of Philosophy:* epistemology: Bayesian.

Chapter 11

AFTERWORD: SOME FUTURE EPISTEMOLOGY

There is progress in philosophy. Some ideas that once seemed promising, even intuitively obvious, we now understand to be very problematic. They can be defended, but only with great ingenuity and at the price of abandoning other intuitively obvious ideas. And some hard problems are settled. I would argue that we now know (yes, know): that there is no argument which will convince an extreme skeptic that we do indeed know most of the things we claim to; that there is no apriori proof of the existence of a traditional God; that attempts to solve Hume's problem by showing in a way that needs no backup from inductive reasoning that the future must resemble the past are mistaken; that our knowledge of other people's minds is not based on the argument from analogy; that prior beliefs about general patterns in nature are needed in order for evidence to support later hypotheses about particular patterns in nature. And others. Notice that many of these conclusions are negative, and notice that they have to be stated in a careful and qualified way in order for it be remotely plausible that we know they are true. This is because the progress that is made in philosophy usually consists in learning the distinctions and qualifications it is necessary to make in order not to get confused about an issue, and in learning the price of a philosophical claim, the other beliefs that you may have to abandon if you want to hold on to the claim. When we understand what concepts we must focus on and what distinctions we must make, and what traps we must avoid, we can see the importance of a new set of problems, which were hiding behind the old ones. They are usually just as hard to solve, but they are the ones that, at this stage of our science and our culture, we have to be struggling with.

In the theory of knowledge we begin with some easily understood issues, which any reflective person will have thought about. Easily understood, but not easily solved. The most significant of them are the following.

Skepticism versus common sense: How much of what we claim to know still appears, when we reflect on it and on our grounds for believing it, to be knowledge?

Criticism versus tolerance: When considering our own versus other people's beliefs, should we evaluate them with an ideal that stresses the importance of publicly available evidence and which is suspicious of beliefs for which evidence cannot be produced, or should we allow that the beliefs of different people may be different in ways that they may not be able to defend to one another?

Grounds for belief: What considerations show that it is reasonable to continue to hold a belief? Does only evidence from perception count, or does support from other beliefs shared by numbers of sensible people carry any weight? Are the only considerations those that make it more likely that the belief is true, or do considerations about what is useful or what makes one's life make sense also carry any weight?

In current epistemology these have been refined into a number of different questions, which we can apply more careful arguments to. Some of the more important ones which have been discussed in the previous chapters are the following.

The diagnosis of skepticism. What is it that gives skepticism its appeal? What is so persuasive about arguments that claim that we do not know things about which our claims to knowledge seem completely secure? Until recently the most common diagnosis of the appeal of skepticism was that it depends of the plausibility of the idea that knowledge needs certainty. If there is any doubt about anything, you don't know it. Skeptics are then presented as arguing that since there is some doubt, however small, even that you have two hands or that the world existed yesterday, you do not strictly speaking know these things. And anti-skeptics are presented as arguing that to the extent that knowledge needs certainty it does not need total certainty. Or to put it differently "certain" means "certain enough": you are certain enough that you have two hands to justify you in carrying out practical activities and so you can reasonably say that you know that you have two hands. (After all, say these philosophers, if skeptics really think they don't know that buses are real why do they step out of the way of them? And the skeptics reply that while it's more likely that buses will flatten you than that they won't, that doesn't mean you really really know they will.)

Recently, other diagnoses have come to prominence. Even if you accept that the certainty that humans can attain is limited, and that we can speak of knowledge when it is based on the certainty that we can attain, you might still think that we know a lot less than we suppose. Remember the "defeaters" discussed in chapter 6 and 7. Suppose that you are looking out your window and see a bird. You would normally take yourself to know that there is a bird there on the window ledge. But your belief wouldn't be true if instead of a real bird it was a toy bird that someone had climbed up and glued onto the ledge. And you have not done any of the research needed to show that this has not happened. But the toy bird possibility is not so unlikely that human enquiry could never establish it: you just haven't bothered to investigate. (And you couldn't investigate all such possibilities.) But there are many possible defeaters like this for almost all of your beliefs, which you haven't bothered to rule out. So, a skeptic can say, none of these beliefs count as knowledge, if we are using the word exactly and literally. And anti-skeptics will reply in a similar way as they did when the issue was certainty. They will say that knowledge requires not that you have ruled out all possible defeaters but that you have ruled out all *relevant* ones. Again the question comes down in part to what it is reasonable to build into the word "knowledge."

Externalism/internalism/naturalism. There is yet another interesting diagnosis of the appeal of skepticism. This one traces it to the mistaken belief that knowledge is a matter of justified belief. The externalist anti-skeptic says "I'll grant for the sake of argument that none of our beliefs are ideally justified. But that does not show that none of them are known. To be known is to be the result of a process that reliably links beliefs and facts. Most of our everyday beliefs are reliably linked to the facts, so most of them are known, even when we cannot give any completely convincing reasons or evidence for them." To this the internalist, whether or not she is a skeptic, replies "but if this is what knowledge is, why should we think that it is important?"

Part of the externalist answer to this question is clear. We are sources of information to one another; indeed we are one another's primary sources of information, at least as important as our senses. As a result we have an interest in knowing when other people's beliefs can be trusted, and this will involve knowing whether their belief-acquisition takes account of various factors relevant to their and our situation, including factors that they are not aware of. Our attitude to the beliefs of others must always be externalist. But, as discussed in chapter 7, this is a very broad attitude. It can range from evaluating thinking processes in terms of factors beyond those that the thinker is aware of, to describing human knowledge in terms that make no special place for reasoning at all.

The theme of a strong externalism is not that reasoning is not real or not important, but that its importance lies outside itself. Reasoning is a way that human beings touch and track the world around them. It is one of the central adaptations of our species (the other is a kind of organized and improvised social life, which itself makes heavy demands on reasoning). Other species know in different ways: knowledge is a natural phenomenon. (I know where my keys are, particle physicists know whether neutrinos have mass, salmon know the rivers that lead to their native streams.) There are many different kinds of knowledge in the world: the knowledge that humans have in everyday life, the knowledge that human scientists tease out of nature, and the knowledge that different other animals gain in an enormous variety of ways. If we understood how all these different kinds fitted together we would not only have useful information about how to combine common sense, science, and speculation, we would have an insight into a fundamental aspect of what it is to be human.

The hope here is for a something between a philosophical doctrine and a new science, which would study the ways in which the world can be known. It would build on psychology, biology, and also what philosophers have achieved in understanding knowledge from the inside. Can we achieve this? How deep an understanding might it give us? We can only find out by trying.

Context. Beliefs can be more and less certain; they can track the facts more or less well. Unknown facts that might defeat them can be more or less relevant. From reading this book you might have thought that in the theory of knowledge we have to find definite thresholds for these factors. How much uncertainty is consistent with knowledge? How well must a perceptual system track the environment for the perceptual belief to count as knowledge? What kinds of fact can defeat a given belief? But in fact these questions can seem extremely naive. They presuppose that there are definite thresholds for certainty and for effectiveness of tracking, and that for each belief there is a list of facts which can undermine it. But there is an obvious alternative. The thresholds could vary depending on whose belief it is, and when, and what their purposes are. Suppose, for example, that a chemist has mixed some chemicals, which usually result in one compound but extremely occasionally can result in another. Does the chemist have enough certainty to know that the usual compound has resulted? One thing that seems relevant is the purpose for which the chemicals are being mixed. Suppose they are being mixed to prepare a demonstration for an audience, and the worst that will happen is that the chemist will be embarrassed by the demonstration not working. Then the chemist does seem to have all the certainty that is needed. But suppose that the chemicals are being mixed to make a vaccine which will be injected into seriously ill children, who will die if the wrong compound is used. Then more certainty is certainly needed, more tests are called for.

An analogy (due to Peter Unger) compares being known to being flat. Kansas is very flat, and Tibet is certainly not flat. But the flattest field in Kansas has bumps that would disgrace even a mediocre mirror. When we are talking about parts of the earth we apply less demanding standards of flatness than when we are talking about mirrors. Similarly, when we are wondering whether we know what compound we have mixed for a chemical demonstration we apply lower standards than when we are wondering whether we know whether we have prepared the right ingredient for a vaccine. Or so one could argue. It would not follow that nothing is really known, just as it is not clear that nothing is really flat. (Kansas *is* flat – just ask anyone who has been there.) The uncontroversial conclusion has to be put more carefully: the standards we use when we are ascribing knowledge vary from one context to another.

What aspects of context matter? There is very little agreement about this. An austere version would have it that we are dealing with conversational contexts, the kinds of things that make an ambiguous word mean one thing in one conversation and another in another. A more liberal version would allow the general purposes of the person whose beliefs are being evaluated to be relevant. An extreme version of this position would allow that if truth weighs much less heavily in one's purposes than achieving spiritual comfort then one can be said to know doctrines for which there is very little evidence but which make ones life bearable. (As long as they are true, that is, but at least the believer could claim to know.) A less extreme version would allow that the purposes of everyday life make different standards appropriate to those that are called for in some scientific enterprises.

What is rationality? A central aim of the theory of knowledge may be taken as an attempt to define rational belief, working out what it would be reasonable to believe by discussing different classes of beliefs separately. But deep ambiguities in the concept of rational belief are now emerging. Might the ideal of rationality be one that we limited humans cannot achieve? The discussion of the Bayesian ideal in chapter 10 raised the possibility that probabilistic thinking may be the right way for perfect beings to operate, but not something that humans can do without making many mistakes. If this is so, how should people formulate less demanding ideals? How many concessions to their limited powers should they make?

Once we begin to separate the strands that make up rationality it becomes very unclear that we can still think of *the* beliefs that it is reasonable to hold in a given situation. (In the terminology of chapter 7, there are many epistemic virtues, and holding a belief might be in accord with some and not with others.) Contrast two extreme pictures of rational belief. On the first picture there is in any situation a single set of beliefs that it would be rational to hold. It is irrational (in a sense which entails wrong, foolish, undesirable) to believe anything that is not in that set. Such a view is often associated with a very definite sense of the power of evidence to give us rational beliefs. Then we can express it by saying that no one should ever believe anything without sufficient evidence. Call this the *compulsive* conception of reason. It contrasts with the **voluntarist** conception, according to which all that rationality determines is what it would be irrational to believe. In any situation, according to voluntarism, there are a few beliefs that it would be irrational not to believe, but most beliefs are such that we can accept or reject them as we choose, as long as we are careful to be consistent. (Bas van Fraassen, discussing these questions, cites US Supreme Court Justice Oliver Wendell Holmes who wrote that in Prussian law everything is forbidden except what is explicitly permitted, while in English law everything is permitted, except what is explicitly forbidden. Prussian law is compulsive, English law is voluntaristic.)

These are the issues behind current debates in the theory of knowledge. They are very real and open questions, and it is not at all obvious what the answers to them are. Moreover, they clearly have implications well beyond epistemology. Well beyond philosophy, in fact. They are relevant to issues about religion, about the relation of science to common sense, to issues about whether there is such a thing as scientific method, and ultimately to large imponderables about our place in the universe. They all represent some kind of break with a core assumption of early thinkers in the theory of knowledge, from Bacon through Descartes to the British Empiricists. All these thinkers assumed that there were easily grasped principles that, if we could follow them, would lead us to all the true beliefs we could have. ("Rules for the direction of the mind" as Descartes called them.) The history of epistemology, and the history of knowledge itself, has shown that this assumption is at best extremely dubious. When we realize this we are led into the debates that I have just sketched. In this way epistemology is like our other beliefs: we begin with assumptions, use them to evaluate evidence and form new beliefs, and then eventually abandon the assumptions with which we began.

Thinking Questions

1   One surface can be flatter than another, but one belief cannot be more known than another. Is this a problem for the analogy between flatness and knowledge?
2   Describe connections between issues about the purposes that should be relevant to belief and issues about voluntarism.
3   Describe connections between issues about the finiteness of human thinking powers and issues about voluntarism.
4   The last paragraph of the chapter claimed that the current issues that had been sketched were relevant to questions about religious belief. What is the relevance?

Further Reading

Stimulating, and controversial, defenses of naturalistic epistemology and of contextualism are given by Hilary Kornblith, "In defense of a naturalized epistemology" and Keith DeRose,

"Contextualism: an explanation and defense," both in John Greco and Ernest Sosa (eds), *The Blackwell Guide to Epistemology* (Blackwell, 1999). For more detail about how I relate the current issues in epistemology to one another see Adam Morton, "Saving epistemology from the epistemologists: recent work in the theory of knowledge," *British Journal for the Philosophy of Science*, 51, (December 2000), 685–704.

Electronic resources: *Routledge Encyclopedia of Philosophy*: Naturalized epistemology; Contextualism, epistemological. *The Stanford Encyclopedia of Philosophy*: epistemology, evolutionary; feminism: feminist epistemology and philosophy of science; epistemology, naturalized; skepticism.

DEFINITIONS

Below there are definitions of some central terms used in this book. A definition is only the first step to understanding a word. A full understanding of a philosophical concept nearly always requires understanding the theories that use the concept, so after reading a definition it is usually a good idea to use the index to find pages on which the word is used.

analytic   analytic sentences are sentences which are true because of the meaning of the words found in them. Analytic beliefs are true because of the concepts involved in them. Contrasted with **synthetic**. It is controversial whether there is a precise distinction between analytic and synthetic sentences or beliefs.

analytic/synthetic distinction   the contrast between analytic truths like "moose are animals" with synthetic truths like "moose don't have stripes." The former are true just because of what the words mean, while the latter are true because of the way the world is. Philosophers who follow Quine argue that either there is no such distinction or that it is vague with many intermediate cases. Note that to accept the distinction you have to do more than believe that truths can be classed into these two categories; you have to believe that in the one category truth results entirely from meaning and in the other it results entirely from physical facts.

aposteriori   aposteriori beliefs are beliefs which cannot be known to be true or false without considering evidence from experience. Usually written "a posteriori." Contrasted with **apriori**.

appearance   the way the world around a person seems to them as a result of the use of their senses.

apriori   apriori beliefs can be known to be true without considering evidence from experience. More often written "a priori."

argument from analogy   the argument that a person can know that other people have minds like her own by noticing relations between her own states of mind and her own behavior and then supposing that other people are in similar states of mind when they perform similar behavior.

ascent routine   the transformation of the answer to a question about the world into an answer to a question about a person's mind. For example if you are asked

"What do you think 33 + 777 is?" you give the answer to the question about your thoughts by finding the answer to the arithmetic problem.

basic beliefs beliefs in terms of which other beliefs can be justified, but which cannot themselves be justified by any other beliefs.

Bayesian the movement in statistics and philosophy which uses conditional probability to measure the strength of evidence.

cognitivist theories which claim that some sentences do not express beliefs which can be true or false. (See **emotivism**.)

coherence the relation between beliefs when they combine to make a unified and logically consistent system.

coherentism the theory that it is reasonable to hold a belief when it increases the coherence of your beliefs.

conditional probability the probability of a proposition given that another proposition has probability 1.

conditionalization changing the probabilities you give to events by accepting some evidence and then giving all events new probabilities equal to their conditional probability on that evidence according to your previous probabilities.

deductively valid argument step-by-step reasoning from premises to a conclusion, such that if the premises are true the conclusion must be true.

defeater a fact of which a person is not aware, whose existence makes some of her beliefs fail to be knowledge. The fact that platypuses lay eggs would defeat someone's belief that no mammals lay eggs. The fact that the gem you pick up comes from a bag of perfect imitation diamonds would defeat your belief that that gem is a diamond, even if it is true and based on what would otherwise be adequate evidence.

emotivism the ethical theory that moral judgments are expressions of emotion rather than beliefs.

empiricism the doctrine that perception provides the ultimate justification for nearly all our beliefs. Moreover, most empiricists hold that this justification is foundationalistic, that is, that there is a one-way relation of evidence between perception and belief.

epistemic virtue an aspect of a person's personality or thinking that helps her acquire knowledge.

error false belief. Contrasted with **ignorance**.

evidence reasons for holding a belief, usually derived from experience.

experiential concepts concepts which can be learned by having particular experiences and seeing what they have in common.

externalism the theory that what makes a belief justified or qualify as knowledge depends on factors outside the person. (Beware: in other parts of philosophy "externalism" and "internalism" are used with similar, but different, meanings.)

fallibilism the theory that any belief could be false, however strong our evidence for it. Stronger or weaker fallibilisms take the possibility that beliefs we are confident of may turn out to be false more or less seriously.

false beliefs which are meaningful but not true (see **true**). So a belief that Jabberwockys blurg glurbashiously is neither true nor false. (Therefore many philosophers' beliefs may be neither true nor false: in a way it is an honor to have achieved falsehood.)

folk psychology   the beliefs, concepts, and ways of thinking which we use in everyday life to understand ourselves and other people.

foundationalism   the theory that a belief is justified only when it is based on a basic belief. (See **basic beliefs**, **justified belief**.)

Gettier examples   examples which show that a belief can be true and justified but not qualify as knowledge.

holism   the same as **coherentism**.

ignorance   not having a belief you need. Contrasted with **error**.

induction (inductive reasoning)   reasoning that begins with particular instances of a general pattern and concludes that the pattern applies to all instances.

inference to the best explanation (IBE)   reasoning from the fact that a hypothesis is the best available explanation of some evidence or belief to the conclusion that the hypothesis is true.

internalism   the theory that whether or not a person's belief is justified depends on factors within that person's mind. Contrasted with **externalism**. (See the warning under **externalism**.)

irrational belief   A belief is irrational when it is rational to believe that it is false. (See **rational belief**.)

justified belief   a belief which is supported by evidence, argument, or other beliefs, so that an intelligent person who had made no mistakes in reasoning and who had that evidence and those other beliefs would hold it. A justified belief is held for reasons which maximize the person's chances of having a large number of true beliefs.

Lehrer's principle   the claim that for a belief to count as knowledge it must be true and based only on other true beliefs.

logical truth   a sentence or belief which is true because of the meaning of the logical words in it (such as "and," "not," "all"). (See **analytic**.)

naturalistic epistemology   the claim that in order to understand when a belief is reasonable and when evidence supports a belief we must understand the way that human beings process information from their environment. This position makes discoveries in psychology and biology relevant to the theory of knowledge.

necessity   the property a belief has when there is no possible circumstance in which it could be false (i.e. a **necessary** belief).

other minds problem   the problem of showing how a person's beliefs that other people have minds similar to hers can be justified.

perception   getting information about the world by use of the senses.

perception, propositional   forming a belief about the environment by use of the senses.

perception, relational   gathering information about a particular physical object by use of the senses.

perceptual appearance   the way the environment seems as a result of the use of the senses.

perceptual beliefs   beliefs obtained by use of the senses.

psychological beliefs   beliefs about thoughts, experiences, memories, emotions and other states of mind.

rational belief   a belief acquired by sensible and clear thinking, which considers possible objections and counter-evidence. (See **irrational belief**.)

rationalism   the theory that many of our beliefs can be justified by the use of our power of thinking alone, without evidence from per-ception.

realism   the theory that we can have true or false beliefs about real things which are independent of our minds. For example scientific realism holds that scientific theories describe objects, such as electrons and genes and gravitational fields, which would exist even if we did not have any theories about them.

reflective equilibrium   a situation where a person's intuitive beliefs about a class of particular situations are consistent with their theories and other general beliefs about those situations.

sense data   information about what a person is perceiving which is so basic that the person has no alternative to believing it.

skepticism   the theory that people have a lot less knowledge than they think they do.

synthetic   a synthetic belief or sentence is one whose truth or falsity depends on factors besides the meaning of the words or concepts. Contrasted with **analytic**.

theoretical concept   a concept which is used in a theory, and which is understood by learning the theory.

true   true beliefs can be defined in two ways. A belief is true when it describes the world accurately. Or, for a subtler definition, a belief that p is true if and only if p. That is, a person who believes that there are UFOs believes truly if and only if there are UFOs, and a person who believes that there are infinitely many twin primes believes truly if and only if there are infinitely many twin primes, and so on. These two definitions should support one another.

unjustified beliefs   beliefs which the person in question does not have adequate reason to hold. Note that one person's belief may be justified though another person may have no adequate reason for the same belief. Note also that justification depends on reasons that the person could use to defend their belief, not on the psychological reasons why they hold it.

voluntarism   the claim that different people with the same beliefs can respond to new evidence by changing their beliefs in different ways. (Warning: in other parts of philosophy "voluntarism" is used with related but different meanings.)

APPENDIX FOR TEACHERS

This third edition has significant changes from the second, which was very different from the first, though the difference may be disguised by the similar titles of many chapters. The book now covers more topics and describes a greater range of philosophical positions, and my own philosophical loyalties are less prominent and more clearly marked. The discussions of moral knowledge, Bayesianism, and naturalistic epistemology were entirely new to the second edition and the chapter on externalism and epistemic virtues is new to the third, in which every chapter has been rewritten.

My intention has been to provide an easily read book for a first course in the theory of knowledge that a teacher would not have to waste time quarrelling with. Students with a minimal background in philosophy, as in a one-semester introductory course, should be able to read chapters of the book on their own without much help or guidance. This should allow the teacher to concentrate on the exposition of classical texts or more difficult contemporary works. There should be no difficulty using this book in combination with either Descartes' *Meditations*, Hume's *Enquiry* or *Treatise*, Russell's *The Problems of Philosophy*, or other classics of the subject. In the further reading section of every chapter I have listed relevant selections from John Cottingham's *Western Philosophy: An Anthology* (Blackwell, 1996) which could be used to accompany the chapter. Paul K. Moser and Arnold vander Nat, *Human Knowledge* (Oxford University Press, 1995) would also supply suitable readings. Equally, there should be no difficulty using it with contemporary standards such as Alvin Goldman, *Epistemology and Cognition* (Harvard University Press, 1986), Alvin Plantinga, *Warrant: The Current Debate* (Oxford University Press, 1993) or chapter 8 of his *Warrant and Proper Function* (Oxford University Press, 1993), Laurence BonJour, *The Structure of Empirical Knowledge* (Harvard University Press, 1985), or Bas van Fraassen, *The Scientific Image* (Oxford University Press, 1980). It would be impossible to use any of these books in an introductory course without also using something much easier to read, to give the students something to hold on to.

A course also needs a reserve of books, usually held on reserve in the library, for students to use when writing essays or preparing for seminar presentations. The works by Descartes, Hume, Russell, Goldman, Plantinga, BonJour, and van Fraassen mentioned above could well have a place in such a reserve, as should Jonathan

Dancy, *An Introduction to Contemporary Epistemology* (Blackwell, 1985), Plantinga, *Warrant and Proper Function* (Oxford University Press, 1993), Robert Schwartz, *Vision* (Blackwell, 1994), Gilbert Harman, *Change in view* (MIT Press, 1986), Peter Unger, *Ignorance: A Case for Skepticism* (Oxford University Press, 1975), John Greco and Ernest Sosa (eds), *The Blackwell Guide to Epistemology* (Blackwell, 1999), and Jonathan Dancy and Ernest Sosa (eds), *A Companion to Epistemology* (Blackwell, 1993). Of course the exact list will depend on the course you give.

In my experience, philosophy students like to appear to understand more than they do. So they semiconsciously fake it, learning sophisticated names and moves by rote, to disguise their bafflement. (I certainly did.) The expectation that intelligent students should be able to grapple with the most difficult issues and the most sophisticated writers at an early stage encourages this pretence, putting students in a situation where only years later can they admit how little they had understood. I would like this book to encourage a style of teacher–student interaction where examples and counter-examples abound, where formulations are tested and the aim is to understand rather than to impress. One device for encouraging this is the questions at the end of each chapter. As explained in the foreword for students, the reading questions test the students' comprehension of each chapter. They are suited for discussion groups accompanying lectures. Students who have done the reading should be capable of at least beginning to answer all of them. Some of them lead beyond bare comprehension and could be the basis for discussion. The thinking questions are more challenging. They could be used as essay topics, to provide more demanding material, and to raise doubts about whether the line in the main text tells the whole story. Sometimes when you think that the discussion in the main body of a chapter misses an important point or evades a difficulty you may find that I raise the problem for myself in a thinking question.

Chapter by Chapter Notes

In each of these I list problems that may arise, teaching techniques that may apply, and sections of *Philosophy in Practice* that could be used or adapted to provide activities, for teachers who prefer an activity- and dialogue-based style of teaching.

Chapter 1   One unstated aim of this chapter is to introduce the rather special senses of "belief" and "know" found in philosophy. These are best not approached very explicitly: that just causes confusion. Instead, if they are used in making other distinctions they come to seem natural. The basic distinctions in section 3 are important; they are just the kinds of thing that students often seem to understand but do not. I'd recommend a class discussion of alternative medicine, astrology, or some other topic that will bring out intuitive differences of epistemic value. Sections 1.8, 1.10, 1.11, 2.1, and 3.2 of *Philosophy in Practice* contain activities that could be used with this chapter.

Chapter 2   Robert Schwartz' *Vision* contains additional material that would fit well with this chapter. The mix of psychological and philosophical ideas about perception may well raise issues about naturalized epistemology that are not dealt with until chapter 9. Sections 1,3,4,5,7,8, and 12 of chapter 9 of *Philosophy in Practice* contain activities that could be used with this chapter.

Chapter 3   The reading questions on this chapter seem harder than average; students may need more patience with some of them. I have tried to present Quine's views so that they are consistent with his later writings rather than sticking by the rather starker "Two dogmas" formulations. I have listed a chapter of Quine and Ullian's *The Web of Belief* under further reading: although Quine and Ullian's chapter is an easy read, students may have to think to find the connections with the more traditional formulations in my chapter. The contrast between Quine's views and Kant's requires a sense of a quantifier alternation (as rehearsed in question 5 of this chapter) which some students have trouble grasping. The examples used to argue that not all apriori beliefs are necessary, in section 2, and the examples used to make it plausible that there could be synthetic apriori beliefs, in section 3, may be more controversial than the text suggests. The idea of a deductively valid argument may require more explanation, if many in the class have done no philosophy before. You may want to expand on these topics. Question 11 covers Duhem's thesis, which you may want to mention. Questions 3 and 15 are in a way a pair. Question 3 is rather hard for a reading question. Sections 2.8, 3.4, 9.8, and 9.10 of *Philosophy in Practice* contain activities that could be used with this chapter.

Chapter 4   This chapter presupposes a very basic understanding of deductive validity, such as would be given in the first three weeks of any logic course, or in sections 5.4 to 5.6 of *Philosophy in Practice*. The discussion of sampling may be harder for some students than the rest of the chapter, though for others it may make things fall into place. Some teachers will want to spend more time exploring possibilities of what Hume may actually have meant than I do. Question 10 should then be compulsory. The discussion of Goodman's problem tries to avoid the panic that it often induces in students by linking it to much more easily grasped examples than the notorious "grue." Grue is introduced in question 11 though. Sections 2, 11, and 12 of chapter 5 of *Philosophy in Practice* contain activities that could be used with this chapter.

Chapter 5   This is a shorter than average chapter and serves to bring together themes from the preceding chapters while taking them to a higher level of abstraction. The ideas of holism and foundationalism, and the error/ignorance distinction, should be connected to the issues in the previous chapters. It is important to avoid identifying holism with ignorance-avoidance, or foundationalism with error-avoidance, even though there is a clear sympathy between each pair of views.

Chapter 6   Though the topic of this chapter is more difficult than average for the book, I have tried to make a simple discussion, in part by separating off some harder issues which have gone into chapter 7. The last section is not difficult, but it is worth pointing out that it represents my views rather than current orthodoxy. My version of the conditional definition of knowledge is worded to avoid Nozick's awkward use of a counterfactual with a true antecedent. One teaching technique to consider with the topic of this chapter is to present the students with thought experiments in which they have to judge whether a person does or does not have knowledge. The examples in this chapter or similar ones would do. The point is that it is more enlightening for students to discover for themselves the remarkable similarity of our intuitions about knowledge and the difficulty of finding the pattern behind the intuitions.

Chapter 7   This is a harder chapter and you may want to skip it. Even if you do, you should refer to it and suggest it as optional reading, as it gives the implicit background for the next two chapters. If you do cover this chapter you may want to include the material in chapter 11 on contextualism at the same time, as the issues are closely linked.

Chapter 8   My characterizations of Cartesian (self-centered) and behaviorist positions are rather extreme. You may want to discuss how more moderate positions can be formulated. I have left conclusions about the force of eliminative behaviorism deliberately indefinite. Students tend to get enthusiastic for or against on this point and it would be as well to leave the initiative to them. My discussion of the reasons against folk psychology as a theory could naturally lead to a discussion of the Wittgensteinian attitude to mental language. Section 12.10 of *Philosophy in Practice* could be used as an activity for this chapter.

Chapter 9   The danger in discussing this topic is of getting bogged down in disputes about moral relativism or about the religious basis of ethics. The comparisons with humor, color, and witches are meant to prevent this. The idea of reflective equilibrium is used in this chapter to show how there can be a non-mysterious cognitivist theory of ethics. A number of other moral theories would have done as well. The point made in the very last section, that we may be able to say "if there are facts of a certain kind then we have moral knowledge" without being certain of the antecedent, and that this conditional can serve many of the functions one would want an assurance of moral knowledge for, is fairly subtle. It does not matter if not all students get the point, as there is enough other material in the chapter for them to get their teeth into. Question 7 may help here, though. Question 11 makes links with internalism/externalism issues in meta-ethics, which are present throughout the chapter but which I did not want to make explicit. Sections 11.4 and 11.5 of *Philosophy in Practice* could be used as activities for this chapter.

Chapter 10   This chapter combines a discussion of the Bayesian approach with an introduction to some ideas of naturalistic epistemology. The reason for combining them is that naturalism is just rhetorical without some psychological or biological facts to give it bite. This book is not the place to give an independent exposition of much psychology or biology, but facts about the psychology of probabilistic reasoning fit in with the rest of the book very smoothly. So I use them and their obvious link with Bayesian issues as the springboard for naturalism. Some students will find even the small amount of mathematics in the chapter off-putting. But others may find that philosophy is rehabilitated in their opinion by even this small quantitative element. To avoid the mathematics almost completely, you could stick to sections 1, 3, 5, 6, and 7. When teaching the material in section 6 on framing effects and similar phenomena you may want to divide the class into groups and run the experiments on them, to make the issues vivid. Then they will not see the results as showing that people are stupid but that they themselves tend to reason in ways that are hard to square with probability.

Chapter 11   The purpose of this chapter is to provide material for a retrospective discussion at the end of a course, in which the ideas that have been raised over a semester are rehearsed and connected. At the same time it should show how a number of areas of current debate in epistemology are related to each other, and how they arise out of the topics dealt with in the book. I have not included any reading questions as the chapter is so short.

Four Epistemology Courses

There are many courses with which this book could be used. Here are very bare outlines of four. I expect that no actual course will be identical to any one of them, but considering these may help you plan your own sequence of topics. For each one I give a sequence of topics linked to chapters of this book, and a list of other books that could be used as additional texts or for further reading. (a) is probably the easiest course and (d) the hardest, in terms of demands on the students' sophistication. I should add that the simplest way to use this book in a course would simply be to read each chapter in order, centering the course on the book and choosing additional readings from Hume, Descartes, and Russell, possibly augmented with Cottingham or Schwartz. I suspect this would work as well as any of the more complex plans below.

(a) *A guide through the theory of knowledge*   The aim would be to understand why epistemology is central to philosophy and what the main ideas in it are Topics: reasonable belief (chapter 1), sources of belief 1: perception (chapter 2), sources of belief 2: reason (chapter 3), problems about induction (chapter 4), escaping traditional constraints (chapter 5), what is knowledge? (chapter 6). And then two out of the following three: knowledge of minds (chapter 8), moral knowledge (chapter 9), Naturalism (chapters 7 and 11). Other books: Cottingham, Plantinga, Russell, Schwartz.

(b) *Epistemology: a historical approach*   The emphasis here would be in the development of ideas about knowledge. Topics: the origins of epistemology (chapter 1), Cartesian ideas (chapter 3), Empiricism (chapter 2), the Kantian revolution (chapters 3 and 5), beyond empiricism (chapters 3, 5, and 11). Other books: Cottingham, Schwartz, Tyles and Tyles (see chapter 1), Woolhouse; Descartes, Hume, Russell. This course could easily be given by reading chapters of this book and the relevant selections in Cottingham's *Western Philosophy*.

(c) *The variety of knowledge*   The aim would be to see the different problems of justification and analysis that arise with different kinds of belief. Topics: belief and justification (chapter 1), perception (chapter 2), mathematics and the apriori (chapter 3), induction (chapter 4), knowledge of minds (chapter 8), moral knowledge (chapter 9), knowledge via theory (chapter 5), knowledge in general (chapter

6), evidence-based knowledge versus common-sense (chapters 7 and 11). Other books: Dancy, Goldman; Hume, Russell.

(d) *Current trends in epistemology* The aim would be to get students to the point where they can appreciate current work in the subject. Topics: the tradition of epistemology (chapter 1), empiricism (chapter 2), breaking with empiricism (chapters 3 and 5), Induction and the Bayesian approach (chapters 3 and the first five sections of chapter 10), the definition of knowledge (chapter 6), Naturalism (chapter 7, sections 6 and 7 of chapter 10, and chapter 11). Other books: BonJour, Dancy, Goldman, Plantinga.

Two More General Courses

An epistemology textbook is often used in a course on "Epistemology and Metaphysics" (or "Knowledge and Reality," or the like). It is very hard to give such a course without tangling with very hard and confusing issues. My advice is to focus on specific issues where the link between the epistemology and the metaphysics is clear. Two obvious choices are phenomenalism, where chapters 2 and 5 of this book would be central, and laws of nature, in which chapters 4 and 10 would be central. (The metaphysical issues arising from epistemological positions very often center on realism about counterfactuals.) A less obvious very general theme would be supervienience, in which the issues in chapter 9 would fit well with a discussion of mind and body.

Issues about knowledge and rational belief fit very naturally with issues about decision. Moreover issues about rational and irrational decision are easy to motivate and teach, even if the orthodox decision-theoretic formalism is not. A course that is rarely taught, but which I would like to see explored, would discuss issues of rational belief and rational action together. The central texts could be this book and Michael Resnik's *Choices: An Introduction to Decision Theory* (University of Minnesota Press, 1987).

INDEX

A number in **bold** indicates that there is a definition or explanation of the word on that page. Some page numbers indicate pages which are relevant to a topic even if the word is not mentioned on that page.